Practical JAMstack

Blazing Fast, Simple, and Secure Web Development, the Modern Way

Frank Zammetti

Practical JAMstack: Blazing Fast, Simple, and Secure Web Development, the Modern Way

Frank Zammetti
Pottstown, PA, USA

ISBN-13 (pbk): 978-1-4842-6176-7   ISBN-13 (electronic): 978-1-4842-6177-4
https://doi.org/10.1007/978-1-4842-6177-4

Managing Director, Apress Media LLC: Welmoed Spahr
Acquisitions Editor: Louise Corrigan
Development Editor: James Markham
Coordinating Editor: Nancy Chen

Cover designed by eStudioCalamar

Cover image designed by Freepik (www.freepik.com)

Distributed to the book trade worldwide by Springer Science+Business Media New York, 1 New York Plaza, New York, NY 10004. Phone 1-800-SPRINGER, fax (201) 348-4505, e-mail orders-ny@springer-sbm.com, or visit www.springeronline.com. Apress Media, LLC is a California LLC and the sole member (owner) is Springer Science + Business Media Finance Inc (SSBM Finance Inc). SSBM Finance Inc is a **Delaware** corporation.

For information on translations, please e-mail booktranslations@springernature.com; for reprint, paperback, or audio rights, please e-mail bookpermissions@springernature.com.

Apress titles may be purchased in bulk for academic, corporate, or promotional use. eBook versions and licenses are also available for most titles. For more information, reference our Print and eBook Bulk Sales web page at http://www.apress.com/bulk-sales.

Any source code or other supplementary material referenced by the author in this book is available to readers on GitHub via the book's product page, located at www.apress.com/9781484261767. For more detailed information, please visit http://www.apress.com/source-code.

Printed on acid-free paper

After writing several books, it actually becomes challenging to come up with a dedication, believe it or not. You've pretty much dedicated one to everyone you ever know at some point.

But, sadly, this was an easy one to come up with:

Dedicated to the enduring memory of John Pfeffer.

A better role model, aside from my parents? Hard to imagine.

A better coach? Absolutely impossible!

Thank you for the memories that will be with those of us who had the honor to know you forever, and for all you taught us, whether you knew you were teaching it to us or not... or, more importantly, whether WE knew you were teaching it to us or not... and even if some of the lessons took some extra time to stick for some of us! It may not be gymnastics like it was back then, but I don't know that I would have written a first book, let alone a thirteenth, without what you ingrained in me during those years.

And now, I'd like to end this dedication with a magic trick...

Table of Contents

About the Author

Frank Zammetti is a technical author of some renown – and by *some* I mean very little. But hey, a guy's gotta eat, right? Frank has been a programmer in one fashion or another, for nearly 40 years, about 25 of those *professionally*. These days, you'll actually find *architect* on his business card, but he's still a code monkey at heart and twiddles bits nearly every day. Frank is – and I believe I have the correct technical term here – a nerd of the highest order: when not making inanimate computing objects do his (likely evil) bidding, Frank can be found watching, reading, or writing sci-fi; building rail guns, Tesla coils, or some other contraption that will probably zap him to death at some point; quoting *Babylon 5*, *Lord of the Rings*, *Chronicles of Riddick*, or *Real Genius* to people for no apparent reason (which, of course, they just *love*); or playing video games to pretend he's a hero (of the space or guitar variety most usually). Frank is also a progressive rock musician (keyboard player) and an avid eater of pizza and all things carbohydrates. He's also got a wife, a dog, and some kids, just to round out the awesomeness, and will always be the one that stands up and exclaims "And my axe!" any time plans are being made (see, I told you, just quotes *Lord of the Rings* for no apparent reason! – what a nerd!).

About the Technical Reviewer

Ferit Topcu is a senior software developer who is enjoying the last years working and exploring the Web and JavaScript. He's been in web development for 7+ years and has worked in different areas from research topics to social media analytics or Internet of Things. In the last few years, he has been working at one of Europe's biggest ecommerce companies, Zalando. Here, he is currently developing and architecting new and existing web applications to improve a new fashion subscription offering, scaling that to thousands of users. In his free time, he enjoys quality time with his two kids, family, and friends.

Acknowledgments

I'd like to acknowledge all my friends at Apress, too numerous to name, who keep allowing me to write these books and putting in the time and effort to make them a reality. The writing is the easy part I often think, and there's a lot of work behind the scenes that goes into putting one of these on store shelves. Nancy Chen, James Markham, Louise Corrigan, and all those I've unintentionally not named just because we'd run out of space too quick – thank you all very much!

I'd also like to acknowledge my technical reviewer on this book, Ferit Topcu. This was our first time working together, and I can only hope you enjoyed the interaction as much as I did. Thanks for keeping me honest every step of the way!

Introduction

Web development. It's kinda crazy!

If you've done it for any length of time, then you will have seen cycles, ebbs and flows, paradigm shifts, and complete changes in technology.

And, I mean, that was just last month!

Because of that, it's always interesting when ideas that aren't entirely new get recycled, repackaged, extended, and expanded to become something novel. I think that's precisely the case with JAMstack.

When you develop a website, or a web-based application, there are many different concerns you have to factor in – speed of development, cost, performance, extensibility, SEO, and many more. It can all really make your head spin whether you're very experienced or are new to it all (that's one of the things I always emphasize to new developers: if you feel overwhelmed, don't let it get to you, just remember that even someone with 25 years of doing this professionally under his belt still feels that way sometimes!).

JAMstack is an exciting thing. In many regards, it's a return to the old ways, but most definitely touched up for the modern age. Of course, it adds some new hotness to the mix too, and the result is something that is having a significant impact on the web development industry.

In this book, I'll do my best to introduce you to the concepts of JAMstack and demonstrate how to use them in various ways. I'll present some real, practical code to use to explain it all, the goal being not just to have a bunch of simple, contrived examples, but to have more significant code you can look at – and which is explained well, more importantly – that is closer to the real world than what many tutorials offer.

In the end, I hope that you'll see the benefit that JAMstack provides, and you'll have a good, solid foundation from which you can build and execute your own visions with.

So please sit back, grab a cold drink (alcoholic or not is entirely up to you!), and let's get into JAMstack!

—Frank

CHAPTER 1

What Is JAMstack All About?

Welcome, dear reader, to the book!

I'm sure you've heard about this JAMstack thing – or else why would you have bought this book?! – and clearly, you're interested in learning about it.

Well, that's precisely what I aim to help you do!

We'll begin by discussing what JAMstack is, how and why it came about, the pros and cons of JAMstack, and what it offers you as a developer and as just an everyday old website user too. Then, before long, we'll get into building some real-world projects (that's where the "practical" in the title comes from) that, while nothing Earth-shatteringly complex, will provide you real hands-on experience with JAMstack. We'll deploy these projects on the Web for all the world to see too, gaining you even more experience and understanding about how JAMstack makes this far more straightforward than it used to be, while also providing many additional benefits including excellent performance, and enhanced security and SEO (Search Engine Optimization). In the process, you'll learn about many concepts and techniques, all the things that make JAMstack so appealing, and gain a solid foundation from which to go forth and build your own projects.

So, sit back in a comfy chair, pour a nice cup of your favorite beverage (and maybe some snacks – a rumbling tummy is bad for learning!), and join me for a journey into a new way of doing web development…

…a new way that, in many ways, is just about as *old* as it gets!

© Frank Zammetti 2020
F. Zammetti, *Practical JAMstack*, https://doi.org/10.1007/978-1-4842-6177-4_1

...But First, a History Lesson!

In the beginning – and by that, I mean the "ancient days" of the mid-1990s – there was the World Wide Web, or WWW, or "the Web." And it was good.

Actually, no, it really wasn't!

We had mostly text-only sites (see Figure 1-1), unless you were on AOL (America Online), which was actually *worse*, in many people's estimation! Graphics were rather primitive, where they were present at all. Animation, when there was any, mostly came in the form of pretty awful animated GIFs, or if you were "lucky," RealMedia video streams that looked like someone was hand-drawing each frame as you watched!

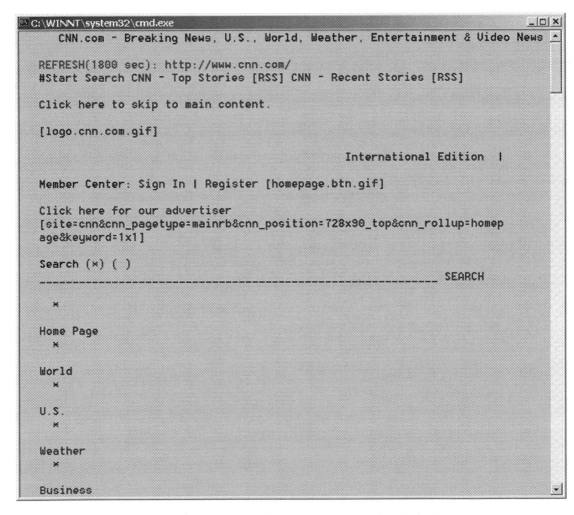

Figure 1-1. *Yes, kiddies, the Web really did used to be nothing but text!*

For most users, though, it was an exciting time because it was their first exposure to online connectivity of any sort, even though it wasn't what many people would realistically subjectively call "good." When it's all you've got, though, and you have no frame of reference for anything else, it looks fantastic. And, it really was in some important ways! Information at your fingertips (albeit more difficult to access than it is in the Google world of today), contact with people all around the world. That's good stuff, even in a primitive form.

And, for us web developers, it was awesome in some important ways too.

Building a website was as easy as opening Notepad on the just-released Windows 95 and hacking together some HTML (Hypertext Markup Language). Then, you'd fire up Netscape Navigator to view it (or edit using Vim on Unix and viewing with Lynx – it doesn't matter, the point is it was just plain text with no special tools involved). You'd make some changes, reload the page, and see your handy work immediately. It was a straightforward but surprisingly effective workflow in those simple, early days.

Then, when you were ready to unleash your handiwork on the world, you would just hop on FTP (File Transfer Protocol), upload your HTML files to a web server, plus whatever images might be needed if you were one of those "fancy" graphical sites, and you were good to go. You might not even have to deal with the web server yourself: sites like GeoCities hit the scene before long and made it even easier to do everything through a simple browser-based interface. Though, GeoCities was its own kind of hell because while it was great in that it let anyone produce content on the Web, it let *anyone* produce content on the Web – gotta take the good with the bad, I guess!

And if you wanted to see how someone did some neat trick you saw on some site? You would just right-click, View Source, and there it was! No obfuscation (usually), no incomprehensible library needed, only "naked" HTML, JavaScript, and CSS (Cascading Style Sheets) to learn from (or, let's be honest: to steal!).

Now, the flip side of this ease is that it was a terrible time in terms of browser compatibility, and CSS was incredibly primitive. JavaScript was a buggy mess that varied from browser to browser, and performance wasn't a primary concern of anyone (although it tended to wind up being pretty good simply because less was being transferred and less was being done on a given web page). Just getting things working and out there was all that mattered to most people. And SEO? Well, search engines were extremely primitive at that point, where they existed at all, so it wasn't much of a concern.

Note   And even earlier on, there literally were no search engines! I can remember buying a book, much like a phonebook, that listed sites in categories, and that, in conjunction with your fingers to flip through it, was the "search engine," in effect!

It wasn't all roses and rainbows, that's the point, whether for users *or* developers.

But still, it was ultimately as simple as a bunch of HTML pages linking to each other, with no complicated tooling to put it together. There wasn't much more to building a website than that early on, and there wasn't much more to hosting it than uploading it somewhere.

Today though? UGH!

You have to install a seemingly never-ending cavalcade of different tools, some of which you've likely never dealt with previously because they seem to come and go like the wind. Some will be general purpose, but some may well be specific to the library or framework you're using (oh yeah: *and you probably are using some library or framework!*). Then you have to execute some obtuse maybe half a dozen commands to produce some skeleton code that has a million different dependencies. As a result, your website has to be developed in a specific, unique way, and you'll struggle to understand it, especially when things go wrong, because you didn't write most of the "meat" of the code that makes up your website yourself. And it's all to produce a website that is as complex sometimes as the space shuttle was! Then, you have to create perhaps an S3 bucket (whatever *that* is). Then you build some Lambda functions and maybe create a RESTful interface (again: what?!). Then you upload the code via SSH (Secure Shell, which might require you to know about certificates) and define your deployment model. You check it all into Git and struggle to understand some complex SCM (Source Code Management) workflow. And so on, and so forth, until your head is smacking against the wall and it actually feels better than the work you're trying to do!

And, at the end of it all, you have a website that quite possibly doesn't even perform all that great because it's loading *so* much content and making *so* many requests to a server that is servicing *so* many concurrent requests, each of them critically requiring some complex processing and rendering logic to occur on the server before the final content is delivered to the browser for display to the user!

It's incredible that anyone can get anything done and that sites perform even as well as they do, despite so many admittedly amazing tools to do a large chunk of the work for you!

At some point, someone threw up their hands and declared: "there *must* be an easier and better way than this!" (see Figure 1-2).

Figure 1-2. *What I imagine Mathias was feeling when he came up with JAMstack*

The time was roughly five years ago (2015-ish), and that "someone" was a guy named Mathias Biilmann, CEO and founder of a company named Netlify, and the "easier and better way" is JAMstack.

Okay, History Is Nice, But What Is JAMstack?!

Put simply: JAMstack is fundamentally a philosophy. It's an approach, a way of thinking, a set of principles, and best practices. It's an architecture, if a somewhat reductive and minimalistic one.

It's not really about specific technologies, per se. Instead, it's about going back to the very basics of web development: pre-rendered HTML documents, and hosting them in a way that doesn't require a vast infrastructure or investment in hosting hardware (whether physical or virtual), at least not directly by you as a developer. Most usually, this last part means a CDN, or content distribution network.

It's the "static web," in other words, much like it was in the beginning. It's client-focused development, where "client" means the combination of the machine and browser that is accessing the website. It's a new way to look at things that provides us a new paradigm that, paradoxically, is a return, in many ways, to the paradigm that started it all!

If you've ever heard of the MEAN stack (MongoDB, Express, Angular, Node), or the LAMP stack (Linux, Apache, MySQL, PHP), then you have a good idea what JAMstack *isn't*: it's not a specific set of technologies that, bolted together, provides a particular foundation to build a website on. At least, none beyond what the Web itself depends on at least, namely, HTML, CSS, and JavaScript. JAMstack doesn't prescribe you use a specific server, or database, or templating language, or anything else. In fact, it doesn't mandate that you use those things *at all* (though you can and, frankly, most likely will for anything but the most trivial of websites).

With JAMstack, rather than every user action resulting in a call to a server that then renders a new page dynamically, all pages in a JAMstack website are static HTML pages that the user navigates between. And yes, if you're wondering if you can do SPAs – single-page apps – under the JAMstack banner, the answer is yes: your site/app will have just a single static HTML page.

Now, that may sound incredibly limiting at first because it seems like JAMstack means you can't have a dynamic site. However, it turns out it doesn't have to be because you still have JavaScript at your disposal, which means that you can always make calls to remote services to get data and insert it dynamically into the page. Also, although your pages are static HTML documents, the *content* it displays doesn't have to be. It's just that the page's markup and the data aren't being constructed on the fly by the server and sent to the client all the time because typically, there is no server when dealing with JAMstack, none you yourself deal with at least. You are essentially pre-rendering pages when working the JAMstack way, just like the server would have, but before the content is served now, so it only happens once at build time. And then, at runtime, you still have JavaScript to introduce even more dynamic content.

So, static in the context of JAMstack doesn't mean unchanging, it just means that when and how changes occur is rethought.

To the extent that JAMstack *is* about specific technologies, the three pillars of JAMstack, as shown in Figure 1-3, are contained in its name, namely, the JAM part: (J)avaScript, (A)PIs, and (M)arkup. As Mathias Biilmann himself put it, JAMstack is

> *A modern web development architecture based on client-side JavaScript, reusable APIs, and prebuild markup.*

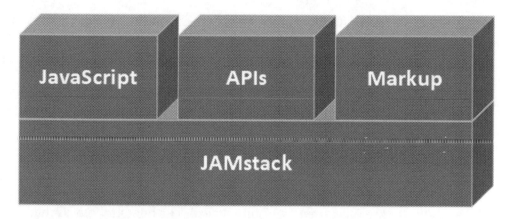

Figure 1-3. *In deference to Spinal Tap, This Is JAMstack!*

But, critically, JAMstack doesn't dictate how you use those. It doesn't demand you use this framework or that, any specific library or toolkit, nor does it push you to architect your app in any particular way. In fact, a JAMstack website doesn't even have to use all three of those pillars. They can use one of those, two of those, or all three of those. And again, *how* they're used is up to you.

Every website is going to use markup, of course, in the form of HTML. But, whether you need JavaScript and APIs (application programming interfaces, which are the remote services your JavaScript calls on to perform more complex functions and access data) is up to your requirements. You can still have a JAMstack website without APIs, and you could even have a JAMstack website without JavaScript, which you'll be seeing shortly, just to drive the point home.

Where this all differs from more traditional web development is largely in the workflow. In a traditional workflow, the process of building the website and hosting the website is, in a sense, tightly coupled activities. When a user requests a page, the target file on the server, be it PHP, a Java servlet, or something else that can produce content at that time, is processed by some engine. This processing most usually involves some complex set of actions like accessing a database, or perhaps calling on a remote system to get some data. Eventually, the data is inserted into a template, and the resultant HTML returned to the browser. There are various forms of caching involved along the way too, many layers to consider before the content gets to the user. Note that the HTML the browser receives never exists as a static entity, which is why I say that building the website, which happens dynamically, is coupled to the hosting of the website. Put another way: it is both built and delivered to the client at the time it is requested.

On the JAMstack (which is frequently how it's termed when you build a JAMstack site: "on the JAMstack"), that HTML file already exists in its final, "servable" form. It was built previously and is hosted, most typically on a CDN rather than a server. When it is requested, no processing is required; it is simply sent to the browser immediately. In that way, the building of the website and the hosting of the website are decoupled: the page was previously built and then is served when requested.

Also typical of the JAMstack flow is that the core content, that is, the precompiled HTML pages, are stored in Git. While using an SCM system isn't a requirement, and using Git specifically isn't a requirement either (it could be Subversion, or other Source Code Management – or SCM – system), it's quite typical. The benefit of this is that, first, your website is version-controlled. This means that it's easy to have collaborators, and you'll be able to view the history of any given file, as well as keep collaborators accountable for those changes.

Another key benefit is that there are services that can be used (which we'll get to see in later chapters) that can monitor for and react to the changes to your Git repo when you push them and automatically deploy them out to a CDN. In the process, cache invalidation is automatically done so that clients get fresh content immediately. As part of this concept, deployments are always done atomically, meaning that the entire website is pushed out as a single unit. You aren't trying to deploy things piecemeal; it all goes live together, as a full snapshot of the site, which means that the content is consistent globally.

Essentially, everything I'm describing here leads to a continuous deployment model: your website is always live and updated almost instantly when using certain JAMstack-oriented services (which you'll see in upcoming chapters), without you lifting a finger to make it happen! Figure 1-4 shows you this basic flow.

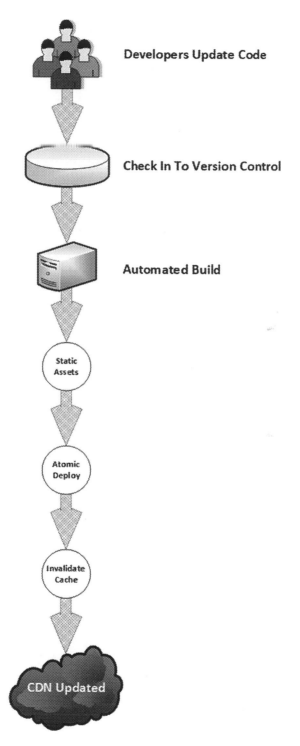

Figure 1-4. *The basic, typical, JAMstack workflow*

At the end of the day, a JAMstack website is likely to be any website that isn't built with a server-side Content Management System (CMS) like WordPress, Drupal, or Joomla. It also likely isn't a single-page app that specifically uses isomorphic rendering techniques to build the views of the website on the server at runtime. And, it probably isn't a monolithic application that runs on a server like Tomcat, WebSphere, GlassFish, or similar application servers, or that uses things like Node or Spring Boot to be its own server, in essence.

Anything else is pretty much fair game on the JAMstack!

Fisher Price's My First JAMstack Website

Now that you have an idea what JAMstack is and how it came about, let's talk briefly about how you actually build a JAMstack website, and we'll start with an example:

- Open Notepad (or your plain text editor of choice).

- Type the following:

```
<html>
  <head>
    <title>JAMstack Hello, World!</title>
  </head>
  <body>
    JAMstack Hello, World!
  </body>
</html>
```

- Save the file and then open it in your web browser of choice.

Yes, you've literally just created a JAMstack website! It's not gonna win any awards, but it might be the simplest example of something that qualifies as a JAMstack app. It uses markup (though not JavaScript or APIs), and it can be hosted on any CDN without any sort of server-side requirements.

Of course, nobody but you can see it as it stands now, but that doesn't change what it is. And, if you *did* upload this to a CDN right now, then you'd have a live JAMstack site!

Naturally, more complex sites require more than this, and frequently you'll find that JAMstack sites are built with what's called a static site generator, or SSG. This is an application that can suck in templates and various forms of source data content, and spit out final, "compiled" HTML files that are ready to be hosted on a CDN for end users. This is something we'll look at in a lot more detail in the coming chapters, but for now, it's enough to know that (a) such a thing exists, and (b) you in no way *must* use them to do JAMstack development.

Advantages, Disadvantages, and Misconceptions

Okay, so you have a little history and historical context now, and you should have a clear picture of what JAMstack is, but why would you want to use it? That's a whole separate question! And, as a corollary, why might you *not* want to use it?

Let's tackle the advantages of JAMstack first because they are simple, obvious if you think about it, and arguably far outweigh any disadvantages there might be:

- **Scalability** – A JAMstack app doesn't require a server to run, which means it can be hosted easily and cheaply on CDNs. That is, in fact, the most common deployment model (note, however, that using a specific server doesn't suddenly make it not JAMstack either). CDNs are inherently scalable facilities that distribute the load around the entire world, and which can adjust to growing load quickly and easily, all without any intervention on your part. The very nature of a JAMstack website means that they are light in terms of resources on the "server" side of the equation (and they often are light on the client side too, although that's actually up to what you do in your code). All of this contributes to making a JAMstack website more scalable and able to handle load efficiently. If you've ever heard the term "serverless," this is what I'm describing: you don't concern yourself with the infrastructure involved in hosting your website – someone else does that for you – it's just a place to put your content, and all the details about actually serving it are mostly abstracted away from you.

- **Cost** – As alluded to in the previous point, JAMstack sites usually require far less delivery-side resources in terms of servers and databases and such. This makes hosting them cheaper, by and large, and sometimes massively so. Obviously, this can vary depending on what your website must do to function, but it is typically true.

- **Security** – Much of the exploits suffered by websites these days are due to flaws on the server-side. Sure, there is a whole class of exploits that are client-side in nature. Still, even those will typically require some sort of breach in server-side security. Cross-site scripting, for example, is generally considered a client-side exploit, but if HTML pages aren't generated on the fly by a server, then it becomes all but impossible to implement such an exploit, just as one example. As such, JAMstack sites are almost always more secure than are non-JAMstack sites. To put it another way, JAMstack reduces the attack surface of your app, and a smaller attack surface is always a very good thing as far as security is concerned.

- **Performance** – A pivotal benefit to JAMstack is that with no server in the mix generating content on the fly, performance can be significantly better on the JAMstack than on more server-bound applications. There will, of course, be some dependency on the client performing well, but that's always true whether on the JAMstack or not. If half of the performance equation – what the server has to do to service a request – is all but eliminated, then assuming the client isn't massively underpowered, performance is automatically going to be better, and there's a good chance it will be to a significant extent. Time-to-first-byte is a common metric talked about here that is used to describe how long it takes before the content provider responds with the first byte of content to a client request. JAMstack boasts an almost instantaneous time-to-first-byte advantage over more traditional server-based architectures.

- **Developer experience** – Most developers that work with JAMstack for even a little while will inevitably tell you that things are just simpler and more straightforward for them. Debugging typically becomes easier because what you're debugging on the client side doesn't change – remember, it's static content when served. That eliminates a lot of questions from the debugging cycle. It's also easier to comprehend the "bigger picture" of a website on the JAMstack for the same reason: when you decouple the build and hosting concerns as previously discussed, you're back to just static pages and not trying to figure out when content gets rendered, what renders it, and how all those pieces get put together in real time. They *aren't* getting put together in real time, which is just easier to understand for any developer!

- **SEO** – Because JAMstack websites are just static content, and because static content is much easier for search engine spiders to crawl and index, they naturally provide better SEO value (though, of course, you still have work to do to make sure the right terms make it into the index). A website that renders content dynamically presents challenges for indexers that a purely static-content site doesn't.

It would be dishonest to say there aren't some negatives to JAMstack. However, they tend to be at least somewhat debatable and not nearly as numerous or as "weighty," so to speak, as the positives. Still, let's talk about the (possible) downside to JAMstack:

- **Developers are required** – Because of the way JAMstack works, a developer must be involved for any content update because it involves rebuilding the entire site (in whatever way the site is built). Now, it's entirely possible for content creators to supply the content in a nontechnical fashion that the build process consumes to produce the static HTML in the end (and you'll see some of that in the coming chapters). So, the developer could just be a glorified button-pusher in a sense! But, it's almost guaranteed that a developer *will* have to push a button in the end. For some use cases, that's going to be seen as a negative because developers ain't cheap!

- **Update frequency** – Largely because of the previous bullet, JAMstack isn't a great choice when you're dealing with a website that needs to be updated frequently. If you were working on a website for a large news organization, like CNN or MSNBC, for example, then JAMstack would almost certainly be a counterproductive approach. There, you would very much want content creators to be able to upload content directly to the system in some fashion (whether a literal upload or via some administrative app creation interface) and have it automatically made available. That pretty much can't happen when working the JAMstack way (it's not 100% impossible, but it's far from optimal to force it into JAMstack). For that, you'd be looking at a more typical server-based approach that reads data from a database or CMS of some sort to produce the always-dynamic site.

- **Steep learning curve** – This is one of those "highly debatable" ones because I, for one, don't really perceive a steep learning curve to JAMstack, but some do. My opinion is that any steep learning curve is almost entirely a direct result of it not immediately being clear what JAMstack is in concrete terms! As developers, we tend to think there's more to a new term than there sometimes is, and I believe JAMstack is an excellent example of that. You think of a "stack" as being some collection of technology, each with its own learning curve that, when combined, makes the whole stack challenging to comprehend at first. That's not the case with JAMstack: we're really going back to basics with it and removing a lot of the complexity. But, our brains have trouble accepting that at first (I know mine did when I first encountered the concept of JAMstack). I hope that this chapter has done a good enough job explaining things that you don't experience this and so find the learning curve not at all steep, at least, not any steeper than non-JAMstack development.

You'll notice "…and Misconceptions" in the title of this section. What misconceptions, you ask? Well, there's one key one, and that's the misconception that JAMstack websites can't be dynamic. It's a logical thought: we are expressly dealing with *static* pages of HTML content, so how in the world can they possibly be dynamic at the same time?

The short answer is mostly down to the A in JAM: APIs. Once that static page is rendered in the browser (and remember that that static page may have been built – one time – from dynamic content), there's absolutely nothing that says you can't use JavaScript to make an out-of-band (or AJAX, as it's commonly known) request to a server, get some data back, and then insert that data onto the page, or perhaps modify the page entirely based on that data. The page absolutely can change, absolutely can be dynamic in that way; JAMstack doesn't stop that from happening.

Note   I've been careful to use the term website in this chapter exclusively, but you'll also see the term webapp thrown around, and indeed, you'll see it going forward in this book. What's the difference, you ask? Well, there is no canonically right answer, but a good rule of thumb is that if a user can manipulate stored data in some way that persists, then it's likely a webapp, whereas a website is more about consuming content that they can't change. Some say that if you must log in, then that makes it a webapp. There might be something to that given that logging in to manipulate stored data makes a lot of sense. But, none of this represents hard-and-fast rules. It's one of those "you kind of know the difference when you see it" things, but the critical point is that on the JAMstack, you can absolutely build both, regardless of how you define the terms. JAMstack puts no limits on that whatsoever; it's all up to what and how you create the thing you apply these terms to.

This misconception is what caused an initial backlash to the JAMstack concept. When developers first learned about it, they threw up their hands and said it'll never work because modern websites are very dynamic, so how can you possibly pre-render them? It's a legitimate concern, until you factor APIs into the mix. We'll be getting into APIs for sure later in this book, and you'll see precisely how they're used to make what would otherwise be static, unchanging – and boring! – into dynamic, flexible, "living" websites.

A Slightly More Advanced JAMstack App

The previous example wasn't much of an example at all, was it? It was, after all, just an almost empty HTML document, and while it may technically qualify as a JAMstack website, it lacks API usage for one thing, and even if it had that, it wouldn't really prove anything as such.

So, let's put together something a tad more robust!

In Listing 1-1, I've thrown together a simple example that uses all three components: JavaScript, Markup, and now APIs. It queries an API provided by the US government census bureau to get the population of the country in 2018 and displays it. It's certainly not a super-advanced website, but it is a bit more than the previous example, and just like that previous simplistic example, it is indeed a proper JAMstack website.

Listing 1-1. A slightly "meatier" JAMstack website

```
<!DOCTYPE html>
<html lang="en">

  <head>

    <meta charset="UTF-8">

    <title>U.S. 2018 Population Grabber</title>

    <style>
      #result { color : #ff0000; }
    </style>

    <script>
      async function getData() {
        let response = await fetch(
          "https://datausa.io/api/data?" +
          "drilldowns=Nation&measures=Population"
        );
        response = await response.json();
        const us2018 = response.data.filter(
          inValue => inValue.Year === "2018"
        )[0];
        document.getElementById("result").innerHTML =
          us2018.Population;
      }
    </script>

  </head>

  <body>

    <input type="button"
      value="Get U.S. 2018 Population" onClick="getData();">
    <h1 id="result"></h1>

  </body>

</html>
```

Hopefully, the actual code is something you can understand easily. If not, then you may need to brush up on some basic web development knowledge first because while this book doesn't assume you're an expert by any stretch, it *does* assume you know the basics of HTML, JavaScript, and CSS.

However, let's run through it at least briefly. It merely makes a call using the JavaScript `fetch()` API when the user clicks the button to the census API, then parses out the population from the response, and inserts it into the page. The response that comes back from that API is some JSON that includes an array where each element is an object, one per year, with population data for it. So, after we get the response as a proper JavaScript object via a call to the `json()` method of the `response` object, the `filter()` method is used to get the object with the `Year` value "2018". Then, the value of the `Population` field in that object is inserted into the `result` element.

That's it! Simple, concise, but a more "proper" JAMstack website in the sense that it uses all three of those pillars we've been discussing. The only real piece missing is hosting it on a CDN. Now, I'm going to hold off on that for now, until the next chapter, where we'll touch on this aspect of JAMstack. However, just to give you a preview, I went ahead and made this example available here: `https://fzammetti.github.io/jamstack1-1`. Exactly how that's done is something we'll get to a bit later, but for now, it's enough to see this example and realize it's the full picture of JAMstack, albeit in just about as simple a way as is possible.

Summary

This wasn't a big chapter, but it arguably is the most important one in the book since it tells you what this JAMstack thing is! We wouldn't have much luck moving forward without that! In it, you learned that the core concepts of JAMstack are JavaScript, APIs, and Markup, which is the basis of the philosophy that is JAMstack. You discovered how this approach yields benefits, including performance, scalability, lower costs, and enhanced SEO while also providing an arguably superior developer experience. You saw some simple examples of all of this just to demonstrate what JAMstack is, at a basic level.

In the next chapter, we'll build a website that, while more involved than the ones in this chapter, is still very simple but which also still represents what JAMstack brings to the table. Critically, we'll get it hosted on the public Internet quickly and easily so you can see the full benefits of JAMstack in action!

CHAPTER 2

Making a Simple Sandwich with JAMstack

With the preliminaries out of the way courtesy of Chapter 1, let's drive home many of the points made there by building a slightly more substantial site using JAMstack principles. Also, this time, let's take it a step further – beyond a somewhat more involved site – and get it hosted on the Web for all the world to see on a CDN. In fact, it's the goal of hosting the website that is the primary focus of this chapter, the main thing I want to get across. Let's get to it!

Let's Impress with a Vanity Site

As mentioned in the opener, the main thrust of this chapter is the part about hosting the site. However, we, of course, need something to host, and it should have a bit more meat on its bones than the simple examples from the previous chapter. Still, we're not going to build something overly complicated since the site itself, in a way, doesn't matter. But, it's essential to truly understand that a JAMstack website is statically built while still allowing some level of dynamic content through scripting, so we'll create something that achieves that: a vanity website.

A vanity website is something a person (usually) builds to talk about themselves. Whether it has a professional bend, in the hopes of landing the next big job, or is just a personal expression of your loves in life – or a combination of the two – it's not usually anything too involved. There's often a home page, some way to navigate to other pages, and then a few other pages that break the content down into some areas as you see fit.

© Frank Zammetti 2020

F. Zammetti, *Practical JAMstack*, https://doi.org/10.1007/978-1-4842-6177-4_2

Since I need a subject for such a site, I decided on someone I know pretty well: me! Plus, don't you just wanna get to know your favorite author a little better? Of *course* you do! So, my vanity website will start on a simple home page, sometimes called a "splash" page, and it will have four other pages to navigate to: My Work Life, My Hobbies, My Family Life, and Get In Touch With Me. The navigation will be in the form of four "nav bars" that slide in from the top, bottom, left, and right of the page as you move your mouse near to them. That provides us some degree of dynamic content (even more than it seems because those nav bars will be added through code rather than being static elements). Some of the pages may have some expandable sections as well, just for fun.

To give you an idea of what this looks like, take a peek at Figure 2-1. This is the home page.

Figure 2-1. Yes, I'm having GeoCities flashbacks too right now

You can also see the My Work Life nav bar has been slid down. Clicking that brings you to the page that talks about my work life, which is just a copy of my resume (or CV – curriculum vitae – for you non-Americans), and which looks like Figure 2-2.

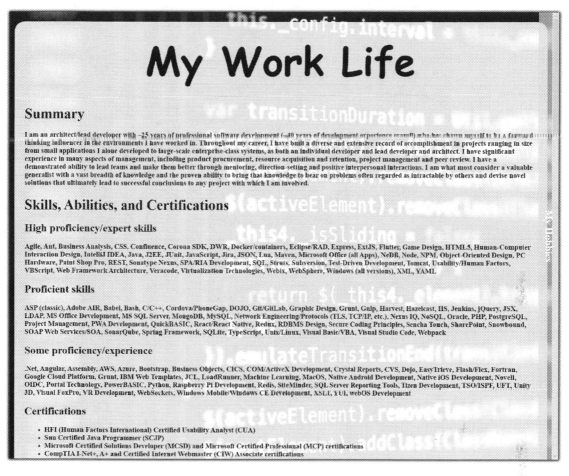

Figure 2-2. *The My Work Life page*

As before, you can see that the nav bar on the right, the one for My Hobbies, has slid into view.

I'm not going to expend a lot of space here to show you all the pages of the site, though hopefully by now, you've already downloaded the source code bundle for this book, so you can go check it out now. In addition, you can access it live here: `https://fzammetti.github.io/jamstack2-vanity`. It's probably not going to win any website design awards, but it gets the job done for our purposes here.

The basic structure of all the pages is similar. There is some background image that fits the theme of the particular page, a semitransparent box with rounded corners for the main content to live in, and of course, the four nav bars around the edges of the screen. On the My Hobbies page, some sections expand and collapse when some text is clicked. Other than those elements, everything is just static text and images.

Basic Site Structure

Now, let's talk about the basic structure of the site in terms of its code. Figure 2-3 shows you the directory structure and the files involved.

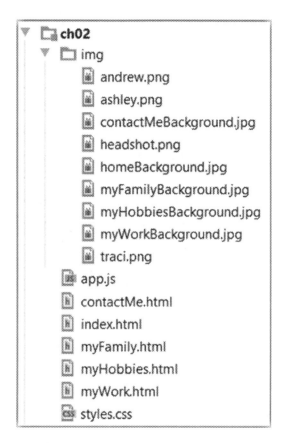

Figure 2-3. *The vanity website directory structure and constituent files*

It's probably self-explanatory, but I'll explain none the less!

Everything starts in the index.html file, which is the home page. From there, the user can navigate to the four pages: My Family Life (myFamily.html), My Work Life (myWork.html), My Hobbies (myHobbies.html), and Get In Touch With Me (contactMe.html). The styles.css file contains shared CSS that is used across the site, and similarly, app.js contains JavaScript used across the site. Each page may have some of its own CSS and JavaScript embedded in it as well, but most of it has been pushed up into the common styles.css file.

In the `img` directory, you find images: `homeBackground.jpg`, `contactMeBackground.jpg`, `myFamilyBackground.jpg`, and `myWorkBackground.jpg` are the background images for each page; `andrew.png`, `ashley.png`, and `traci.png` are pictures of my family for the My Family Life page; and `headshot.png` is my stylized headshot from the home page.

That's it! Not much at all, as promised!

The Code, Bit by Bit (Well, uhh, Mostly)

Now, we'll look at the code for the site. It is, by and large, plain and mostly basic HTML, CSS, and JavaScript. As such, I'll explain it enough for you to get the overall picture of how it's put together, and go into a few details where it makes sense, but I may skim over some bits of it too, and the listings you see following this will be cut down a little bit to save space. I encourage you to take a look at it in more detail on your own after you finish this section, but even if you don't, I don't think you'll have any problem understanding things. And, again, this whole chapter isn't so much about the site itself as it is the hosting of it later, but I couldn't not describe the website and its code to at least some degree, so let's do that now.

styles.css and app.js

The `styles.css` and `app.js` files, as mentioned earlier, are shared styles and code, stuff that is used on all the pages. As such, rather than look at them as individual files, I'm going to simply show you the styles and code they contain as we encounter them. However, for the `app.js` file, you must understand the basic structure of it, which is simply this:

```
const app = {
...code...
};
```

Yeah, that's it! It's a single object that contains all the code for the app. So, for example, there's a `start()` function that you'll see later. What you'll find, if you look at the `app.js` file, is this:

```
const app = {
  start : function() {
    ...code...
  },
  ...more code...
};
```

In other words, the whole thing is just a JavaScript object with functions in it (thereby making them methods of the object) in it, as well as a few variables (which makes them properties of the object). Obviously, that means that if we want to execute that `start()` method, we have to call `app.start()`, qualifying the method name with the object name, and you'll see that throughout the code.

So, like I said, as we encounter the variables and methods being used in the rest of the code, we'll look at them at that point.

Similarly, `styles.css` is just a stylesheet with a bunch of style classes, so as they are used, we'll see their definition at that point so that you have context for everything.

index.html

So, the first file we need to look at is obviously the starting point, `index.html`, shown in Listing 2-1.

Listing 2-1. The index.html file

```html
<!DOCTYPE html>
<html lang="EN">

  <head>

    <meta charset="UTF-8">
    <meta name="viewport"
      content="width=device-width,initial-scale=1">

    <title>All About Me</title>

    <link rel="stylesheet" type="text/css"
      href="styles.css" />

    <style>

      .contentInner2 { height : 571px; }

      .background {
        background : url(img/homeBackground.jpg);
        background-size : cover;
      }
```

```
  .headshot {
    float : left;
    padding-right : 20px;
  }

</style>

<script src="app.js" type="text/javascript"
  charset="utf-8"></script>

<script>app.currentPage = "home";</script>

</head>

<body onload="app.start();">

  <div id="content" class="content background">
    <div class="contentInner contentInner2">
      <img src="img/headshot.png" alt="Frank W. Zammetti"
        width="640" height="571" class="headshot" />
      ...Introduction text...
    </div>
  </div>

</body>

</html>
```

As you can see, it's just some basic markup (which I've trimmed down a bit to save space, which I'll be doing with most of these source files), and as such, I'm only going to describe the elements that are of particular importance to making this whole site work. I'm also going to skip the JavaScript at first, but we'll get back to it shortly!

First, you'll find that all the pages have a background image of some sort, and as a result, they all have a background style class defined. This will be applied to a main content <div>, as you can see here. Those <div>s have some common base styling applied via the content class, which is found in styles.css, which was imported in the <head>:

```
.content {
  position : fixed;
  width : 100%;
  height : 100%;
  left : 0;
  top : 0;
  overflow : auto;
}
```

The goal here is simply to cover the entire screen with the content.

In the case of index.html, we also have my headshot to deal with, so there's a style class named, not surprisingly, headshot, for that. It ensures that the image appears to the left of the text and that there is some space between the image and the text.

All pages – and this one is no exception – have another <div> inside the first that has style class contentInner applied. That style is as follows:

```
.contentInner {
  margin-top : 20px;
  margin-left : auto;
  margin-right : auto;
  width : 1024px;
  font-size : 14px;
  color : #ffffff;
  background-color : rgba(0, 0, 0, 0.5);
  border-color : rgba(0, 0, 0, 0.5);
  padding : 20px;
  border-width : 4px;
  border-radius : 20px;
}
```

The basic goal here is to have a semitransparent box with rounded corners that our content can live in so that it is readable over the background images. It also provides for some spacing around it and padding inside of it so that we have nice spacing and separation everywhere.

After that, it's just straightforward markup, so hopefully nothing that you need explained there, aside from the fact that we have a style applied to the <body> element as follows:

```
body {
  padding : 0;
  margin : 0;
  overflow : hidden;
  color : #ffffff;
  font-weight : bold;
}
```

That just ensures that we start with no padding or margin around the page, that there is no scrolling of long content (that will be handled by the inner <div>), and that the default font color is white and is bold. These may be overridden as needed, of course, but these apply in *most* cases, so it makes sense for them to be common.

Now, let's get into the JavaScript. You'll also find that every page has a small bit of embedded JavaScript to add a property currentPage to the app object (which is present as a result of importing app.js before that). This is used in the nav bar code later, as you'll see.

In the <body> of the document, and all pages, this one included, make a call when the onload event fires to the app.start() method. The code for that is as follows:

```
start : function() {

  app.myWork = app.createNavBar("myWork");
  app.myHobbies = app.createNavBar("myHobbies");
  app.myFamily = app.createNavBar("myFamily");
  app.contactMe = app.createNavBar("contactMe");

  document.onmousemove = app.mouseMoveHandler;
  window.onresize = app.resizeHandler;

  app.resizeHandler();

},
```

Several tasks must be accomplished every time any page loads. First, the four nav bars have to be created, which is accomplished by a call to app.createNavBar(), passing it the name of which of the four nav bars to create. That method's code is this:

```
createNavBar : function(inWhich) {

  let whichLink = inWhich;
  if (inWhich === app.currentPage) {
    inWhich = "index";
  }

  const navBarOuter = document.createElement("a");
  navBarOuter.setAttribute("href", `${inWhich}.html`);

  const navBarInner = document.createElement("div");
  navBarInner.setAttribute("id", inWhich);
  navBarInner.setAttribute("class", `navBar ${whichLink}`);
  const navBarText =
    { contactMe : "Get In Touch With Me",
      myHobbies : "My Hobbies",
      myFamily : "My Family Life",
      myWork : "My Work Life",
      index : "Home Page"
    };
  navBarInner.innerHTML = navBarText[inWhich];
  navBarOuter.appendChild(navBarInner);
  document.body.appendChild(navBarOuter);

  return document.getElementById(inWhich);

},
```

These nav bars are created in code rather than being static elements on the page simply to reinforce the point that in a JAMstack app, JavaScript is very much the coin of the realm, so to speak, for dynamic content. This particular dynamic content requires that we build an <a> element, a link the user can click to navigate to a page, and then inside that <a> element is a <div> that is the visual representation of the nav bar itself. Each of the <div> elements has two style classes applied that are found in styles.css. The first is navbar, which imbues some common styles to all nav bars:

```
.navBar {
  position : absolute;
  z-index : 1000;
  text-align : center;
  line-height : 40px;
  font-size : 20px;
}
```

All of the nav bars must be positioned absolutely so that we can position them explicitly and later move them. Setting a high z-index ensures they appear over all the content of any given page. All of them get the same text-align, line-height, and font-size settings as well so that their text is centered, regardless of the orientation of the nav bar, and that the text is sized consistently.

Then, each nav bar has its own style class too, named to match the name passed to the app.createNavBar() method, for the values that aren't common between them:

```
.myWork {
  width : 100%;
  height : 40px;
  background-color: rgba(255, 0, 0, 0.75);
}
```

The nav bar for My Work Life needs to stretch horizontally across the screen, and it is red (each nav bar is a different color).

```
.myHobbies {
  width : 40px;
  height : 100%;
  background-color: rgba(0, 255, 0, 0.75);
  writing-mode : vertical-rl;
}
```

The My Hobbies nav bar is on the right, so it needs to be 40 pixels wide and stretch from the top of the page to the bottom, and this one is green. However, the text needs to be oriented vertically too, which is where the writing-mode settings come in.

```css
.contactMe {
  width : 100%;
  height : 40px;
  background-color: rgba(0, 0, 255, 0.75);
}
```

The Get In Touch With Me (or "Contact Me") nav bar is at the bottom, and is blue, so it's not much different than the myWork style class.

```css
.myFamily {
  width : 40px;
  height : 100%;
  background-color: rgba(255, 255, 0, 0.75);
  writing-mode : vertical-rl;
  transform : scaleX(-1) scaleY(-1);
}
```

Finally, the My Family Life nav bar on the left is the trickiest. While its width, height, and background-color should be obvious by now (this bar is yellow), and the writing-mode makes sense, what's the deal with the transform? The issue here is that without it, that text will appear vertically, as we want, but the top of the letters will be facing right, just like it does in the My Hobbies nav bar. To my eyes, that seems weird. With My Hobbies, the letters are facing "outward," so to speak, but for this one, without the transform, it would be facing "inward." It just looks weird to me (remove the transform to see what I mean). So, this transform does a vertical and horizontal mirror, which puts the top of the letters on the left, so that it appears to be facing outward, just like My Hobbies does. This just looks more natural and correct to me, but that's all the transform is about.

Now, getting back to the code, finally, we need that app.currentPage variable I mentioned earlier! The goal here is that if I navigate to, say, the My Hobbies page, I need a way to get back to the home page. Since we don't have a nav bar for that specifically, I decided that the nav bar for the page you're on, being not needed at that point obviously, will instead become a Home Page nav bar. So, if inWhich matches app.currentPage, then we change inWhich to "index" so that the nav bar will link to index.html (since the value of inWhich matches the filename of the target page, minus the extension, which is added via the code).

Hopefully, the code that creates the `<a>` and the `<div>`, nests the `<div>` inside the `<a>`, and appends the `<a>` to the page is straightforward since it's just basic DOM manipulation code. The only "tricky" thing is the text to display on the nav bar, which is taken from that anonymous object in the line that sets `innerHTML` on `navBarInner`. As you can see, the properties of that object match the possible values coming into the function via `inWhich` ("myWork," "myHobbies," "myFamily," or "contactMe" – or the special value `"index"` when the current page is the one requested), and the value is the actual text to insert as `innerHTML`.

Once the elements are appended to the page, a reference to the outer `<a>` element is retrieved and returned so that the caller can cache it. This is just a small micro-optimization that allows us to avoid having to do `document.getElementById()` calls a lot later, since that's more expensive than caching the reference in our own code.

Jumping back into the `app.start()` function, the next thing we need to do is hook up an event listener for the `mousemove` event. This is how the nav bars will trigger to slide into view. Let's leave the code of the `app.mouseMoveHandler()` for last because it's actually where the bulk of the code is, and it will probably help to see some other things before then.

Now, one thing to consider is what happens if the user resizes the browser window. Given how the nav bars are constructed, we'll need to do some work when the `onresize` event fires, and the `app.resizeHandler()` takes care of that:

```
resizeHandler : function() {

  app.myWork.style.top = "-40px";
  app.myHobbies.style.left = `${window.innerWidth}px`;
  app.myFamily.style.left = "-40px";
  app.contactMe.style.top = `${window.innerHeight}4px`;

},
```

I didn't say it was anything too involved, and it's not! In fact, all it really does is ensures that the nav bars are off-screen, which they might not be after resizing the window if this wasn't done. Since the bars are 40 pixels in height or width, depending on their orientation, we just have to push them up, down, left, or right 40 pixels, depending on where each is. No biggie!

And, in fact, the final line in the `app.start()` method is a call to `app.resizeHandler()`, which ensures the nav bars start where they're supposed to: off-screen.

Okay, so now, let's go back to that app.mouseMoveHandler() method that I skipped earlier:

```
mouseMoveHandler : function(inEvent) {

  if (!app.firstMouseEventDone) {
    if (inEvent.x > 80 &&
      inEvent.x < (window.innerWidth - 80) &&
      inEvent.y > 80 && inEvent.y < (window.innerHeight - 80)
    ) {
      app.firstMouseEventDone = true;
    } else {
      return;
    }
  }

  if (inEvent.y < 80) {
    if (app.slideWhich !== "myWork") {
      app.slideIn("myWork");
    }
  } else if (inEvent.x > (window.innerWidth - 80)) {
    if (app.slideWhich !== "myHobbies") {
      app.slideIn("myHobbies");
    }
  } else if (inEvent.x < 80) {
    if (app.slideWhich !== "myFamily") {
      app.slideIn("myFamily");
    }
  } else if (inEvent.y > (window.innerHeight - 80)) {
    if (app.slideWhich !== "contactMe") {
      app.slideIn("contactMe");
    }
  } else {
    if (!app.slideInterval) {
      clearInterval(app.slideInterval);
      app.slideInterval = null;
    }
```

```
    app.slideWhich = null;
    app.resizeHandler();
  }

},
```

First, let me explain the overall logic here. Any time the user moves within 80 pixels of an edge of the screen (80 rather than the 40 pixels the nav bars actually are so that it's a larger and easier to hit target), we want the associated nav bar to slide into view. When they move the cursor out of that 80-pixel area, the nav bar should go away. That's the high-level goal here. But, the first `if` statement deals with a problem that arises from this. Picture what happens if the nav bar at the top slides into view, the user clicks it, and it navigates to that page. Where is the cursor (probably) going to be on that next page? There's a good chance it'll be right where it was, inside the nav bar trigger area. So, that nav bar will show up the first `mousemove` event that fires. While not a huge problem, but it's not ideal either. So, instead, we'll have an `app.firstMouseEventDone` property on the app object. This will start off set to `false`, so that the first `if` statement will execute. Then, we do a check of the mouse coordinates. Once we see it outside all nav bar trigger areas, we'll set `app.firstMouseEventDone` to `true,` so on the next `mousemove` event, we'll get past this first `if` statement. The result is that no `mousemove` events will trigger a nav bar slide until we've seen the mouse outside any nav bar area, so we can't get that initial "accidental" nav bar trigger event.

Now, once we're past that check, we're into the core logic, and it's quite simple. We do a check of the x and y mouse coordinates on the `inEvent` object on each `mousemove` event. When we see it within 80 pixels of any edge of the screen, we call the `app.slideIn()` method, passing it the name of the nav bar to slide in. We'll look at that method next, but let's continue on here. If we find the mouse coordinates aren't within 80 pixels of any edge, then the `else` block does a check to see if a nav bar is currently sliding into view. As you'll see shortly, the slide is handled with an interval, a reference to which is stored in `app.slideInterval`. If that's not `null`, we know a nav bar is sliding into view. But, since we're not inside a nav bar trigger zone anymore, that nav bar should be off-screen again. So, we cancel the interval and make sure `app.slideInterval` is `null`. Regardless of whether a nav bar was sliding or not, we then set `app.slideWhich` to `null`, which is a value that tells us which nav bar is currently visible (or sliding into view, which is the same thing for our purposes), and we also call `app.resizeHandler()` to ensure all nav bars are off-screen.

Of course, many `mousemove` events can fire that are not within a nav bar trigger zone when the user is navigating around the page, which will result in that `else` block executing repeatedly, and that's fine. It does no harm to keep moving the nav bars off-screen even if they already are, so we keep the code simpler this way.

Now, back to that `app.slideIn()` method:

```
slideIn : function(inWhich) {

  if (app.slideInterval) {
    clearInterval(app.slideInterval);
    app.slideInterval = null;
  }

  app.resizeHandler();

  app.slideWhich = inWhich;
  app.slideVal = 0;
  app.slideTicks = 0;

  switch (app.slideWhich) {
    case "myWork": app.slideVal = -40; break;
    case "myHobbies": app.slideVal = window.innerWidth; break;
    case "myFamily": app.slideVal = -40; break;
    case "contactMe":
      app.slideVal = window.innerHeight;
    break;
  }

  app.slideInterval = setInterval(function() {
    switch (app.slideWhich) {
      case "myWork":
        app.myWork.style.top = `${app.slideVal}px`;
        app.slideVal++;
      break;
      case "myHobbies":
        app.myHobbies.style.left = `${app.slideVal}px`;
        app.slideVal--;
      break;
```

```
      case "myFamily":
        app.myFamily.style.left = `${app.slideVal}px`;
        app.slideVal++;
      break;
      case "contactMe":
        app.contactMe.style.top = `${app.slideVal}px`;
        app.slideVal--;
      break;
    }
    app.slideTicks++;
    if (app.slideTicks === 40) {
      clearInterval(app.slideInterval);
    }
  }, 5);

},
```

Okay, the way this begins is to make sure no nav bar is currently sliding into view, just as was done in app.mouseMoveHandler(). This *should* be redundant at this point, but better to be sure. Similarly, ensuring that all nav bars are off-screen *shouldn't* be necessary either, but we'll do it again, just to be sure.

Next, we have to reset some properties on the app object and record some starting values. First, we need to know which nav bar is sliding into view, so app.slideWhich is set to the inWhich value that was passed in. Then, we have app.slideVal and app.slideTicks. The app.slideVal property is the current location of the nav bar that's sliding into view, and app.slideTicks is how many ticks of the interval that we'll kick off later have occurred. With each tick, app.slideVal will be either incremented or decremented, depending on which way a nav bar is sliding from, and it will become the new left or top style value, again depending on orientation. When app.slideTicks hits 40, that's how we'll know it's time to cancel the interval.

Next, we need to set the starting value of app.slideVal. You'll notice this basically mimics what app.resizeHandler() does in terms of the values, which is exactly as it should be: the nav bar is starting off-screen, and we need to know that value to alter it accordingly with each tick.

With those preliminaries out of the way, it's time to start the interval and record a reference to it in `app.slideInterval`. This fires every five milliseconds, and what it executes is an anonymous function. This function looks at what nav bar is sliding into view and then alters the `top` or `left` style property of the nav bar according to the value of `app.slideVal`, and it adjusts that value accordingly with each tick. Here, you can see why I cached the references to the nav bars earlier: we don't need to call `document.getElementById()` on every tick, every five milliseconds, so we get better performance this way by avoiding a (slightly) more expensive call.

Finally, the value of `app.slideTicks` is incremented and then checked. When it hits 40, the interval is canceled, and the nav bar is now fully in view and ready to be clicked by the user.

That covers all the code in `app.js`, and all but one of the styles in `styles.css` (which we'll come back to when we first use it). So, now, let's move on to the first of the four pages: My Family Life.

Note   From here on out, I'm going to be cutting these files down, specifically removing a lot of the boilerplate stuff that is the same as in index.html.

---

myFamily.html

Next up is the My Family Life page, as contained within the `myFamily.html` file, specifically the content inside the `<div>` with the `innerContent` style class applied (which is the pattern you'll see in all the remaining files):

```
<div class="pageHeader">My Family Life</div>

<div class="familyContainer">

  <div class="traciPic"><img src="img/traci.png"
    width="480" height="680" alt="Traci"></div>
  <div class="traciText">
    ...descriptive text...
  </div>
</div>
```

```
<div class="andrewPic"><img src="img/andrew.png"
  width="480" height="680" alt="Andrew"></div>
<div class="andrewText">
  ...descriptive text...
</div>

<div class="ashleyPic"><img src="img/ashley.png"
  width="480" height="680" alt="Ashley"></div>
<div class="ashleyText">
  ...descriptive text...
</div>
```

```
</div>
```

First up, we have some header text, and this uses the final style class from `styles.css`, the pageHeader class:

```
.pageHeader {
  font-size : 80px;
  font-family : cursive;
  font-weight : bold;
  text-align : center;
  padding-bottom : 20px;
}
```

This just provides us a large bit of text, suitable as a header, written in a cursive-like style, and centered on the page with some padding below so it is separated from the content.

And, that content is what follows! In simplest terms, it's three sections, one for my wife and one each for my two kids, all nested within a <div> with the familyContainer style class applied. This is one embedded in the <head> of this page and is defined like this:

```
.familyContainer {
  display : grid;
  grid-template-columns : repeat(2, 1fr);
  grid-template-rows : repeat(3, 1fr);
  grid-column-gap : 0;
  grid-row-gap : 40px;
}
```

The goal here is to lay out the page in a zigzag pattern, one person on the left, then one on the right, and then the last one on the left again. CSS Grid is used to accomplish this.

Then, as I said, each person is a block of code where each has an image, enclosed within a <div>, and then some descriptive text in another <div>. The image <div> and the descriptive text <div> each have a style associated with them. For my wife, Traci, they are

```
.traciPic { grid-area : 1 / 1; }
.traciText {
  grid-area : 1 / 2;
  padding-top : 20px;
  font-size : 24px;
}
```

That puts here to the left. Then, Andrew, winds up on the right with these:

```
.andrewPic { grid-area : 2 / 2; }
.andrewText {
  grid-area : 2 / 1;
  padding-top : 20px;
  font-size : 24px;
}
```

Finally, Ashley winds up on the left again:

```
.ashleyPic { grid-area : 3 / 1; }

.ashleyText {
  grid-area : 3 / 2;
  padding-top : 60px;
  font-size : 24px;
}
```

I'm assuming here that you have some familiarity with CSS Grid, but if not, let's take a quick detour to explore it, if for no other reason than it's supercool!

A Quick Detour: CSS Grid

There are lots of ways to lay out a website, or parts of a website, each with their own pluses and minuses. But, given that we're trying to use relatively modern techniques in this book, we're going to go with the newest darling on the street: CSS Grid.

Virtually any web page layout can be described in terms of a grid (in fact, I'm not sure there's any that *can't* be). It's all just columns and rows in the end, whether there's only one of each (read: just a single block of content) or whether there are nested grids inside nested grids. All of it just rows and columns.

Let's start with some simple markup, Listing 2-2:

Listing 2-2. CSS Grid example markup

```
<html>
  <head>
    <title></title>
  </head>
  <body>
    <div class="container">
      <div style="background-color:#ff0000;">A</div>
      <div style="background-color:#00ff00;">B</div>
      <div style="background-color:#0000ff;">C</div>
      <div style="background-color:#ff00ff;">D</div>
      <div style="background-color:#ffff00;">E</div>
      <div style="background-color:#00ffff;">F</div>
    </div>
  </body>
</html>
```

When loaded in your browser, you'll simply see six rows of content, stacked one right on top of the other, as shown in Figure 2-4.

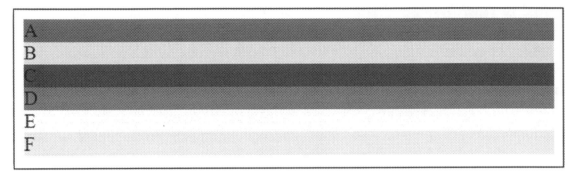

Figure 2-4. You can't see the colors on the printed page, but trust me, they're there

To introduce CSS Grid to the mix, in order to create a more interesting layout, we start with a container element, which we have here. Then, on this element, you define the grid, that is, the rows and columns contained within the grid. The container element already has a class attribute, so we just need to define that style rule:

```
.container {
  display : grid;
  grid-template-columns : 150px 50px 100px;
  grid-template-rows : 100px 100px;
}
```

Now, if you reload the page, you'll see two rows of items with three columns in each, as shown in Figure 2-5. The six <div> elements get dropped into each of the areas defined by the intersection of the rows and columns.

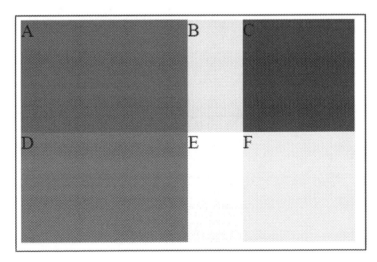

Figure 2-5. Our beautiful, beautiful grid

What's even better is when you start to add some styling to one or more `<div>`s to tell them where in the grid they should live. For example, let's add some style to element E:

```
<div style="background-color:#ffff00;grid-column:1/4;grid-row:1/1;">E</div>
```

Now, reload the page, and you'll find that the first `<div>` shown, E, extends across the entire grid, as seen in Figure 2-6. The meaning of the `grid-column` and `grid-row` attributes is that it tells the grid what columns and rows the element should cover, but it does so using the grid lines, not the boxes that make up the grid.

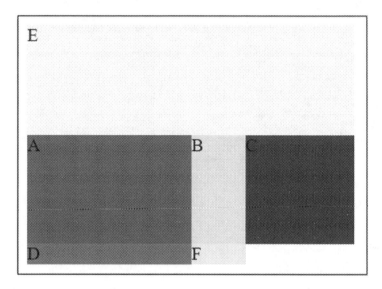

Figure 2-6. *A more interesting grid (well, I think so at least!)*

In other words, when you have three columns, you have four grid lines: the two between the three columns, of course, and the one before the first column and after the last one. So, here we're saying that this `<div>` should stretch from that first grid line to the fourth one, the last one, which results in it covering the entire row. Figure 2-7 should, expect, make this all clear.

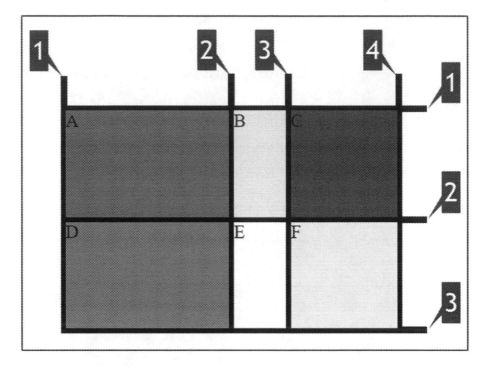

Figure 2-7. *The numbers across the top are the column lines; the ones down the side are the row lines*

Also, because `<div>` E now takes up the entire first row, `<div>`s A, B, and C use the second row, which pushes D and F down. Sometimes, it takes a little tweaking to get your grid to work precisely the way you want it to, but when you do, you'll find that laying out pages is a piece of cake with CSS Grid.

It's also important to realize that you can nest grid. So, say we want to have some grid layout within `<div>` B, we can absolutely do that, and you do it in exactly the same way: apply the `display:grid` style to a container `<div>` (along with the grid-template-columns and grid-template-rows as appropriate) inside `<div>` B, and then define the grid in exactly the same way, but now that grid will be constrained to `<div>` B.

It's also important to realize that you don't have to apply a CSS Grid to the page as a whole. You can do it for just a subsection, which is precisely what is done on the My Family Life page to lay out the three sections for each member of my family.

CSS Grid offers a great deal more flexibility than I've shown here, but if this is your first encounter with it, then hopefully this is enough to give you the general idea. Especially if you've got some web development experience already, you're likely thinking this is very cool and will make life a lot easier, and you couldn't be more correct!

myWork.html

The My Work Life page, found in the `myWork.html` file, is even simpler than the My Family Life page (and again, trimmed down for size):

```
<div class="contentInner contentInner2">

  ...lots of content...
```

Now, here, you'll see that in addition to the `contentInner` class applied to the second `<div>`, there's a new `contentInner2` class applied, which is embedded in the `<head>` of this page. That class is

```
.contentInner2 {
  color : #000000;
  background-color : rgba(255, 255, 255, 0.9);
  border-color : rgba(255, 255, 255, 0.9);
}
```

The problem here is that while `contentInner` gives us a dark box for our content, that doesn't look good on this particular background. Instead, it works better if the box is white and if the text in it is black. So, that's what's done here, effectively overriding the defaults in `contentInner`.

If you look at the content of the page – which is just my resume as of the time of this writing – you'll encounter a list of projects I've done at my current employer. This is a basic `<ul>`, with each project being a `<li>`:

```
<li><span class="project">Payment System</span> -
```

A description of the project follows that. But, when you just have a big, long `<ul>` like that, the individual items bunch together. So, to deal with that, I decided that the project name would have a line above and below it. The `project` style class does that:

```
.project { text-decoration-line : overline underline; }
```

And that wraps it up for this page!

myHobbies.html

In the `myHobbies.html` file, you'll find the My Hobbies page:

```
<a href="javascript:void(0);" class="heading"
  onclick="app.toggleSection('music');">
  Frank's Musical "Career"
</a>

...content here...
```

It begins like all the others, with a header and the same basic structure in the `<body>`. There are four main sections: my music "career," my fiction writing, my Twitter feed, and my Facebook page. For the first two, the user can click some text and expand a section to see more details, and for the last two, there are obviously links off-site.

Each of these uses the heading class for the heading text:

```
.heading { font-size : 24px; }
```

Yep, nothing but some bigger text! You may be wondering why I didn't use an `<h1>` element for this, and the simple answer is that it doesn't play well with the `<a>` element in terms of styling, and I frankly couldn't figure out how to get the CSS to do what I wanted (something that isn't all that unusual with CSS sometimes). So, rather than fight the browser, I just introduced by own class for this, which does the trick.

When this text is clicked, the `app.toggleSection()` method is called, which is actually embedded in the `<head>` of this page, *not* in `app.js` (it's just added to the `app` object to avoid global-scope pollution):

```
app.toggleSection = function(inID) {
  const e = document.getElementById(inID);
  if (e.style.display === "none") {
    e.style.display = "";
  } else {
    e.style.display = "none";
  }
};
```

The actual act of expanding or collapsing the section is as simple as toggling the `display` style property between an empty string (which defaults it to block, or visible, essentially) and `"none."` The section to expand is passed in as `inID`.

When a section is expanded, there is an `<hr>` at the bottom, to avoid it visually running into the next section, and there's a style class for that in the `<head>` too:

```
hr { margin-bottom : 20px; }
```

That ensures the separation we need.

Now, in each of these expanding sections, there are also subsections, to break up the content. This is again just some text with a style class applied, subheading in this case:

```
.subHeading { font-size : 18px; }
```

It's no different than text with heading applied, just slightly smaller (and although these aren't linked, so an `<h2>` would have made semantic sense, since I already broke that with the main headers, I figured I might as well be consistent at least and break it for these too!).

Finally, for my Twitter feed and Facebook pages, there are some links off-site that need to be addressed. I styled them with the following:

```
a { color : #ff0000; }

a:hover {
  color : #ff0000;
  background-color : #ffff00;
  cursor : pointer;
}
```

That way, they stand out a bit, and the browser's default behavior for links is overridden, so that visited links don't blend into the background by accident.

contactMe.html

The final page to look at is the Get In Touch With Me page, which is in the `contactMe.html` file. But, here's the thing: once I remove the common stuff on this page, as I've done for the others, guess what's left? Nothing but some content text! So, there's no real point in showing it here. Have a look in the download source bundle – just so you can see I'm not lying! – but there isn't anything special to see here, so since we've now examined the code for this relatively simple vanity website, let's get into the stuff that this chapter is really all about: hosting!

A Brief Introduction to SCM

One of the big concepts in JAMstack is that, by and large, your site should be stored in an SCM and then pushed out to a CDN from there. As I've said before, you don't *have* to do this, but it *is* extremely common – *so* common, in fact, that it's a core principle of JAMstack despite being basically optional.

You're probably already familiar with the SCM concept in general, but if not, let's very briefly talk about what it is.

SCM – an acronym for Source Code Management – is a tool that provides a place to store source code and, critically, track the changes in it over time. It provides a history of those changes and the ability to compare different versions to see what changes occurred. This history is sometimes called "versions" of the source code, and hence SCM is often referred to as "version control" (they are essentially synonyms, in fact).

A single developer can use SCM, but it really starts to shine when multiple developers are working on a shared code base. Then, the notion of merging comes into play. This is what happens when the edits that multiple developers make to the same piece of code conflict. A developer will need to merge the changes such that the work of both is preserved (or one overrides the other, whatever is appropriate). Most any SCM system will automatically merge any changes that don't conflict, so if two developers didn't edit the same line of code, for example, then merging is done automatically. When merge conflicts do occur, the SCM will report that to the developer and will usually provide some tooling to resolve the conflict. More complex conflicts will require more intervention and perhaps other tools, though.

The reason SCM is beneficial is that as the team of developers grows, so too does the overhead of communicating and coordinating between them. You spend more time having conversations like "hey, I'm gonna work on feature A in source file B, you work on feature X in source file Y, but DO NOT touch file B!". That's a recipe for disaster. SCM allows you to (mostly) avoid such conversations because using SCM sidesteps such conflicts that simultaneous changes can result in by automating (as juch as possible) the merging of changes. To be sure, there's still management to be done to try and avoid even those conflicts because an SCM can't do your job for you entirely. But it *can* help you avoid a big mess if you don't do it!

In the bad old days, before SCM, it was not at all uncommon for one developer to trash the work of another because they were, perhaps, editing files on a network share. There was no history of who did what, so one developer might implement a fix for a bug, and then another developer, who was editing the same file at the same time for another bug, would effectively overwrite the bug fix of the first when they saved their changes. A proper SCM system helps avoid this situation, or at least make it easier to deal with.

Also common in those bad old days was working on a source file for a while, then realizing that something you did previously was actually the right answer, but by then, it's gone because you had been continually overwriting the same file. SCM also helps with this situation via history (it's true that developers, before SCM, would often make multiple copies of a file, appending some version number to the filename as they worked, which is a poor man's form of history).

When you work with an SCM, you will "commit" changes to a central location called a repository (usually shortened to just "repo"). This is where the history is maintained. Each commit will (if you're doing it right!) have a message attached that describes what changed. This helps you and other developers later to understand what was done to the code over time (you can always just compare each successive version, of course, but that's a lot of manual effort that a commit message makes unnecessary if done right). Note that this central location doesn't necessarily have to be on another machine, a server of some kind usually, but most of the time, it is. Although, when we talk about Git, a specific SCM, in the next section, you'll see that the location of the repo is… more complicated.

One last thing that a good SCM provides is the notion of branches. Conceptually, a branch is a copy of the code base. When you commit, you can tell the SCM where to commit to. That might be a branch, or it might be a special "main" branch (this all depends on the specific of the SCM you use). The point of a branch is that you can be working on some code, a new feature perhaps, "on the side," without risk to your main code base. When your work has progressed far enough, you can then merge the branch into your main code base so that everyone then has that new feature to work with. Branches are good when the work you're doing will take a while, since the alternative is frequently committing incomplete work into the main code base, which can cause trouble if your work isn't fully baked yet.

Branches are also typically used for releases. When it's time to ship the code, you will frequently "cut a branch" for that release. New development will continue on in your main code base branch, and that release branch will remain untouched. If bugs are discovered that need to be fixed before the next release, you can make the change in that release branch and release a new version of the branch (perhaps making yet another branch). In this way, you can even "roll back" an entire release if need be.

One topic I won't get into in this book is the idea of SCM workflows. This is a very expansive topic and one, frankly, where there is a lot of debate about best practices. You may hear about something called "Git Flow," for example, which is a popular workflow when using the Git SCM. But, there's no hard-and-fast rule that says you *have* to use that methodology, and indeed there are pluses and minuses to it, as there are for the other competing strategies. I invite you to explore this topic on your own, because it certainly is a fascinating topic if nothing else, but for our purposes here, it's not especially relevant anyway.

Come Git You Some (SCM, That Is!)

Now that you have a basic notion of what SCM is, let's talk about that one specific SCM I mentioned earlier: Git. At this point in time, it is the effective de facto standard in SCM in the software development industry, so it makes sense that we'd talk about and use it. This is instead of other options you might hear about, like Subversion or Mercurial, which, while popular in their own right, aren't the clear thought leader as of this writing, Git most definitely is that.

Git is a product of a mind you've probably heard of before: Linus Torvalds. Yes, the same guy that brought the world the Linux operating system also brought us Git. Around 2005, some drama, let's call it, arose in the Linux kernel development community. At that time, they were using an SCM called BitKeeper. At the end of the day, the company that owned BitKeeper wound up revoking the free-of-charge usage the team had been using. This prompted Linus to develop his own SCM, and thus, Git was born.

Git had several key goals, including speed, a simple design, strong support for nonlinear development (read: branches), it had to be distributed in nature (more on this later), and able to handle large projects, namely, the Linux kernel.

Now, to be clear, some will argue that not all those goals were met. Personally, Git, to me, is far from a simple design. Even if the internal design might be somewhat simple, the part that you, as a developer, interact with can quickly become anything but. However, that's just my personal opinion, and you'll find no shortage of the opposite opinion. And, ultimately, it's your opinion that matters most! My experience in terms of Git speed also hasn't been all roses and rainbows, but I've also found that to depend on several factors that are project and setup specific, so I'll just call it a mixed bag overall and say that it *is* speedy, with certain qualifications.

On other fronts, though, Git succeeds completely in several important ways, and probably at the top of that list is being distributed in nature.

Most SCMs, like Subversion that I mentioned before, are centralized. This means that there is a single "source of truth," a single repo, sitting out on a server somewhere. When you want to work on the code, you must first pull down a copy from that server (which is termed "checking out," though note that unlike some older SCMs, the act of checking out in either Subversion or Git *does not* lock the checked out content, meaning others can check it out and edit it at the same time). Or, if you already have a copy, you'll have to refresh your copy from the central repo to make sure you have all the latest changes (failing to do so can quickly lead to merge conflicts that you'll have to resolve). It's important to understand, though, that your local copy is a snapshot of the code *at that time*. It's not a snapshot of the entire repo; it doesn't include all the history associated with it.

As you're working, everything you do is on your machine until you commit to that central repo. If your laptop blows up in the middle, your work is lost. It also, more importantly, means that if your server blows up (perhaps because a Terminator from the future and his human compatriots fears your work is going to spawn a humanity-destroying artificial intelligence in the future and so go all Rambo on your data center), and assuming nobody had a backup, then all that code is lost. Your entire business could be wiped out in an instant.

A distributed SCM, on the other hand, is different in that when you "clone" a repo (note the different term: "checkout" vs. "clone"), you *are*, in fact, getting a *complete* copy of the repo, *including* history. It is, quite literally, a *clone* of it! There is still effectively a single source of truth, a centralized repo, but every developer also has a copy of it. Much safer, don't you think?

Another key difference is that when you're working with a purely centralized SCM, and you want to commit some code, you must have connectivity at that time. There's no other choice. With a distributed SCM, though, things are essentially done in two phases. You still commit, which is the first phase, but now those changes are only committed to your local copy. You still have history, and commit messages, and all of that (even branches, if you want!), but it's entirely local. The second phase is called "pushing," which means sending all the commits that you've done since the last time you synchronized with the central repo, up to that central repo. No one will see anything you've done locally until you push. But, now, you could be on a train with no connectivity and still be able to work on your code, under full version control, on your local machine. Yes, indeed, there is still the risk of losing your local-only code due to a hardware failure or something catastrophic like that until you've pushed. Still, it's better than not even having the notion of version control without connectivity at all, which is effectively the case with a purely centralized SCM.

Installing Git and the (Very) Basics of Operation

Installing Git will, of course, depend on your OS. If you're on a Linux machine, you'll use your system package manager (Yum, or Apt, or whatever else) the same way you install any other package. On Windows, you'll need to hit up a website to get the download package. In all cases, here's the site to go to: `https://git-scm.com/`. You'll find instructions and download links for virtually any OS, and I leave the actual installation as an exercise for the reader.

Once it's installed, we're going to do everything from a command line. There are GUI clients available for Git, of course, but most people start using Git from the command line, and I think that makes a lot of sense. It's better to understand the basic operations in that manner, so you truly understand what the GUI tools are doing for you later.

So, let's talk about some basics!

Note   It is assumed that whatever OS you're using that you have Git in your path. Simply drop to a command prompt and execute the git –version command and ensure it shows you the version of Git installed. If it works, great, you can move on! If not, consult the installation documentation to see what steps you need to do to make it work (usually nothing more than adding it to your path environment variable).

Creating a New Local Repo

The first step will be to set up a directory for a project. There are two ways a new project can begin life: either from scratch or starting from an existing remote repo. We'll talk about the first option here.

All you need to do is create a directory to be the home for your project, then go into it on a command line, and execute this command:

```
git init
```

That's it! You now have yourself a local Git repo!

Cloning an Existing Project

The second way to begin a project is by cloning an existing remote repo (referred to simply as "the remote"). That's a simple command:

```
git clone <repo_url>
```

You will now have a local repo that is a full, complete, and exact replica of the remote, including all history and branches. Obviously, what the URL is will depend on where the remote is. A common source for repositories – probably the *most* common, in fact – is a site called GitHub. We'll get to that later, but the bottom line is it's just a URL that the server the repo is on will provide.

Your initial context for any work you do, the target branch, if you will, is whatever the repo defines as the active branch, which in most cases will be a branch called master, and it's the only branch that always exists in a repo. It's the branch everything you do with Git will go to unless you explicitly change the context.

Staging New Files

Regardless of how your local repo was created, from scratch or a clone, you can now begin adding files to it. This is, in fact, a two-step process: staging and committing.

Staging a file moves it into a special "staging area" in the repo. This is just a list of the files that will be committed later, whether new or altered. Let's say you want to add a new Java source file to your project, call it `MyClass.java`. You create it and edit it like you do any other file with whatever tools you like. At this point, though, Git is unaware of it. To change that – to "stage" it – you issue this command:

```
git add MyClass.java
```

You can add multiple files at once:

```
git add MyClass.java MyOtherClass.java
```

You can also add an entire directory:

```
git add .
```

This will recursively add all files in the current directory.

Committing Your Changes

Staged files are ready to be committed whenever you are. This saves them permanently to the repo (but remember, still only the local repo). To commit (everything currently in the staging area), you simply do:

```
git commit -m "Testing"
```

It is good form for every commit to have a commit message describing the code you're committing, and that's what the -m switch does. Supply the message after it, and every file that is staged will be committed.

You can also commit individual files:

```
git commit MyOtherClass.java -m "Committing more stuff"
```

If there were multiple files in the staging area, only MyOtherClass.java would be committed, and the rest would remain staged.

You, of course, can continue to edit files that are staged, no problem there. However, if you edit a file that has already been committed, you will need to re-add it to the staging area.

Checking Repo Status

How do you know what's in the staging area? There's a command for that:

```
git status
```

This will show you all the files in the staging area, as well as any files that were previously committed and have been modified. You will need to add those to the staging area again to be able to commit them; Git won't automatically do that for you.

This command shows some other information, including what branch you're on, but what files are modified and staged is the most important information it provides.

Pushing to a Remote Repo

What about when it's time to push your changes to a remote? That's easy:

```
git push -u origin master
```

That may look a little complicated at first, but the explanation is simple. It's just saying that you want to push all your changes from the master branch in your local repo into the master branch of the remote repo. The word origin here is a default name that the repo gets when you clone. Yes, it's possible to give the repo a different name, but that's infrequently done.

If you happen to have multiple branches in your local repo and you want to push all of them to the remote, you can do:

```
git push -u origin
```

Not too tough, right?

Pulling Changes from a Remote Repo

The final piece of the puzzle is getting changes that others have made in the remote into your local repo. That's called "pulling," and the command for it is pretty obvious:

```
git pull origin master
```

Just like when pushing, you're saying that you want all the remote changes from the remote branch of the origin (the remote repo) in your local master branch.

Those, in a ridiculously small nutshell, are the basic Git operations you'll need going forward. This is just the tip of the enormous iceberg that is Git, but it's enough to get going if this is your first exposure to Git.

Note   While branching and merge conflicts are common operations, I'm going to leave them for you to discover on your own because they will fall outside the scope of the needs of this book. They don't really come up much when you're a single developer (certainly that's true of merge conflicts, though branching is really up to you and how you want to work).

Hosted Git: GitHub

In our previous look at Git, I talked about a remote repo a few times, but what does that really mean? Simply stated, it's a Git repo hosted on some remote server. You could do this yourself, and your company probably will, but there's another popular option in the world, probably the most popular option at this time, in fact, and its name is GitHub.

GitHub is a product of GitHub, Inc., which is now owned by Microsoft. GitHub is a service that hosts Git repos and then adds many features on top of it. One such feature is called merge requests. When things started with Git for Linux kernel development, a developer would have to pull the kernel repo and make their changes. But then, they wouldn't be allowed to push to the repo directly (unless Linus himself granted them that right, and few get that right, even today). Instead, they would have to produce patch files and email them to Linus and the other kernel maintainers. They would vet it and, if they accepted it, would apply the patch themselves.

This is a bit of a bottleneck in the process, so with GitHub, you instead can submit your changes to the repo but without actually having them pushed into the repo. Instead, you would push them into your own copy of the repo, called a fork. Then, you send a pull request to the owners of the original repo. They again vet the change and, if accepted, pull the change from your repo into theirs. It allows a project to have the same sort of tollbooth, so to speak, in front of their project, but the workflow is considerably more streamlined (more so with the user interface that GitHub provides).

And, a user interface is one of the other huge features GitHub provides. When you host your repo there, you can go browse the repo through a standard web browser and can perform all sorts of operations on it like creating, deleting, and merging branches; adding new files; and editing existing ones.

Getting started with GitHub is a piece of cake. All you need to do is go to `www.github.com` and sign up for a free account. No string attached! You will, at the time of this writing, just need to provide a valid email address, select your email preferences (whether you want announcement emails sent to you and such), solve a little puzzle to prove you're a real human (you *are* a real human, aren't you?!), select some interests and your goals with GitHub, and validate your email address. Once you've navigated that gauntlet, you're good to go! You can immediately create a repo if you like, then pull that repo (the GitHub UI will provide you the URL), start creating and editing files, and then push it to the repo. You can then browse the repo, right there on the GitHub site, and see your changes. Very neat!

If you are going to collaborate with others, GitHub provides a whole security wrapper around your project where you can grant access to others of varying levels, like whether they can push directly to the repo, or whether they have administrative privileges to the project, and so on. But, for what we're going to do here, none of that is necessary, so you should definitely take some time to explore GitHub on your own after signing up for an account. Oh, did I mention that you *should* sign up for an account? Because you should! You're going to need it as we move forward. Obviously, if you already have an account, then you're all set already.

Either way, let's move on to talk about why GitHub is even something we're talking about, which is hosting our little vanity site to make it available for the entire world!

Let's Throw a Party: Hosting the Site

One key component of the whole JAMstack concept is site hosting. Usually, when not talking about JAMstack, you would host your site on a server somewhere, whether it was your own or sitting in a web hosting provider's data center. And, the server might be a physical machine or a virtual one in a server farm. But either way, you wind up with your own server. Maybe you would just have an Apache or Nginx web server, or maybe you'd have a Java app server like Tomcat or WebSphere, or some combination of those, or perhaps Node.js. The variations are limitless. But, they all are the same thing: a server that runs some server software to serve your website.

One thing you may also have, sitting in front of your server in a sense, is a CDN. A CDN, or Content Distribution Network, serves as a cache, in a sense. Your website, or maybe portions of it, is stored on a CDN. When a user goes to access your site, the CDN, which is a large, distributed network of machines, usually all around the world, kicks into action. It looks for the nearest server to serve your content from, and does so, leading to better performance for your users.

This works great for static content like images and pages that don't change, but of course, if you have something like PHP or JSP, something that runs code to produce content, then a CDN (usually) won't work. So, for more traditional websites, those that rely on more capabilities on the server, a CDN can't do the entire job for you, you can't host your entire website on a CDN.

But, wait, isn't JAMstack, by definition, all static? Why, yes, it is! So, does that mean you can host your entire JAMstack website on a CDN and reap all the benefits that brings?

It sure does!

Hosting a JAMstack website on a CDN is, while not a requirement of JAMstack, definitely a pervasive thing to do. In fact, it's probably the de facto standard way to host a JAMstack website.

But, what does all this talk of CDN have to do with GitHub? Sure, your website could be stored in a Git repo on GitHub, and yes, that allows you to browse the code, but it doesn't actually serve the website. A user can't go and access the website in a "live" way on GitHub.

That is, until you bring in another of those value-added services that GitHub builds around Git: GitHub Pages.

A CDN for All Seasons: GitHub Pages

GitHub Pages is a way to take a Git repo stored on GitHub and serve it to the world (assuming it's a website). You'll wind up with a special URL that anyone can access, and instead of seeing a Git repo and the GitHub user interface around it, they will instead see your website, just as if it was hosted on its own dedicated server.

And, it's better than that, because GitHub Pages is, in essence, a CDN! Git, Inc. has built that network of servers around the world and the plumbing needed to choose the best place to serve your content from. It takes care of replicating your repo as necessary around the world, so you get the speed benefits of hosting your site on a CDN.

What's great about this too is that any changes you push into your repo are live on your site right away (well, maybe with a small delay, like a few minutes, but still, that's basically immediate for all intents and purposes). There is no special procedure for you to make your changes live. Simply push to the repo (or edit files directly through the GitHub UI if you wish), and once you commit (and push, if working remotely) those changes, you're done; they're up around the world for all your users to see.

Experienced developers will recognize that this is effectively "developing in production," which is generally a huge no-no. That's why it's not at all uncommon to have a workflow built up around GitHub Pages (or whatever other CDN you might use) where you develop on your local machine and then only push to the repo when you're ready (and you may well be working in a branch all that time, and then only merge to master when you're ready for the changes to go live). All of that is on you as a developer, though. The bottom line is that when you make a GitHub repo a GitHub Pages repo, the changes you push to the repo go live immediately.

So, how does one "make a GitHub repo a GitHub Pages repo"? Because that implies that not all repos on GitHub are servable as a website through GitHub Pages, and that's exactly correct. Let's talk about the actual steps you have to take to make this all work. It ain't much, I promise!

The Mechanics of Getting the Site "Out There"

So, the first step to using GitHub Pages is simply to create a repo. I assume at this point that you've set up a GitHub account, so go ahead to github.com and sign in if you aren't in already. You'll see a plus sign at the top with a down arrow next to it. Click that, and you should see New Repository in the list. Click that.

Now, you need to give the repo a name. Usually, this can be just about anything, but when you want the repo to be served as a website using GitHub Pages, the name has to be in a special form: `<username>.github.io`, where `<username>` is your GitHub username. Enter anything else, and it'll be a plain old Git repo that can't be served as a website.

At that point, your repo will be created. Next, click the Settings link with the gear icon next to it that should be sitting near the top of the repo page that you'll find yourself on after creating it. Scroll down to the GitHub Pages section. Here, you have the opportunity to select a theme for your site, which will actually start building it. But, *this is completely optional*! And, in fact, let's *not* do it here. However, note that this section also shows you the URL for your website, which is useful information, obviously! Notice too that you can also have your site coming from a branch rather than master, so you have some flexibility there.

Rather than using a theme, though, just go back to your repo and look for the Create New File button. Click that and name the file index.html. Go ahead and create a simple HTML document, like this:

```
<html>
  <head>
    <title>My first GitHub Pages website</title>
  </head>
  <body>
    It's alive! IT'S ALIVE!!
  </body>
</html>
```

Of course, you're free to do whatever you like, but the point is it doesn't need to be much. Once you're done, click Commit New File, and then give it a few minutes to update across the GitHub Pages CDN. After a few minutes, use the link you saw on the Settings page, and you should see your website, just like any other website on the Web.

The final task is, of course, to get the actual vanity website there. That couldn't be easier! All you need to do is clone the repo to your workstation, delete the index.html file so that you have an empty repo, and then copy in all the files for the vanity site. Commit everything, then push it, and give it a few minutes (the GitHub Pages documentation says it can take up to 10 minutes in fact, but I've observed it usually only takes a minute or two). Before long, you should see the vanity site at that location.

And that's it! You now have a proper JAMstack website hosted on a CDN, available to anyone, anywhere! As you can see, there's really not much to getting to this point, but that's precisely the point of JAMstack: it's a much simpler and easier workflow, and there's less barrier to entry.

Of course, GitHub Pages is just one option for hosting on a CDN, and we'll see another later, but I felt that this was a good and simple first step. And, note that you can only have a single website like this when using a free account (as of this writing anyway). If you pay for a GitHub account, you can have more, and you can also give them URLs using domain names you purchase. You aren't stuck with these `*.github.io` URLs if you toss a few dollars to the company. But, as a free service, it's pretty great, isn't it?

Summary

In this chapter, you took your JAMstack knowledge to the next level by building a not-all-that-complex vanity website but one which shows all the basic tenets of JAMstack (except for APIs). Further, you learned about SCM and Git, in particular, got introduced to GitHub and GitHub Pages, and you took that website and hosted it there for all the world to see.

In the next chapter, we'll build another website, but this time we'll do it with a special piece of tooling that, while not directly part of JAMstack, very much goes hand in hand with it: the static site generator Gatsby.

CHAPTER 3

Bringing in the Big Guns: Gatsby

So, we're two chapters in, and by this point, you should have a good idea with JAMstack is all about, and you've had some experience building and finally hosting a simple JAMstack website.

But, so far, we've built all of this by hand. While that's fine for a relatively simple website such as the vanity website, it is, perhaps, not the most efficient way to go. Why write code when we have excellent tools that can spit it out for you?

That's what this chapter is all about! The JAMstack concept, you'll recall, at its core, is about static websites. There are some fantastic tools available for producing these, or just the skeleton of one that you can then build on to create a more advanced site. That's precisely what we'll do in this chapter (the producing the skeleton part, that is), so let's start by discussing the tools I'm alluding to, shall we?

What Is a Static Site Generator?

At the risk of claiming the title of Captain Obvious: a static site generator is a tool (or set of tools) that generates static sites.

Yeah, I know, obvious, isn't it?

To be a bit more precise, though, a static site generator (which from here on out I'll abbreviate as SSG) takes in templates in some form, possibly (usually, even) combining it with data of some kind, and spits out HTML. The most common template form is Markdown, though there are other options, depending on the SSG you use.

Contrast this with a CMS, such as WordPress, which produces the HTML at runtime, for each client request. We're doing JAMstack here, so that's not what we want! An SSG produces its static content at compile time (or build time, they are synonymous in this context), thus avoiding that performance penalty. In this way, it's a bit like when you write something in Microsoft Word and then print to a PDF file to make it more easily consumable by others.

© Frank Zammetti 2020

F. Zammetti, *Practical JAMstack*, https://doi.org/10.1007/978-1-4842-6177-4_3

Although you can (and in probably most cases will) edit the source that an SSG creates, that may not be true. It all depends on how robust the SSG is and what your needs are. The critical point, though, is that you *can* do so. Using an SSG doesn't inherently limit anything you can ordinarily do with a static website. In fact, a strong argument can be made that it will significantly help you produce such a website because an SSG usually provides a strong foundation for your website. Many of the more mundane details, the boilerplate kind of stuff, will be done for you – tweakable, of course, as your needs dictate.

Also, note that using an SSG doesn't automatically imply you're on the JAMstack. True, you *probably* are just by the nature of what an SSG is, but it's entirely possible to use an SSG to create a "skeleton" website that you then use as the basis for a more traditional dynamic website. But, this is a bit atypical and, ultimately in a way, defeats the very purpose of using an SSG in the first place. You always gotta choose the right tool for a given job, and an SSG may not be the right tool if you know you need a dynamic website.

The benefits of using an SSG are the same benefits you get from JAMstack, assuming what it produces remains a static website, namely, performance, security (primarily owing to not needing a database), better response to traffic spikes, lower cost, version control of your content, and now a new one: less coding! Something that produces code for you obviously is going to decrease the burden on you to create the code from scratch. You can get a website created with an SSG in a minute or two (assuming the SSG is installed and ready to go) and then get it hosted on a CDN like GitHub Pages in just a few minutes more.

There are probably dozens of SSGs out there to choose from, but we're going to focus on one, in particular, one that may well be the most popular of the bunch: Gatsby.

Enter Gatsby

Gatsby is an SSG that melds together several common front-end development technologies into a cohesive whole, including React, GraphQL, and Webpack. When you generate a website with Gatsby, all those things come together to provide you a rich developer experience and a website coded in a way that makes it easy to extend it to meet your specific needs.

In fact, you could drop the term "static" from the equation, and you'd still be left with a powerful tool for front-end development generally. But, obviously, Gatsby is undoubtedly geared toward creating static pages, that's ultimately the goal.

Gatsby uses the notion of *starters* to build sites. A starter is essentially a prepackaged project with all the essential files for a particular type of website. There are a variety of starters to choose from for various needs. Want to create a blog? There's a starter for that (many, in fact!). Want to create an image gallery website? There's a starter for that. Want to create a portfolio website to showcase your talents? There are starters for that. In fact, you'll always start with a starter, even if it's a very basic, bare-bones starter that you'll then build out yourself. You'll always have a solid foundation with Gatsby, regardless of how much of the work you want to take on yourself.

Gatsby is a command-line tool that is easy to install and use. When you use it, the final output is a directory structure that contains, among other things, an HTML file. That file is the entry point to your website. Then, you'll also find any static resources that make up the website, be they images, stylesheets, or of course, other HTML pages to navigate to, are produced.

Gatsby uses GraphQL to read in data from a variety of sources, including Markdown, JSON, and more, and merges that data into your templates (we'll get into what those are in the context of Gatsby shortly) to produce the static pages. This represents the Gatsby data processing layer, and it's the key thing that makes your static websites dynamic (at compile time, that is – JavaScript still provides the dynamic content at runtime, of course).

Gatsby also has a vibrant ecosystem of plugins that allows you to extend its functionality easily, all driven by simple configuration files. There are plugins provided by the Gatsby team, and there are also third-party plugins out there that you can use as you see fit.

I've mentioned React and GraphQL a couple of times now, and those may be things you aren't familiar with. That's okay! You're going to get an introduction to both of them throughout this book. In fact, there's a whole chapter coming up focused on React to get you up to speed quickly (there isn't one dedicated to GraphQL just because I don't think it really requires an entire chapter, at least not for the extent we're going to be using it in this book, but there *is* a section dedicated to it near the end of this chapter).

Gatsby websites are (usually) React websites. React is at the heart of much of Gatsby (it might be possible to force the issue and not use React, but that would be highly unusual even if you could manage it). However, you don't *have* to use GraphQL. By default, you *probably will*, and it might even be considered a bit atypical not to use it. But, it turns out Gatsby kind of pushing you to use these two things is actually a good thing anyway, as I hope you'll agree with after we're played around with Gatsby a bit.

Speaking of which…

Installing Gatsby and Basic Usage

Now that you have an idea what Gatsby is, let's get it installed and start churning out some websites with it!

Before you can install Gatsby, you have to install Node and its package manager NPM (Node Package Manager), as well as Git. Let's deal with Node and NPM first. If you are unsure if you have those installed, go to a command prompt or terminal prompt, whichever is appropriate for your system, and execute this:

```
node -v
```

You should see a version reported. If you do, then you're all set.

Note   At the time of this writing, the latest Long-Term Support (LTS) version available of Node was 12.6.2. I suggest ensuring you have that version installed if you can, and definitely make sure you don't have an older version. For NPM, the version should be 6.14.4 or higher.

Next, execute this command:

```
npm -v
```

You should again see a version.

If either or both of these don't work, that means that either you don't have Node and NPM installed, or else they aren't in your path. So, if you're sure they are installed, then you'll need to add them to your path in whatever way is appropriate for your operating system. If you know that they aren't installed, or you are unsure, head on over to the Node website at nodejs.org and follow the directions there to install it for your system. Note that Node automatically comes with NPM, so you should be all set after the installation (of course, execute the preceding commands again to be sure).

For Git, execute:

```
git --version
```

As with Node and NPM, if you see a version, you're probably good to go (the version at the time of this writing was 2.26.2). If you need to install it, the website for that is git-scm.com. You'll find instructions and downloads for whatever type of system you have.

Now, once you have Node, NPM, and Git all ready to go, it's time to install Gatsby! That's as easy as executing the following command:

```
npm install -g gatsby-cli
```

If you are unfamiliar with NPM, it's a tool that pulls down JavaScript packages from a central repository (npmjs.com) and makes them available to run on your system. The gatsby-cli is one such package, and it's the command-line interface (CLI) tool that is your primary interface to the world of Gatsby. The -g switch tells NPM to install this package globally so that it can be run from anywhere. Leaving that off will install it in whatever the current directory is, and you'll find a node_modules directory is created – get used to seeing that directory because that tells you you're dealing with an NPM/Node project.

It will take a little time to download and install, but once it does, you're actually ready to use Gatsby! To prove it, execute:

```
gatsby –version
```

You should see something like:

```
Gatsby CLI version: 2.12.7
```

In fact, that version there is the current version as of this writing, so please ensure you install at least that version. Note that Gatsby puts out a new release seemingly almost daily, so you will almost certainly see a higher version than that. Unless it's a major version change, the expectation is that it will be compatible with the code for this book (you can also direct NPM to install a specific version if you run into issues - just do a search for how to install a specific version of an NPM package to find out how).

Now, with Gatsby installed, let's go ahead and create a website! To do so, simply execute this command:

```
gatsby new my_first_gatsby_website
```

This will take some time as Gatsby clones a repo from GitHub and prepares your project from it by executing npm install, which is perhaps the most common NPM command. It takes care of installing all the packages that Gatsby, and the website itself, depends on. This will create a directory named my_first_gatsby_website in whatever directory you were in. Gatsby will also helpfully tell you what to do: navigate into that new directory and start the website up like with:

```
gatsby develop
```

This, again, will take some time, as Gatsby builds your site and starts up a development web server with your brand-new website ready to be served from it. Hit up the URL `http://localhost:8000`, and you should see something like Figure 3-1.

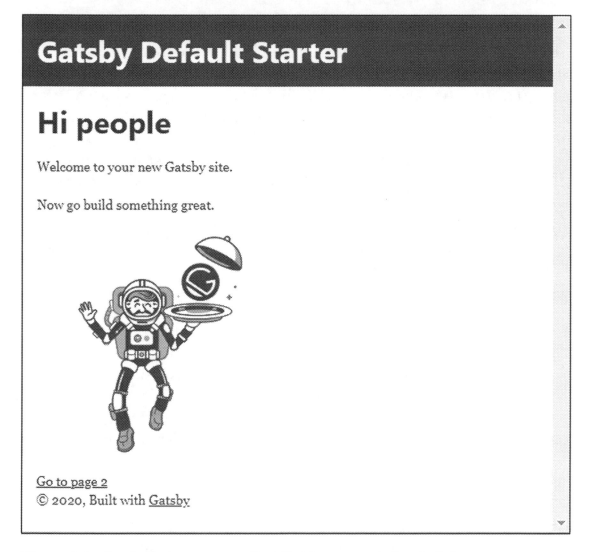

Figure 3-1. *Say hello to your very first Gatsby-generated website!*

Go ahead, click the "Go to page 2" link there, and see that it really is an actual, working (albeit very simple) website. This particular site uses what's called the Gatsby Default Starter. This provides all the necessary plumbing you are likely to need, and it's a good starting point if you are intent on mostly developing your website from scratch.

Now, let's take a look at what was actually produced, at least at a high level to start with.

Note   The code for this project is not included in the source code bundle for this book because I'm expecting that you are going to generate it yourself. That is, after all, the whole point of this section, to make sure you have the tools installed and working that you'll need to use Gatsby, and generating this project is the final check.

Gatsby Project Structure

Gatsby projects have a well-defined structure, and if you take a look at the project you just generated, you'll see that structure. In detail, and at a high level, those elements, in the form of directories and files, are as follows:

- **/.cache** – This is a directory where Gatsby itself keeps internal data that is cached during its work for speed. You are not intended to edit anything here, and you shouldn't check it into source control.

- **/.git** – This is your Git configuration directory and is controlled by Git itself, not Gatsby.

- **/node_modules** – This is where all the packages installed by NPM are stored. This is controlled by NPM and shouldn't be checked into source control (a developer cloning and building your project for the first time would see this directory automatically generated).

- **/public** – This is where the output of the build process goes and is where the content that is served when you start the development server. You should virtually never edit anything here directly.

- **/src** – This directory is where the source of your website goes. Under it, you will find some subdirectories. First will be a `components` directory. This is where you'll find React component definitions. There will also be an `images` directory, and I'll give you just one guess what's in that one! Finally, you'll have a `pages` directory, and the files here will automatically become pages in your website, and the paths to them will be based on their filenames.

- **gatsby-browser.js** – This file contains configuration for usages of the Gatsby browser API, which can be used to customize or extends default Gatsby settings that affect web browsers in some way.

- **gatsby-config.js** – This is the primary Gatsby configuration file and certainly the one you'll deal with the most (it may be the *only* one you ever deal with). Here, you can specify metadata about your website such as site title and description, what plugins you want Gatsby to use, and so on.

- **gatsby-node.js** – This configuration file deals with usages of the Gatsby Node API, which allows you to tailor the build process to your needs (Gatsby uses Node in at least parts of the build process).

- **gatsby-ssr.js** – The Gatsby Server-Side Rendering API can be incorporated if you need to use Server-Side Rendering, and this configuration file is how you control that.

- **package.json** – This is an NPM/Node configuration file that contains information about your project that NPM and Node need to work. The most important thing here is the list of NPM packages that your project depends on.

- **package-lock.json** – This is a file used internally by NPM to manage your dependencies, and as such, you should not touch it.

In addition to the described directories and files, which should always be present, others may be present too, depending on the starter you use and your needs:

- **/plugins** – You may sometimes need to have plugins that are local to your machine and not hosted as an NPM package. If that should happen, this directory will be present and will contain those plugins.

- **.gitignore** – This is the standard file where you can specify files and directories that Git should ignore.

- **.prettierrc** – Some starters use the Prettier tool to make their source code looks good. This configuration file controls that, if so.

- **.prettierignore** – Like .gitignore, if you have files you don't want Prettier to mess with, then you can specify them here.

- **LICENSE** – This is a standard license file that most GitHub repositories contain.

- **README.md** – Like license, this is a standard file often found in Git repositories and is intended to describe your repository and project (this is what you see on GitHub below the repository contents).

Any other structure is pretty much up to you, with some caveats that you'll learn about later that result from some of the built-in functionality that Gatsby provides for navigation and other things, and from the use of React.

Starters

A starter is perhaps the most fundamental concept in Gatsby, and it's a simple one: it's a boilerplate website that Gatsby copies and customizes (along with you, obviously!) to make your website. That's really all there is to it!

Gatsby offers official starters for a variety of types of websites, including things like blogs, simple "hello, world" websites, and more. In addition, the Gatsby community offers a whole host of other starters, and you can always make your own too.

Starters get installed with the `gatsby new` command that you saw earlier. You simply append the URL of the starter's Git repo to the end of it (or don't, in which case the default starter is used, as you saw before).

For example, if you want to create a blog, you might use the gatsby-starter-blog starter:

```
gatsby new blog https://github.com/gatsbyjs/gatsby-starter-blog
```

In short, that command clones a Git site from somewhere, installs all the dependencies it specifies, and starts you with a clear Git history. Your project is in no way connected to the source Git repo, it is completed stand-alone ("ejected," in Gatsby parlance) and ready for you to do whatever you like with it, like pushing it to your own GitHub account, for example.

Plugins

As mentioned earlier, plugins allow you to extend Gatsby in many different ways. They are JavaScript packages that implement the Gatsby plugin API, and they roughly break down into three types:

- **Functional** – These plugins, in some way, extend what Gatsby can do fundamentally. For example, `gatsby-plugin-react-helmet` is a plugin that provides drop-in support for server rendering data added with React Helmet (where React Helmet is a component which lets you control your document head using their React component – we won't be using this in this book, but it's a good example of a functional plugin).

- **Source** – When a Gatsby project is built, part of the process is building up a series of File nodes, one per file in the project. A source plugin is responsible for creating these, which then allows the files to be manipulated by transformer plugins. The `gatsby-source-filesystem` plugin is an example of this, a plugin that uses files on the local file system that the project is in for creating File nodes.

- **Transformer** – As mentioned earlier, the data that is merged into templates can come from many sources, and it is transformer plugins that are used to convert that source data into a form Gatsby can use. An example is the `gatsby-transformer-remark` plugin. This is a plugin that knows how to take in Markdown File nodes produced from Markdown files processed by a Source plugin and converts it to MarkdownRemark, a form Gatsby can handle internally.

Plugins open up a world of possibilities to the Gatsby developer and allow you to do a great deal with little more than some JSON configuration files. Plugins are installed with NPM and configured in the standard Gatsby configuration files.

Note   This is probably as good a time as any to mention that this whole chapter is a very quick look at Gatsby only, and it's not meant to be a deep dive into it. As we build some projects, you will, of course, start to see a lot of this put into practice, and I'll expand on things as needed. But, I definitely won't be touching on everything Gatsby can do – you'd need a whole book for that all by itself – but my goal is to give you a sold big picture of it and then give you some hands-on experience that can be a good foundation for what you do going forward.

Themes

Themes in the context of Gatsby are a special type of plugin that adds various types of preconfigured functionality and data sourcing, and/or UI code to a website. It does this by having its own `gatsby-config.js` file and is effectively a subproject, so to speak, as a result.

Because themes are plugins and are based on JavaScript, that means that they can be packaged and distributed using tools like NPM or Yarn and hosted on sites like GitHub. As a result, you can also manage the version of a theme in use through the standard package.json file. That way, it becomes a snap to update your theme if and when you want to (or, let NPM do it automatically by specifying a version in package.json that always gets the latest available when dependencies are installed).

The benefit of a theme is that it abstracts out of your own code default configuration and shared functionality into a sharable package. This becomes a big benefit if you are creating multiple websites. Imagine doing so and basing them all on the same starter. When you do this, your websites are no longer "connected" to the starter. They are considered "ejected," meaning that if the starter is changed, that change won't flow down into your projects. You would need to update each site individually.

However, if your websites use a theme, then that theme can be changed, and then that change filtered down into all the websites just by updating its dependencies. The theme will be updated (since, remember, it's just a packaged dependency like any other), and you'll be all set.

You can either use themes provided by others or build your own, just like starters and templates.

You might be scratching your head a little bit wondering what the difference between starters, plugins, and themes is. They are all clearly similar and related ideas. The key difference is how they are intended to be used. Starters are meant to be a starting point for a website, and both themes and plugins are installed into a website created from a starter. Themes are intended to be responsible for some particular part of a website, maybe an about page, or a header, or something like that (or multiple pieces at once). Plugins are intended to effectively extend Gatsby in some way.

In theory, you could construct an entire website from plugins alone, or from themes alone (remember that themes are plugins at the end of the day). And, a starter could consist of nothing but themes and/or plugins. That probably wouldn't be a pleasant experience and wouldn't fit with what each of these things is intended for, but it would be doable.

The Gatsby Build Process

At a high level, Gatsby takes source files, "builds" them in some way, and produces the static HTML files we're ultimately after. It can do this in two fundamental modes: development and build mode. You've already seen the development mode: the `gatsby develop` command does that. When your site is ready for a real deployment, you can execute `gatsby build` to get the final artifacts. This will perform various optimizations and cleanups, all to get your code into a final, "gold" state, ready to deploy.

When you run in development mode, previous HTML and CSS files aren't deleted, which speeds things up. Then, at the end of the process (which is called the "bootstrap phase"), Gatsby starts up the development server with your updated assets in it.

In build mode though, after the same bootstrap phase – which this time *does* include deleting your previously build files – instead of starting that server, it instead kicks off some Webpack tasks.

If you aren't familiar with Webpack, let me give you a (very) brief introduction to it (keeping in mind that most of its inner workings are hidden from you behind Gatsby, so you don't need to be a Webpack expert, but I think a little context doesn't hurt).

A Brief Introduction to Webpack

In the good old days of web development, things were simple. You created a directory, maybe some subdirectories, if you were a bit more organized. Into it, you poured all your resources: a stylesheet or two here, a sprinkling of images, some HTML files, and a heaping helping of JavaScript files. Then, a single HTML file served as your entry point, and it would go out and load, by way of script tag references, to load all your JavaScript files, as well as your CSS files and images.

Now, at a fundamental level, that's precisely still how things work technically, but over time the picture has gotten... messier. Developers will frequently make use of a large number of smaller, more focused libraries and toolkits. What we build is orders of magnitude more complex with far more moving parts, things you need to include.

Of course, people have realized that this isn't efficient. Each networked request is a new connection to the server, and many of those requests must occur serially, so nothing happens until the resources are loaded (and processed in some way). And worse, what if a script file is loaded at the start that isn't needed until the user performs some specific action? What if they never perform that action? You've just wasted a bunch of time and bandwidth and maybe slowed the whole site down for something that you didn't wind up even needing!

And that's before we even talk about how you have to self-organize the code! Think of things like ensuring scripts are loaded in the proper order, and that everything that one script depends on is both included and loaded before it's used and that code that references other code can find one another at runtime.

And all *that* is before we talk about newer JavaScript tricks like modules, the problem of cross-browser development, and the desire to use more modern coding techniques while still supporting older browsers (to a point at least), not to mention ensuring your website is optimized.

As this evolution has occurred, before long even, developers were looking for a way out of this mess. That's when the notion of bundles was born.

In simplest terms, a bundle is a conglomeration of various resources that a web page needs to function. The obvious component of a bundle is JavaScript, but in some cases, it also includes CSS and even images, encoded for use in data URLs (if you aren't familiar with the concept, that's where an image, or other files, is Base64-encoded and included as a string as the source, most commonly, of an `<img>` tag using the data: prefix). A bundle most frequently is a single file, though no rule says it must be (well, I would argue that a bundle is always a single file, and if you have multiple files, then you, in fact, have multiple bundles – but either way the basic concept is the same). The benefit of a bundle is that it is, usually, just a single request across the network, plus the fact that when creating a bundle, you can layer on other optimizations like code minification and compression and such.

How does one create a bundle? Well, at the most fundamental level, you could do it manually by merely concatenating all your JavaScript files together into one. Do that, and you've got yourself a bundle! But, in that case, it's a bundle of only JavaScript, no other resources like CSS or images, and perhaps, more importantly, is that when you do that, you have to take on responsibility for ensuring everything is in the right order and that there are no conflicts. IIFEs, or Immediately Invoked Function Expressions, are a way to solve these problems. If each thing you concatenate is inside an IIFE, then there are no worries (well, mostly at least) about scope collisions. Plus, that way, the order no longer matters. The problem with this solution, though, is that any time a single file changes, you have to rebundle everything.

Plus, it becomes difficult to determine if things are being included that are no longer necessary (the term "tree shaking" refers to determining when an included dependency is not actually being used, and that's more difficult in this approach than what Webpack does, as you'll see). Aside from that, there is also sometimes code that shouldn't be in the bundle for other reasons, maybe because it's only for development or because it's only needed in specific versions of the page. Then, you'll probably need to create some sort of simple tooling (maybe just some shell scripts) to exclude things that aren't necessary (and consider if you use a library like, say, React: what if there are parts of the library you don't use? It would be nice if you could leave those out and make the bundle smaller, thereby improving load performance, wouldn't it?).

Further, when thinking of JavaScript, wouldn't it be nice if you could use modules to organize your code and know it would work across all browsers? That's not the case today: not all browser versions support them, and those that do have some variances to deal with. If you could organize your code with modules and not have to worry about your code working across all browsers, you'd have the best of all possible worlds, right?

For all these reasons, a good tool that can do bundling intelligently is a must, and that's where Webpack comes in.

Webpack isn't the only bundler out there, but it has quickly become the de facto standard and is, by probably most web developers, considered the best. Although it used to have a reputation for not being exceptionally easy to work with, that has changed with the latest version.

Webpack can do a lot more than merely bundling code, though. For example, it can transpile TypeScript and even knows how to work with React, and it's unique `.tsx` files. So, in the end, Webpack can be more than a bundler; it can be a right and proper and full-featured build tool for your web applications. Most of this is optional and can be added on as you need it, so at the start, Webpack is rather simple, but it is highly extensible so can meet your needs every step of the way.

Gatsby uses Webpack behind the scenes to do all of this when you do a build (not a development build). It creates a bundle that has been optimized and made "production-ready." You don't need to do anything special, Gatsby knows how to use Webpack on your behalf, so you don't even have to configure it yourself (though the gatsby-node.js file does give you a mechanism to do so if you have special needs).

That, very briefly, is what Webpack is all about.

Breaking Down the Code

Now that you have some idea about how Gatsby builds your website and how it's structured, let's look at the code that was generated for us and see what makes this website tick!

The Main Gatsby Configuration File

When you generated the simple website earlier from the default starter, you got a
gatsby-config.js file in the process. This is the main Gatsby configuration file that
you'll interact with most. Let's take a quick look at what was generated:

```
module.exports = {
  siteMetadata: {
    title: `Gatsby Default Starter`,
    description: `Kick off your next, great Gatsby project
      with this default starter. This barebones starter ships
      with the main Gatsby configuration files you
      might need.`,
    author: `@gatsbyjs`,
  },
  plugins: [
    `gatsby-plugin-react-helmet`,
    {
      resolve: `gatsby-source-filesystem`,
      options: {
        name: `images`,
        path: `${__dirname}/src/images`,
      },
    },
    `gatsby-transformer-sharp`,
    `gatsby-plugin-sharp`,
    {
      resolve: `gatsby-plugin-manifest`,
      options: {
        name: `gatsby-starter-default`,
        short_name: `starter`,
        start_url: `/`,
        background_color: `#663399`,
        theme_color: `#663399`,
        display: `minimal-ui`,
        icon: `src/images/gatsby-icon.png`,
```

```
        },
      },
    ],
}
```

As you can see, it's just a chunk of JSON (JavaScript Object Notation) that defines an ES6 module, which hopefully is familiar to you. You can see two main branches here: the `siteMetadata` branch and the `plugins` branch. The siteMetadata branch contains common pieces of data that will be used throughout your website. You'll see how this is used very soon. The `plugins` branch is where the plugins Gatsby requires to build your website are specified. Some plugins, like gatsby-transformer-sharp (which is responsible for creating nodes from image types that are supported by the Sharp image processing library) and gatsby-plugin-sharp (which exposes several image processing functions provided by the Sharp image processing library), don't require any configuration details. Others, like gatsby-plugin-react-helmet, require configuration details and so have an `options` element associated with it.

Note   I'd say the meaning of these options is probably fairly obvious based just on their names, but the bottom line is that for any plugin you may need to configure, you'll need to consult the Gatsby documentation. Those can be found here: `https://www.gatsbyjs.org/docs`. One of the things you'll find there is the plugin library, and there each of the official plugins is detailed, including its configuration options.

Other branches you can see include the following:

- **pathPrefix** – Sites sometimes aren't hosted at the root of a domain, and in those cases, you may need a prefix on the URLs. This branch allows you to specify those.

- **polyfill** – Gatsby code uses ES6 Promises. However, not all browsers support that. You can, therefore, provide your own polyfill for it by setting this to false and providing the polyfill elsewhere.

- **proxy** – This allows you to configure the development server to proxy unknown requests to your specified server.

- **developMiddleware** – This is associated with usage of the proxy branch and allows you to configure Express middleware. The development server is a Node web server built using the popular Express library. That library offers the notion of middleware, which is basically little bits of code that can execute as part of the request servicing pipeline to do various things like parsing the request for JSON data, or log the request, and so on. This branch lets you set that up, if needed.

- **mapping** – As part of Gatsby building your site, nodes are created to represent files and other important pieces of information. You may sometimes need to manipulate the mappings between the various node types, and this branch allows you to do that.

Of all of these, I would say that `siteMetadata` and `plugins` are far and away the ones you're most likely to be concerned with. You may never need the others at all, but at least you have an idea of what can go in this configuration file, and if you have more advanced needs, you'll have some notion of what to look for in the Gatsby documentation (which, by the way, can be found here: `www.gatsbyjs.org/docs`).

Note   The gatsby-browser.json, gatsby-node.js, and gatsby-src.json configuration files are by default devoid of any actual content with this starter, so we'll skip them here. We may come back to them as we build some projects later, but by and large, it's the gatsby-config.json file that will matter to you 99% of the time, and you may never need to touch the others at all.

---

index.js

The first actual source file we're going to look at, found in the `src/pages` directory, is the main entry point for our website: `index.js`. All Gatsby sites start in this same place. It may look odd to start with a JavaScript file and not an HTML file, but that's because Gatsby sites are built with React.

If you aren't familiar with React, don't worry, we're going to cover it in some depth in the next chapter. But, as a very brief introduction, React is a JavaScript library for building UIs. At the heart of React is the notion of *components*. Components are chunks of JavaScript that spit out HTML (and CSS and its own JavaScript). Put a bunch of components together, and, at runtime, you will wind up with a whole HTML document that is your UI.

What this means in practice is that you write something like:

```
<MaterialButton color="red"
  onClick={() => alert("clicked");}>Click Me</MaterialButton>
```

That `<MaterialButton>` element is a React component. It's just a tag like any other HTML or XML tag, but one that React recognizes (yes, you can have plain old HTML tags mixed in when building with React as well, and this is quite typical). It has two properties, or just props for short: `color` and `onClick`, for defining its color and what to do when it's clicked, respectively. At build time, this will get translated into something like:

```
React.createElement(
  MaterialButton,
  { color : "red",
    onClick : function() { alert('clicked'); }
  },
  "Click Me"
);
```

And then, at runtime (or at build time, when donig a final Gatsby build execution), this code will execute, and React will produce the appropriate HTML/CSS/JavaScript in place of that `<MaterialButton>` tag that makes a button appear, with the specified styling, and makes it do something when you click it.

Now, a button may not seem like a big deal since that's easy to do in plain old HTML. But, imagine you want something more complex, like a grid. Building that yourself can be tricky. With React, though, it might be as simple as putting `<Grid>` in your code, and you'll have a fancy grid on your page when you load it.

Now, if you're paying attention, you may be thinking, "Wait, how can I put something like `<MaterialButton>` in a JavaScript file? That's not JavaScript, that's HTML!" And, you'd be right to think that! That's because in the context of Gatsby, when you see a `.js` file in the `src/pages` directory (which, remember, is where `index.js` is), what you're actually looking at is something called JSX, which stands for JavaScript XML. This is a special language created for React that lets you effectively embed HTML in JavaScript. I know, that sounds weird when you first encounter it, but what it means is that you can write `<MaterialButton>` instead of calling methods of React directly, like `React.createElement()`, which is the key method that React exposes to create any component. To be sure, you can create a React UI with nothing but JavaScript calls, but that becomes a burden quickly, and so JSX was born.

Now that you have some context, let's get to that `index.js` file, which you now know is actually JSX:

```
import React from "react"
```

First things first: things are not going to work without React being present, so it is imported. We're dealing with ES6 modules here, which makes it very nice, as opposed to explicitly `<script>` tags in an HTML document.

```
import { Link } from "gatsby"
```

Next, we import a React component that Gatsby itself provides: the Link component. As the name implies, this is used for creating links between the pages of your site. You'll see it used shortly.

```
import Layout from "../components/layout"
import Image from "../components/image"
import SEO from "../components/seo"
```

Next, we see three components that are supplied by the application itself imported. Application-level components live in the `/src/components` directory. The `Layout` component is a component that is the parent of all others and represents the main layout of the site. With React, everything is a component that lives in a tree structure, which means that there must be some component that is the parent of all others. That's what the Layout component is. The `Image` component is for producing the Gatsby astronaut image you see on the page. This component takes care of lazy-loading optimized and reduced-size images. Finally, the `SEO` component is responsible for allowing you to embed additional information in the `<head>` of the document via *meta tags* to help with search engine optimization (SEO) and providing additional data to people when your site is shared on social media and other usage cases.

We will look at the code for all these components shortly, but before we do, there's more to this `index.js` file to see:

```
const IndexPage = () => (
  <Layout>
    <SEO title="Home" />
    <h1>Hi people</h1>
    <p>Welcome to your new Gatsby site.</p>
    <p>Now go build something great.</p>
    <div style={{
      maxWidth: `300px`, marginBottom: `1.45rem`
    }}>
      <Image />
    </div>
    <Link to="/page-2/">Go to page 2</Link>
  </Layout>
)

export default IndexPage
```

First, keep in mind that what you see here is an ES6 module. That's what this code is creating. As such, at the very end, something has to be exported. What's being exported here is a React component. The line

```
Const IndexPage = () => (
```

is what's called the functional approach to creating React components. Without getting too far into React, since that's what the next chapter is for, every React component must ultimately provide at minimum a `render()` method. This method must always return a React component (well, not *always* – but as I said, see the next chapter!). Here, it's returning a `Layout` component – which, hey, you saw that imported! That's the top-level component I mentioned. But, Components can have children, and here there's a bunch: an `SEO` component, a plain old HTML `<h1>` element, two `<p>` elements, a `<div>` element, an `Image` component, and a `Link` component.

The `Link` component is one Gatsby provides and is actually a lot more powerful than it at first seems. It replaces the standard HTML `<a>` tag and allows you to link to internal pages of your website easily. In fact, it is *only* for internal pages! You should not use `Link` for links to other sites (it actually won't work if you try – you should use the normal `<a>`

element for off-site links). Critically, it includes a preloading mechanism that fetches the resources for the target page even before the user clicks the link, boosting performance significantly.

The to prop specifies the name of the page you want the Link to go to, and by default, it assumes it is a React component defined in a file named XXX.js where XXX is the value of the to prop, in the src/pages directory. This is a little weird because the default starter uses a value of /page-2/. However, what's going on becomes clear if you change the to value to simply page-2. It will still work because Gatsby knows that your component is defined in the file page-2.js in src/pages automatically. The slashes, on both ends, are optional (if you have subdirectories under src/pages, then you would need to use their names and appropriate slashes to reference them).

There's also that SEO component, which takes care of embedding that information I described earlier into the <head> of the page, but that produces no visual output, so we can kind of ignore it for our purposes here and now.

Now, if you look at that code and then compare it to the screenshot from earlier, it should start to make some sense. Most of the text you see in the screenshot is here, and you can see how the Image component is replaced with the actual image at runtime, and you can see that a hyperlink was generated by the Link component. That demonstrates that React is, in fact, generating markup and backing CSS and code for the components specified in the source files.

The only things missing are the header on the page and the copyright footer. It turns out those are produced as part of the Layout component, and that's where we're headed next.

layout.js

The Layout component is contained in the aptly named layout.js file, and it begins with some imports:

```
import React from "react"
import PropTypes from "prop-types"
import { useStaticQuery, graphql } from "gatsby"
import Header from "./header"
import "./layout.css"
```

Once again, we know we need React, no surprise there. PropTypes is a supporting component of React that allows you to specify the types of props of your components. For example, if the color prop on the MaterialButton you saw earlier is supposed to only accept a number from one to nine, you can use PropTypes to define that so that rather than just blowing up in some unexpected way, you'll get more useful debug information from React at runtime. Using PropTypes is always optional, but it is generally good form to do so.

The useStaticQuery and graphql imports are provided by Gatsby and are the gateway into its data access layer using GraphQL. I'm going to get into that later on in this chapter, but for now, it's sufficient to know that it allows you to write queries to get data from various sources (the gatsby-config.json file in the case of this component) and expose that data to your JavaScript code.

Finally, the Header component is imported, along with its stylesheet. It may seem kind of weird that you can import a stylesheet just like you do a JavaScript file (well, JSX file actually, as you know!), but that's the magic of Webpack underneath, allowing you to treat them the same.

Next, we see the Layout component definition begun:

```
const Layout = ({ children }) => {
```

Recall that the Layout component has a bunch of components and elements underneath it in the index.js code. Those need to be passed into this component to do its thing, hence the children argument.

Next up, we get the data that is needed:

```
  const data = useStaticQuery(graphql`
    query SiteTitleQuery {
      site {
        siteMetadata {
          title
        }
      }
    }
  `)
```

As I mentioned, we'll get into GraphQL shortly, but I'd bet this is pretty self-explanatory. Gatsby's data layer knows that `site` refers to the `gatsby-config.json` file (since that's the file that defines your site!). From there, it's really just a matter of constructing a tree to get to the data we want, in this case, that `siteMetadata` element and then the `title` element within it. This is all retrieved and stored as a JavaScript object referenced by the `data` variable, which we can use later, as you'll see.

When we construct a React component in the functional way like this, the content inside the outer parenthesis is taken to be the `render()` method. Hence, everything you write is implicitly returned. That's the case in `index.js`. However, here, because we needed to do that query first, we have to now explicitly `return`, and that's what we see next:

```
return (
    <>
    <Header siteTitle={data.site.siteMetadata.title} />
    <div
      style={{
        margin: `0 auto`,
        maxWidth: 960,
        padding: `0 1.0875rem 1.45rem`,
      }}
    >
      <main>{children}</main>
      <footer>
        © {new Date().getFullYear()}, Built with
        {` `}
        <a href="https://www.gatsbyjs.org">Gatsby</a>
      </footer>
    </div>
  )
}
```

Remember that the render() method must always return a single React component (or HTML element, or a few other possible things). Well, that's a problem here because the Header component and the <div> element that follows are sibling – the <div> is not a child of the Header. This normally isn't allowed since there wouldn't be a single thing being returned. One way to solve this problem is with React fragments. This allows you to return multiple things from render() without having to add extra nodes to the DOM, which is what happens any time a component has a child. The <> denotes a fragment. Inside it, we have the Header and the <div>, at the same level (and the <div> has a <main> element and a Footer component inside of it, but that's kind of irrelevant in terms of the fragment), just like we want.

Now, for the Header, you can see where the data fetched by that query is used now, and if you look at the gatsby-config.json file, you'll see that the text inserted there is exactly what you see in the screenshot. This, in simplest terms, is how the Gatsby data layer works (whether the data comes from gatsby-config.json like this, or maybe from Markdown files, or any other source Gatsby supports, it's all used in the same basic way).

You can see here how the children argument is inserted, wholesale, into the <main> element, and so becomes part of the fragment returned. Remember that children is everything from index.js, since it's all nested inside the Layout element and so is passed into its render() method automatically.

Now, too, you can see where the copyright footer comes from. At this point, you should be able to mentally put the pieces together in your mind and relate the earlier screenshot to this code.

All that's left in this code is the use of PropTypes, which is used by attaching a propTypes property to the Layout object:

```
Layout.propTypes = {
  children: PropTypes.node.isRequired,
}
```

This simply says that the children prop of the Layout component is required. Give this a shot: go into index.js and delete everything inside the <Layout></Layout> block and reload the page (which should happen automatically, in fact – how awesome is that?!). Look in your browser's developer tools console, and you should see an error "Warning: Failed prop type: The prop 'children' is marked as required in 'Layout', but is value is 'undefined.'" Now, if you put the content back and instead delete this block from Layout.js so that there are no PropTypes defined for children, you'll find that the error displayed is quite unhelpful, certainly far less so than that very explicitly error message. That's the benefit of PropTypes!

Finally, the Layout component is exported, as we know a module must:

```
export default Layout
```

And that wraps up the code for this component. There's more interesting stuff to look at, like the Header component, which is where we're headed next.

Note   There is also a layout.css file associated with this component. However, there really isn't anything special in it; it's just a lot of plain old CSS. And, the majority of it isn't used by default and is just there in case you need it. As such, and because it really is quite long, I'm going to leave that as something for you to investigate on your own. I don't think you'll find any surprises there though, that's the key point.

---

header.js

Next up is the Header component, which you know displays the big "Gatsby Default Starter" text with the purplish background at the top of the page.

```
import { Link } from "gatsby"
import PropTypes from "prop-types"
import React from "react"
```

First up is the usual suspects in terms of imports. Let's move on quickly since you've seen this enough by now. After that is the render() method:

```
const Header = ({ siteTitle }) => (
  <header
    style={{
      background: `rebeccapurple`,
      marginBottom: `1.45rem`,
    }}
  >
    <div
      style={{
        margin: `0 auto`,
        maxWidth: 960,
```

```
      padding: `1.45rem 1.0875rem`,
    }}
  >
    <h1 style={{ margin: 0 }}>
      <Link
        to="/"
        style={{
          color: `white`,
          textDecoration: `none`,
        }}
      >
        {siteTitle}
      </Link>
    </h1>
  </div>
</header>
)
```

Remember that in the Layout component, the site title that was queried with GraphQL from the gatsby-config.json file was passed into this component via its siteTitle prop, and so you can see it passed into the method here. An HTML <header> element is what is returned (which is another thing that can be returned from the render() method). The markup is relatively straightforward within it: a <div> inside it, with an <h1> within that, and a Link component inside that so that the user can click that text to return to the home page (the to value for the Link being just a forward slash accomplishes that since Gatsby knows what the home page is: it's always index.js). The text of the link is the siteTitle that was passed in.

By the way, I haven't said this before, but here's another quick preview of a React concept: any time you see {something}, that's an expression. This can be any valid JavaScript expression, the name of a variable fitting the bill. React will interpret the expression at runtime and insert the result in place of this token. That's how siteTitle is inserted, as well as how the styles are applied to the various elements. But, for those, the expression being evaluated is a JavaScript object, which is itself always in the form {stuff}, so that's why we have to have {{stuff}} – the outer braces demarcate the expression and the inner ones the JavaScript object. But again, don't get hung up on this yet, the next chapter will go into it all.

After that, we have some PropTypes to define:

```
Header.propTypes = {
  siteTitle: PropTypes.string,
}
Header.defaultProps = {
  siteTitle: ``,
}
```

This is defining two things, firstly that setTitle must be a string and then that siteTitle will be an empty string if not supplied (not that it's not marked required like children in the Layout component was).

After that, we just have our export:

```
export default Header
```

And that's one more component in the books!

The next component we need to look at is image.js, and it begins, as always, with some imports:

```
import React from "react"
import { useStaticQuery, graphql } from "gatsby"
import Img from "gatsby-image"
```

You know what React is all about, and this component needs some GraphQL, so we need to import that, as well as useStaticQuery to go along with it. This component makes use of the Img component from the gatsby-image module as well.

```
const Image = () => {
  const data = useStaticQuery(graphql`
    query {
      placeholderImage: file(relativePath: {
        eq: "gatsby-astronaut.png"
      }) {
        childImageSharp {
          fluid(maxWidth: 300) {
            ...GatsbyImageSharpFluid
          }
        }
```

```
      }
    }
  `)

  return <Img
    fluid={data.placeholderImage.childImageSharp.fluid} />
}

export default Image
```

The basic idea here, in the end, is to return an Img component. But, the image will be a child of a fluid container, meaning one that can stretch with the width of the browser window, so we want the image to be fluid as well. To accomplish this, we first write a GraphQL query to get a reference to the gatsby-astronaut.png image. But, wait a minute! How does Gatsby know where the image is? How does it know it's in the images subdirectory? Well, this line in the query

```
file(relativePath: { eq: "gatsby-astronaut.png"})
```

seems to be saying look for a while with a filename equal to (eq) gatsby-astronaut.png and return it as the value of the placeholderImage property in the query results (again, all of this will make more sense when we look at GraphQL just a few pages from now). That is indeed what it means. But what is relativePath, and what is it relative to? It goes back to the gatsby-config.file, and the gatsby-source-filesystem plugin defined there:

```
{ resolve: `gatsby-source-filesystem`,
  options: {
    name: `images`,
    path: `${__dirname}/src/images`,
  },
}
```

This plugin can find files on the local file system at build time. Notice the path property there? That's the answer. We're providing the path there, and from that point on, all references to local files using this plugin, which is done with the file() call – that's what it winds up being in the query – look up the filename specified relative to that directory.

The `childImageSharp` part of the query makes use of the `gatsby-transformer-sharp` and `gatsby-plugin-sharp` plugins. These are plugins for manipulating images. Here, the `maxWidth` option tells these plugins that the maximum width of the image should be 300 pixels. What happens is those plugins will generate some number of images, based on screen width breakpoints, so ensure the image appears best at all resolutions. The appropriate image will be selected at runtime and will be the value of the fluid element in the query results. This is then used when constructing the `Img` component, and the result is that an appropriately sized image will be used displayed depending on the width of the browser viewport, up to a maximum width of 300 pixels.

While this particular starter sets up the code in this component to be specific to this image file, it's more typical to set it up so that it can render any image, and then use a prop on the `<Image>` tag to specify the filename. That, plus a whole lot more configuration options, makes this one of the more powerful components Gatsby offers. Here's the documentation page that dives into all the details, since covering it all here would take up a lot of space (and can differ depending on which starter you use – remember, the default starter is meant to be just about as simple as can be, not necessarily set up with maximum flexibility): `www.gatsbyjs.org/tutorial/gatsby-image-tutorial/#relative-image-paths-and-gatsby-configjs`.

seo.js

The next component up on the hit parade of components is the SEO component:

```
import React from "react"
import PropTypes from "prop-types"
import { Helmet } from "react-helmet"
import { useStaticQuery, graphql } from "gatsby"
```

Yep, all the same imports you're used to, plus a new one: `Helmet`. This is a React component for working with the `<head>` of the HTML document (head… helmet… get it?!) that React will construct at runtime, to create meta tags in it in this case. Note that we aren't concerned here with learning every last detail of some of these components, we're just looking to get the bigger picture. Some of the details will be seen in more depth later, but some just aren't especially relevant to your work except in very specific circumstances. Here, knowing all the details of the `Helmet` component isn't necessary to use the SEO component.

```
function SEO({ description, lang, meta, title }) {
  const { site } = useStaticQuery(
    graphql`
      query {
        site {
          siteMetadata {
            title
            description
            author
          }
        }
      }
    `
  )
```

This component begins with a GraphQL query that gets some data out of the gatsby-config.json file, specifically the title, description, and author properties of the siteMetadata element. Hopefully, by now, even before we're delved into GraphQL in detail, you're starting to get a sense of how these queries work, which was precisely my goal.

Next, a metaDescription variable is defined:

```
const metaDescription = description ||
  site.siteMetadata.description
```

As you can see, this allows us to either pass a description into this component, or else it will use the description retrieved by the query, whichever is present (preferring the value passed in if they're both present thanks to the || operator).

Next comes the value returned by the implicit render() method:

```
return (
  <Helmet
    htmlAttributes={{ lang }}
    title={title}
    titleTemplate={`%s | ${site.siteMetadata.title}`}
    meta={[
      { name: `description`, content: metaDescription },
```

```
      { property: `og:title`, content: title },
      { property: `og:description`,
        content: metaDescription
      },
      { property: `og:type`, content: `website` },
      { name: `twitter:card`, content: `summary` },
      { name: `twitter:creator`,
        content: site.siteMetadata.author,
      },
      { name: `twitter:title`, content: title },
      { name: `twitter:description`,
        content: metaDescription,
      },
    ].concat(meta)}
   />
  )
}
```

As you can see, it's just a Helmet component, supplied by React. The meta prop
defines the meta tags to create. The values of these come from the query results, or the
props passed into this component, and that metaDescription variable that was defined
earlier.

After that, we have some PropTypes to define:

```
SEO.defaultProps = { lang: `en`, meta: [], description: `` }
```

First, default values for props not supplied are defined. After that, the expected types
are described:

```
SEO.propTypes = {
  description: PropTypes.string,
  lang: PropTypes.string,
  meta: PropTypes.arrayOf(PropTypes.object),
  title: PropTypes.string.isRequired,
}
```

The `meta` prop one is interesting. It's telling us that prop is expected to be an array of objects. Did you notice the `concat(meta)` at the end of the expression that is the value of the `meta` prop for the `Helmet` component? That value is an array, and each element in the array is an object, one for each meta tag to create. There are some statically defined tags there, but this component also allows us to pass in one or more objects via the `meta` prop too, and those just get appended onto that array. In this way, we can create arbitrary meta tags when the `SEO` component is used without modifying the code in this file.

Finally, as always, the component is exported:

```
export default SEO
```

And that wraps up another component. Now, we just have two more pages to look at (which are themselves components, of course).

page-2.js

When you click the link to go to page 2, you land on a page produced by the React component found in the `src/pages/page02.js` file:

```
import React from "react"
import { Link } from "gatsby"
import Layout from "../components/layout"
import SEO from "../components/seo"
```

First, we've got a set of imports that you know all about now. Then, a very simple component definition:

```
const SecondPage = () => (
  <Layout>
    <SEO title="Page two" />
    <h1>Hi from the second page</h1>
    <p>Welcome to page 2</p>
    <Link to="/">Go back to the homepage</Link>
  </Layout>
)

export default SecondPage
```

Well, that shouldn't hold any surprises at this point since it's really the same as index.js but even simpler! So, I'll assume you got this one, and we'll just finish off the code with another simple one: 404.js. But, before that, let's talk about one other thing first: TypeScript support.

using-typescript.tsx

One neat thing about Gatsby is that you can use TypeScript right out of the box, if you prefer that to JavaScript. To demonstrate this, but default, you'll find a page using-typescript.tsx has been created:

```
// If you don't want to use TypeScript, you can delete this file!
import React from "react"
import { PageProps, Link, graphql } from "gatsby"

import Layout from "../components/layout"
import SEO from "../components/seo"

type DataProps = {
  site: {
    buildTime: string
  }
}

const UsingTypescript: React.FC<PageProps<DataProps>> = ({ data, path }) => (
  <Layout>
    <SEO title="Using TypeScript" />
    <h1>Gatsby supports TypeScript by default!</h1>
    <p>This means that you can create and write <em>.ts/.tsx</em> files for
        your pages, components etc. Please note that the <em>gatsby-*.js</em>
        files (like gatsby-node.js) currently don't support TypeScript yet.</p>
    <p>For type checking you'll want to install <em>typescript</em> via npm
        and run <em>tsc --init</em> to create a <em>.tsconfig</em> file.</p>
    <p>You're currently on the page "{path}" which was built on {data.site.
        buildTime}.</p>
    <p>To learn more, head over to our <a href="https://www.gatsbyjs.org/
        docs/typescript/">documentation about TypeScript</a>.</p>
    <Link to="/">Go back to the homepage</Link>
  </Layout>
)
```

```
export default UsingTypescript

export const query = graphql`
  {
    site {
      buildTime(formatString: "YYYY-MM-DD hh:mm a z")
    }
  }
`
```

The .tsx extension denotes that this is a JSX page that uses TypeScript. Throughout this book, I will not be using TypeScript, but I wanted to point out that you can without doing anything in Gatsby. Just create the appropriate source files with the appropriate extensions and you're good to go with TypeScript.

404.js

Any good website provides an HTTP 404 error for when the client requests a nonexistent resource. Gatsby websites are no different, and that's where the 404.js file comes into play:

```
import React from "react"
import Layout from "../components/layout"
import SEO from "../components/seo"

const NotFoundPage = () => (
  <Layout>
    <SEO title="404: Not found" />
    <h1>NOT FOUND</h1>
    <p>You just hit a route that doesn&#39;t exist...
      the sadness.</p>
  </Layout>
)

export default NotFoundPage
```

Just like page-2.js, it's a straightforward component since there's not much to do in this situation but to show a cute message to try and assuage the hurt feelings of your user!

On That Funky GraphQL Stuff

Now, you've seen GraphQL in action a bunch of times so far, but I've been promising we'd get into it in more detail. I always keep my promises, so it's time to fulfill this particular one right now: it's time to meet GraphQL in full (more or less)!

GraphQL was created by Facebook – who also happens to have created React – as a method for loading data into React components. The idea is that the components should pull data into them, not have data pushed into them. A key consideration was that they should only pull what they actually need.

Consider a basic REST (Representational State Transfer) endpoint for getting a list of ship crewmembers from a famous starship (that won't be explicitly named due to copyright concerns!) and some data about them. It might look something like this:

```
https://starshipregistry.com/ncc-1701/crewmembers
```

If you make an HTTP GET request to that URL, it might return some data in the form of JSON like so:

```
{ crewmembers : [
  { id : 1234, name : "James Kirk",
    missions : 143, birthdate : "2233-03-22",
  },
  { id : 5678, name : "S'chn T'gai Spock",
    missions : 281, birthdate : "2230-01-06",
  }
] }
```

That's pretty straightforward. But, imagine that you're building a UI to display the ship's crew manifest, and image that there are a lot more crewmembers (that unnamed ship needs a large crew to run!). You just want to display their id and name. Further imagine that you don't care about the number of missions they've been on, or the date of their birth. But, using this endpoint means you're going to get that data regardless. Your code will simply throw that data into the 'ole bit bucket, wasting bandwidth, client, and server resources.

If you instead had a GraphQL endpoint, you could query for exactly what you need despite more being available. A similar GraphQL query might look like:

```
query getCrewmembers {
  crewmembers {
    id
    name
  }
}
```

When executed, what you'll get back would be

```
{
  crewmembers : [
    { id : 1234, name : "James Kirk },
    { id : 5678, name : "S'chn T'gai Spock" }
  ]
}
```

You only get back exactly what you request now – as signified by the definition of `crewmembers` in the query – which can be a lot more efficient when scaled up to many crewmembers. The caller is in control, so it gets exactly what it needs, no more, no less, regardless of what the server could provide.

To dissect the query a little bit, the word `query` is the query operation type. GraphQL defines several types (`query` for fetching data, `mutation` for operations that change data, and `subscription` for when you want the server to push data to the client). Still, Gatsby only uses the `query` type, and in fact, you can omit this word from your queries as a result. The word `getCrewmembers` is the operation name. You can give a query any name, and it's entirely for your own purposes, or you can omit it entirely, in which case the query is considered anonymous. The query fields follow that, and these are the data fields you want from the data. The word `crewmembers` here is a top-level, or root-level, field. As you can see, fields can have other fields nested within them, according to the data hierarchy you're querying.

GraphiQL

Before I go any further in discussing GraphQL, I need to make you aware of something: GraphiQL. Figure 3-2 shows what this is, but to put it in words, it's a graphical environment where you can execute GraphQL queries against the data of your website in real time without writing any code. It's a great way to test and experiment with queries to get them just right, and the best part is you get this automatically for free with Gatsby!

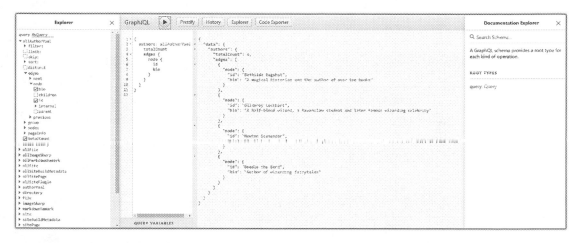

Figure 3-2. *Lights... camera... GraphiQL!*

Every Gatsby website you generate will include this capability by default. In fact, when you started up the simple website you generated earlier, it told you about it, and that it's available at the URL `http://localhost:8000/___graphql`.

On the left is the Explorer, which is a list of all the data available on your site. You can drill down into it, and as you do, you'll see queries appear to the right of that. You can hit the "play" button, the circle with the triangle in it, to execute your query. The results will be shown on the right. You'll also find documentation of the schema you're working with on the far right, and you can navigate that to find what you're interested in.

You can also, of course, enter a query entirely from scratch. Whether you start from the Explorer or just start typing, you'll get some basic IntelliSense along the way, highlighting error and helping you complete your query.

Finally, that Code Exporter button up top spits out ready-to-use JavaScript that you can plop into your site's code immediately and start using the query.

How sweet is that?

This is possible because as part of the Gatsby build process, Gatsby looks at all the files in your project, and all the data within them, and creates a data store from them. You are effectively looking at the data store in the GraphiQL Explorer on the left. Information from the `gatsby-config.json` is present under several branches of the tree. Also present will be any files you specifically tell Gatsby to read, as well as nodes for all the pages of the website. You are then able to query any data you need from this store using GraphQL, and GraphiQL lets you play with those capabilities without writing any code.

Arguments and Filtering

Now, getting back to GraphQL itself, one thing not shown in that query, something that comes up quite often, is the notion of arguments. Arguments allow you to operate on a given requested field in some way, perhaps filtering on it or sorting by it. You can pass arguments to any field, which means that you can make one trip to get the data (be it from a server or not), something else that makes GraphQL more efficient.

By way of example, say we want only to include crewmembers who have been on more than 200 missions. Then, we might do:

```
query getCrewmembers {
  crewmembers(missions: { gte: 200  }) {
    id
    name
  }
}
```

The information in parenthesis after the `crewmembers` field are the arguments. Now, you'll only get one result back since only one crewmember has been on 200 or more missions (`gte` means great than or equal to). We are effectively filtering the data (in reality, the server providing the data is doing so based on the arguments, and only sending back what we asked for).

Gatsby uses the Sift library underneath for its query abilities, so you need to check the docs for that library to see all the details (`https://github.com/crcn/sift.js/tree/master`). But, in short, the operators are as follows:

- **eq** – Short for equal, must match the given data exactly.

- **ne** – Short for not equal, must be different from the given data.

- **regex** – Short for regular expression, must match the given pattern. Note that backslashes need to be escaped twice, so /\w+/ needs to be written as "/\\\\w+/".

- **glob** – Short for global, allows using wildcard * which acts as a placeholder for any nonempty string.

- **in** – Short for in array, must be an element of the array.

- **nin** – Short for not in array, must NOT be an element of the array.

- **gt** – Short for greater than, must be greater than the given value.

- **gte** – Short for greater than or equal, must be greater than or equal to the given value.

- **lt** – Short for less than, must be less than the given value.

- **lte** – Short for less than or equal, must be less than or equal to the given value.

- **elemMatch** – Short for element match; this indicates that the field you are filtering will return an array of elements, on which you can apply a filter using the previous operators.

However, using filtering in Gatsby requires a slightly different syntax than this, and to demonstrate that, we're going to quickly get another Gatsby website up and running. This time, however, we're *not* going to generate it from scratch. Instead, we'll just grab an existing app, courtesy of the Gatsby documentation. To do so, create a directory, then go into a command prompt, and execute this:

```
git clone https://github.com/gatsbyjs/gatsby.git
```

After a minute or two, you'll have the full source code of Gatsby itself sitting in that directory. We don't actually care about most of it at the moment, though out of curiosity you may want to poke around a little. The only thing of interest right now is in the `/examples/graphql-reference` directory. That's a full Gatsby app for playing with GraphQL and which the Gatsby documentation itself references.

Now, before you can fire that app up, you'll need to install all the dependencies it has. This step is done automatically for you when you generate a website, but here that's not applicable. Fortunately, it's easy to do that. First, navigate to the `/examples/graphql-reference` directory at a command prompt, and then execute this command:

```
npm install
```

NPM will download all the dependencies listed in `package.json` and get everything all set up for you. After that, execute the usual `gatsby develop` command and you'll be able access GraphiQL immediately. Do so, and then execute the following query:

```
{
  allAuthorYaml {
    totalCount
    edges {
      node {
        id
        bio
      }
    }
  }
}
```

This is querying against the author.yaml file in the /content/authors subdirectory. Any time Gatsby reads in a file, it gets a name in the Gatsby data store named according to the filename and extension with the word "all" prepended (and camel case used). So, author.yaml becomes allAuthorYaml. You have to tell Gatsby how to read this file and deal with it, and that's done in gatsby-config.json. In it, you'll find some plugins defined, most importantly being these two:

```
{
  resolve: `gatsby-source-filesystem`,
  options: {
    path: `${__dirname}/content`,
    name: `content`,
  },
},
`gatsby-transformer-yaml`
```

The first tells Gatsby to read all the files in the content directory, and its subdirectories. The path option tells the plugin what directory to read and the name plugin gives this instance of the plugin a unique name (allowing you to have multiple plugin instances to read multiple directories or files). The second is a plugin that extends Gatsby to be able to read YAML (Yet Another Markup Language) files. With these in place, Gatsby reads the author.yaml file, parses it, and adds it to the data store.

Now, back to the query, the first element we want is totalCount, which is a special keyword to Gatsby and Sift that requests the total number of elements in the file. After that, we dig down into the data of the file. If you take a look at the author.yaml file, you'll see this:

```
- id: Bathilda Bagshot
  bio: A magical historian and the author of over ten books
- id: Gilderoy Lockhart
  bio: A half-blood wizard, a Ravenclaw student and later
      famous wizarding celebrity
- id: Newton Scamander
  bio: English wizard, tamed Magizoologist and author of
      Fantastic Beasts and Where to Find Them
- id: Beedle the Bard
  bio: Author of wizarding fairytales
```

Unlike JSON, the elements representing authors don't have explicit names. As a result, we have to use the generic naming convention that Gatsby always produces, which is based on *edges* and *nodes*. Edges represent collections of connected things and nodes represent the things in the collection. Knowing that, we can construct a query to filter out "Bathilda Bagshot", because that's a dumb name!

```
{
  allAuthorYaml(
    filter: { id: { ne: "Bathilda Bagshot" } }
  ) {
    totalCount
    edges {
      node {
        id
        bio
      }
    }
  }
}
```

Execute that query, and you'll find that you only get three authors back now, minus the one with the annoying name. We're simply saying to give us all the contents of the allAuthorYaml node in the store, but filtering out the one with an ID field not equal (ne) to "Bathilda Bagshot".

Limiting and Skipping

Limiting and skipping is something else that arguments open up to you. Let's say you only want to return the first two results from a longer list of matches. You can do so simply:

```
{
  allAuthorYaml(limit: 2) {
    totalCount
    edges {
      node {
        id
        bio
      }
    }
  }
}
```

Likewise, if you want to skip the first two results, you can do:

```
{
  allAuthorYaml(skip: 2) {
    totalCount
    edges {
      node {
        id
        bio
      }
    }
  }
}
```

Makes sense, right?

Sorting

It's not just about somehow limiting what data you get back though; with arguments, you can also sort your results:

```
{
  allAuthorYaml(sort: { fields: [id], order: DESC } ) {
    totalCount
    edges {
      node {
        id
        bio
      }
    }
  }
}
```

Now, you'll see Newton Scamander, Gilderoy Lockhart, Beedle the Bard, and Bathilda Bagshot (ugh, Bathilda!), in that order.

These are the core concepts that GraphQL presents. There are some other somewhat more advanced topics, but I'll cover those as needed as we progress through the code of the projects later.

What GraphQL Is and Isn't

It's important to understand, though, that GraphQL isn't a specific product. It isn't a specific server or even a library. It's a specification of a query language (that's what the QL means) only. You can go off and code your own GraphQL server if you like, perhaps using Node and the popular Express module, or you can find an implementation like Apollo and stand up a server quickly and easily.

But, because of the fact that it's a specification and not a specific thing, it means that you can use GraphQL in ways other than as a service endpoint on a server. You can create an implementation of it in your own code and use it to query virtually anything (notice that the preceding query says nothing about the form of the data that underlies what the server provides), and that's exactly what Gatsby does.

Types of Queries

When dealing with Gatsby, there are two basic types of queries you'll run into: page (or "normal") queries and static queries.

Recall that with Gatsby, all your pages are React components. Would it then surprise you to learn that page queries are associated with pages? I should hope not! The key thing to remember about page queries is that they can only be made in the top-level page component. The problem this presents is that if you need the data in some child component, then you'll have to pass that data down through the component hierarchy tree in some way, and this can be a bit tricky in React.

Something else to remember about page queries is that they can take variables. Variables in GraphQL are a special form of argument in this form:

```
query getCrewmembers {
  crewmembers(limit: $limit) {
    id
    name
  }
}
```

An argument value starting with $ like that means that the value can be passed in at runtime. This is handy when you want to reuse this query, perhaps to fetch updated data from a remote service (because of course, you can do that too with GraphQL in a Gatsby website just fine, so long as the remote service speaks GraphQL).

Page queries are constructed simply:

```
export const query = graphql`
  query HomePageQuery {
    site {
      siteMetadata {
        description
      }
    }
  }
`
```

You then use them like so:

```
const HomePage = ({ data }) => {
  return (
    <div>
      { data.site.siteMetadata.description }
    </div>
  )
}
```

Gatsby is smart enough to execute the query when this component renders and passes it to the `render()` method automatically; you don't need to do anything special other than using the data.

By contrast, static queries – as clearly hinted at by their name – cannot take variables. In addition, static queries are used in specific components; they aren't forced to be in a page component.

As of Gatsby version 2, static queries are available and have become the more prevalent type of query. You create them using a feature of React called a hook, and one in particular: `useStaticQuery`. You've seen this used earlier as we looked at the code. Simply put: it takes your query and returns the requested data. You store it in some variable inside your component and use it however you wish. It's that simple! You just have to remember that the query cannot change, cannot be dynamic, and so cannot use variables. Note, however, that the query could be executed multiple times due to the nature of React, but the point is the query itself is static even if the data changes.

Defining a static query looks the same as defining a page query except that you wrap it in the use `useStaticQuery` hook, as you saw earlier. There is also a `StaticQuery` React component that you can use instead, but that seems not to be something most developers do, so I'm going to leave that for you to discover on your own should you ever want to. It's fair to say that `useStaticQuery` is effectively the de facto way to do queries nowadays in Gatsby and should probably be your first choice unless you have a specific need to do otherwise.

Summary

In this chapter, you learned quite a lot! First, you got a first look at the static site generator, Gatsby. You learned how to install it, basic usage, and commands, and you generated a simple site with the starter template and tore through the code of it to see what makes it tick.

As part of this exercise, you got a brief look at React, and a more in-depth look at GraphQL, how websites are structured with Gatsby, and a little bit on how you configure things.

In the next chapter, we'll dive deeper into React, since while it's not a part of JAMstack itself, it's a key component of what Gatsby does. And besides, it's probably the most popular front-end library going today, so it makes sense to delve a little deeper into it before we jump into building the next project.

CHAPTER 4

A Deeper Dive into React

In the last chapter, as part of generating a simple Gatsby app and tearing it apart, you got a look at React. If you're already familiar with React, then, by all means, feel free to skip this chapter.

But, if you have never worked with React before, given that it's a key part of the Gatsby puzzle, it makes a lot of sense to look at it in some detail. This won't be an exhaustive deep dive, because entire books could be (and have been!) written about React. My goal is to give you a lot more detail than the last chapter about what I view as the core concepts you need to be effective with React. When you get down to it, there's actually not as much to it as you might think.

So, without further ado, let's get to it!

A Brief History of React

React, which is sometimes referred to as React.js or ReactJS (but I'll stick with React because, like the Dude, I'm into the whole brevity thing), is a product of everyone's favorite (or the exact *opposite* of favorite – there seems to be no middle ground) company: Facebook. React, in simplest terms, is a library for building web-based user interfaces.

It all started back in around 2010 when Facebook developers – who, despite any feelings about the company you may have, are quite talented – began to run into many issues with code maintenance. That's nothing unusual in the modern web development world: especially when building single-page apps (SPAs), it's easy to make a massive mess of things if you don't have robust architecture and disciplined adherence to it.

As you bring more developers onto a team, maintaining discipline and proper architecture becomes exponentially more difficult. Developers like to *develop*, and they like to go their own way on things often (programming is as much art as it is science, after all). Facebook faced this issue and found that their development velocity was slowing down immensely. Their delivered quality was suffering for it too; all of which are bad for a company trying to make a buck.

© Frank Zammetti 2020
F. Zammetti, *Practical JAMstack*, https://doi.org/10.1007/978-1-4842-6177-4_4

In 2010, the engineers introduced XHP into their PHP stack. XHP is an extension to PHP that augments the syntax and, so the argument goes at least, makes your PHP code easier to read. Perhaps the most significant thing it provided is the notion of composite components, which allows for an interface to be broken down into mostly independent but easily integrated units of functionality.

Then, in 2011, the first notion of what would become React emerged in large part based on some of the core concepts of XHP: FaxJs. This was a project created by an engineer by the name of Jordan Walke. FaxJs had several critical characteristics we now see in React, including the following:

- Views are automatically updated any time their state changes. This is termed a *reactive* interface, and it essentially means that when the data the interface deals with changes, the interface is updated appropriately to reflect it, all without the developer having to write code to do so explicitly.

- High performance is a key consideration right from the start. While FaxJs achieved this in large part thanks to a string concatenation approach, React instead uses something a little more robust: virtual DOM. I'll come back to this in the next section.

- Perhaps most importantly, FaxJs at a high level was based on the notion of components. Everything you did was a component, and then you composed these components into the interface seen by the user. A component, in simplest terms, is a fully self-contained unit of code, in this context, one that creates some element of a UI.

Possibly the big turning point in the history of React was in 2012 when Facebook started running into many problems managing the ads displayed on the site. Since ads usually are served by someone else's server, and you aren't in complete control of what they are, it's easy for them to break your site. So, the engineers at Facebook started looking for a solution, and FaxJs jumped out at them.

At that point, Jordan Walke started working on an initial prototype, and, before long, React emerged.

But just creating React and even using it internally wouldn't have changed the world even if it helped Facebook tremendously. No, something else had to happen, and that something else was in April of 2012 when Facebook acquired Instagram. This was important because Instagram wanted to use React, but at that point, the library was tightly coupled, relatively speaking, to Facebook's site itself and its code. And, of course, it was entirely internal for Facebook and maintained by, for the most part, one (brilliant) person. No, if Facebook was going to let others, even a new acquisition and subunit of the company, start to use React, they would have to open source it, and they would have to build a community around it to continue driving the ball down the field.

The primary driving force of this shift was a guy named Pete Hunt. Pete, along with Jordan, got React open sourced in May of 2013. Interestingly, at its initial release, there was much skepticism about React, and many people, for various reasons that it wouldn't be any real benefit to get into here, saw it as a bit of a step backward. It didn't take long, however, for the momentum to shift as people got a better look at it and some experience with it, and by the end of 2013, things were looking a lot better for React.

During 2014, several things occurred to shift the currents in React's favor. For one, React Developer Tools were released as an extension of Chrome Developer Tools, giving React developers a robust development toolset to use to develop and debug their React apps. Second, a significant number of conferences and meetups were held to expand exposure to React. Third, many editors and IDEs begin to introduce native support for React.

All of this began to take React mainstream.

The years 2015 and 2016 are when it really started to go mainstream. Flipboard, Netflix, and Airbnb all using React most definitely helped a lot. You always want to see big companies using a given technology to validate it before you jump on the hype train. Many more conferences and the release of more robust React tooling helped a lot in those years too.

Since the end of 2017, React has continued to grow and is now one of, if not *the*, most popular library for building client-side web applications.

Note   I keep emphasizing the client-side nature of React, and that's primarily because that's how we're going to use it in this book. But it's worth noting that React can also render content on the server side. That's a whole other topic of conversation that I won't be covering in this book, but I wanted to make you aware of it. Should you wish to Google for it, the somewhat obvious term applied to this is Server-Side Rendering, or SSR. It's not exclusive to React, but React makes it considerably better.

Yeah, Okay, History Nerd, That's All Great, but What Is React?!

You might be surprised to see how little there fundamentally is to React. It doesn't ship with a bunch of interface widgets like grids and buttons and sliders and such, as many more "robust" toolkits do. It doesn't provide a rigid structure to your application, like many frameworks do.

At a very high level, the point of React is to make it easy to reason about the structure of your interface at any given moment in time. This is accomplished by way of components, which you can think of as self-contained pieces of the interface. Combine a whole bunch of widgets, and you have yourself a user interface.

Note   What's the difference between a library, toolkit, and framework? This is a frequent question that developers ask, and there isn't necessarily a definitive answer, at least not entirely. The difference between a library and a framework is relatively concrete and can be simply described via the Hollywood principle that says, "Don't call us, we'll call you." A library, like the ever-popular jQuery and like React now, puts your application code in control. You call it to perform functions; it doesn't do anything on its own automatically for you. A framework, of which Angular is a well-known example, is more like Hollywood in that it calls your code and is primarily in control at execution time. Inversion of control (IoC) is sometimes invoked to describe the difference too: control is inverted with a framework to the extent that your own code isn't in control (mostly); the framework's code is. A toolkit, by contrast, is somewhat nebulous and doesn't have a clear, definitive definition. However, it has nowadays come to be synonymous with the term UI toolkit, which basically means a library that is specifically focused on providing UI elements, or widgets. React pretty clearly falls into the library category. There's always some overlap between these things too. React pretty clearly falls in the library category, but it does have some elements of a framework in places. At the end of the day, this is all really just an academic aside, but an interesting one!

Getting into a little more detail, but still trying to stay within the realm of "simplest terms," React supplies just four things, four *pillars*, if you will: the aforementioned components (more precisely, an approach for building them), props, state, and style (some might argue this fourth shouldn't be included since it's outside React itself, but I think it's reasonable to include it).

Well, you might consider there to be a fifth thing too, given that it's so fundamental to React, and that's virtual DOM.

If you've ever done any web development (and I assume you have, for the purposes of this book!), you are familiar with the Document Object Model, or DOM. This is an inverted tree structure that represents all the elements on the page. It consists of a document object at the top that has children, which corresponds to the `<html>` element. There's also a head and body element in the tree, which corresponds to the familiar `<head>` and `<body>` HTML tags. Then there are a multitude of children under those, perhaps many `<div>` elements under `<body>`, an `<h1>` under one of them, a text node under that, and so on.

Anytime you use the JavaScript DOM API (or other means) to alter something on the page, or anytime the user does something that results in a change, the DOM is updated, and the browser uses the DOM to render the changes. Depending on the nature of the change that triggered it, the DOM might change a lot, forcing the browser to re-render a big chunk of the page, which can be quite slow despite the best efforts of the browser vendors. Or, it might be a relatively small change that doesn't require as much effort because not all changes result in the same amount of work. Changes that don't impact the flow of the page – think of things like changing the color of text – are less expensive. Things like inserting a new `<div>` to show a message impact page flow though, meaning the layout of the page, and are thus more expensive. The latter is explicitly what you want to try and avoid as much as possible as a rule.

It's the fundamental nature of the DOM and how the browser uses it that causes performance problems because many changes make it complicated and expensive to update what's on the screen. Making matters worse: there's not really one DOM under the covers. The browser parses the HTML document and creates a DOM tree, a tree in which every tag on the page corresponds to a node in the tree. But there's also a second tree called the render tree, created alongside it. This includes all the style information related to the tags. These trees are merged by the browse during the render process.

Every time the style information is merged in, a process called *attachment* occurs. This results in a call to the appropriately named `attach()` method. That's where problems come in because every call to the `attach()` method is synchronous. Every time a new node is inserted, `attach()` is called. Every time one is deleted, `attach()` is called. Every time the state of an element is changed, `attach()` is called. All of that might be bad enough, except for one additional fact: changes in one element can lead to changes in others, perhaps many others, because the layout has to be recalculated and re-rendered. Those are those flow changes I mentioned earlier. And again, each of these operations, which could be in the hundreds or thousands depending on what was done, incurs a synchronous call that also happens to be potentially expensive to execute.

Houston, we have a problem! Fortunately, we have a solution, too: virtual DOM.

In the case of a virtual DOM, the browser doesn't use it to render anything directly or to calculate anything. It's a layer of abstraction, a secondary DOM tree effectively, one created and controlled by application-level code. It sits on top of the browser's own DOM, yet it's still a DOM like you're familiar with conceptually, in terms of it being a tree. But, in contrast to the real DOM, virtual DOM is made up of simple, lightweight POJOs (Plain Old JavaScript Objects, to paraphrase the term that began in the Java world).

The critical difference is that anytime you make a change to the virtual DOM via some user action or programmatic event, some code is executed before the browser is aware of anything. That code uses various diffing algorithms to try and batch the necessary changes so that all those changes can be done in the actual browser DOM in one pass. This is in contrast to the more typical situation where each change is done individually, including all the attachment, reflow, and re-rendering. It also works to ensure that as little of the real DOM as possible is updated, which makes it much more efficient. This means that the code, which is React itself in this case, can calculate the differences between the existing virtual DOM and whatever changes your code made intelligently. That way, it can make the minimal number of changes to the actual DOM and do them all at once, making the performance much better than changing the browser's DOM directly and often iteratively. It's a much more efficient approach, especially when page complexity increases. (It may not matter so much for small pages, but the benefit can come into play pretty quickly as a page gets more complex).

None of this impacts your ability to learn React. You could use it just fine without knowing anything about virtual DOM, but I do think it helps (and there are a few cases where knowing how the magician behind the curtain does the tricks might actually be necessary).

For the more curious among you, it's interesting to realize that virtual DOM is nothing new. You could always do what React does essentially, by creating a DOM fragment using JavaScript DOM API methods and then inserting the fragment as a single unit into the DOM. That's been done for a long time before React and is undoubtedly more efficient than adding each node that the fragment contains into the DOM individually, because while layout and re-rendering might be more significant, they'll only have to be done once per update. And, if your code is efficient, it already considers modifying things as little as necessary up-front, so the browser must make fewer of those synchronous calls, even in the context of a single update. Also, if you've ever done any game programming, you might recognize that virtual DOM is essentially a form of double buffering. The changes destined for the screen are rendered into a buffer first, and then the buffer is moved en masse to the screen, leading to better performance and smoother animation. It's the same concept.

So, why use virtual DOM, and React, if you could do it directly with DOM methods yourself? You do it to centralize the code that manages DOM fragments, and that deals with diffing the current DOM from the updated DOM (which is how the number of changes is minimized – only those things that really are changed by the update are actually updated). The virtual COM approach, as implemented by React, also means that many parts of your app can update the DOM at once and that centralized code manages that and, assuming it's implemented well, make it as efficient as possible (and avoid potential conflicts, of course).

Writing robust virtual DOM code isn't necessarily easy, and fortunately, you do not have to do it when you use React. So, this is all just presented as an interesting technical aside, not something you have to be directly conscious of as we move forward.

Let's now talk about each of the other four pillars of React in turn, and in the process, let's build ourselves an elementary React app to see it all in action!

The Real Star of the Show: Components

Let's start things off by creating ourselves a plain old HTML document, like that shown in Listing 4-1.

Listing 4-1. A basic HTML document to start building our simple React app with (if you don't understand this already, then, Houston, we have a problem!)

```
<!DOCTYPE html>
<html>
  <head>
    <meta charset="UTF-8" />
    <title>Intro To React</title>
  </head>
  <body>
  </body>
</html>
```

Yep, that ain't exactly rocket science! Now, to it, let's add two lines into the <head> of the document to bring React into the fold:

```
<script crossorigin src="https://unpkg.com/react@16/umd/react.development.js">
</script>
<script crossorigin src="https://unpkg.com/react-dom@16/umd/react-dom.
development.js"></script>
```

Here, I'm using a CDN to download the main React code (react.development.js) as well as the react-dom package, which you can think of as the bridge between React itself and the browser's DOM. React can talk to different renderers, which are the bits of code that produce the visual output. It might be possible to have a renderer that produces, say, bitmap images for display in a desktop operating system, allowing you to write desktop apps with React. The react-dom package is one such bit of code, but one targeting the browser DOM and HTML. Note that for both, I'm specifying the development builds rather than the production builds, which are also available. This aids in debugging during development since the code isn't minified and munged and whatnot.

Note   For performance, it would usually be better to move the two react imports to the bottom of the document, as well as the code in `start()`, and not call it onload. That's page optimization 101. I did it this way because I think it's slightly easier to grasp what's happening in a more deterministic fashion. In this example, the page loads fast enough anyway that the difference won't matter much either way.

If you reload the page at this point, nothing will happen, because we're not using React yet. React will just happily sit there in the background, not bugging us! So, now, let's introduce some React action, as shown in Listing 4-2.

Listing 4-2.   Our first usage of React!

```html
<!DOCTYPE html>
<html>
  <head>
    <meta charset="UTF-8" />
    <title>Intro To React</title>
    <script crossorigin src="https://unpkg.com/react@16/umd/react.
    development.js"></script>
    <script crossorigin
    src="https://unpkg.com/react-dom@16/umd/react-dom.development.js">
    </script>
    <script>
      function start() {
        const rootElement =
          React.createElement("div", { },
            React.createElement("h1", { }, "Bookmarks"),
            React.createElement("ul", { },
              React.createElement("li", { },
                React.createElement("h2", { }, "Etherient"),
                React.createElement("a",
                  { href : "https://www.etherient.com" },
                  "The home page of Etherient"
                )
              ),
```

```
              React.createElement("li", { },
                React.createElement("h2", { },
                  "Frank's Home"
                ),
                React.createElement("a",
                  { href: "https://www.zammetti.com" },
                  "The web home page of Frank Zammetti"
                )
              )
            )
          );
        ReactDOM.render(rootElement,
          document.getElementById("mainContainer")
        );
      }
    </script>
  </head>
  <body onLoad="start();">
    <div id="mainContainer"></div>
  </body>
</html>
```

Warning   You might encounter a problem with the loading of the two react files from CDN related to CORS (cross-origin resource sharing). I ran into it with Firefox, but it won't happen for every user or in every browser. If you do find that the example doesn't work though, and you see errors in your developer tools console talking about CORS, the easy solution is to download the two files from the URLs shown here, save them to the same directory as the example file, and then change the two <script> tags in the example to reference the local copies rather than from CDN. You'll also likely need to remove the `crossorigin` attribute to make it finally work. I'm just throwing this out there as a general warning in case it comes up, but hopefully it won't for you as it seems to be dependent on many factors specific to any given machine.

This results in the screen shown in Figure 4-1. It's nothing complex, but it gets the point across pretty well.

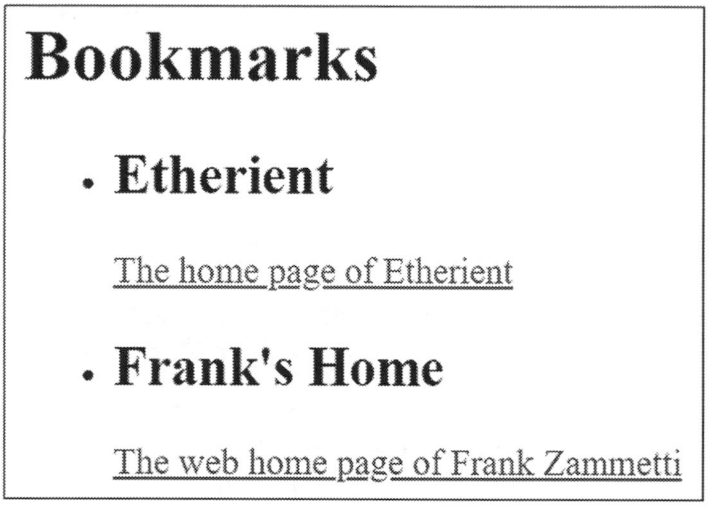

Bookmarks

- ## Etherient

  The home page of Etherient

- ## Frank's Home

  The web home page of Frank Zammetti

Figure 4-1. *Our first React app gets its close-up*

Okay, so what's going on here?! To start, we have a function `start()` called when the page loads. This function uses what is probably one of the most important things React offers, the `React.createElement()` method. The method signature for it is

```
React.createElement(type, {props}, ...children);
```

This method constructs a new React element, which is the smallest building block of the visual interface of a React app. These are POJOs (a term that originally came from the Java world and which stands for Plain Old Java Object – but it applies just as well to JavaScript: Plain Old JavaScript Object, meaning an object that doesn't extend from any base class other than `Object` itself) and thus are cheap and fast to create, as compared to DOM nodes, which trigger all that render activity we talked about earlier (assuming they are inserted into the DOM immediately, that is). React takes care of updating the DOM to match all the elements that are a part of that virtual DOM (and then creating real DOM nodes from the elements and inserting them as appropriate).

It should be noted that, typically, you'll be working with React components. Components are composed of elements. The type you specify can be a tag name, as shown here, or it can be a React component type, or a React fragment, which allows you to create multiple nested elements at once.

In this start() function, React.createElement() is used to build up a tree of elements, all of which are children of the top-level <div> element that the variable rootElement holds a reference to. Each call to React.createElement() after that first one is creating a child of the element above it in the tree. Then, when that tree is built up, the ReactDOM.render() method is called, passing it a reference to that top-level element as well as a real DOM node to render it to. The ReactDOM.render() method takes that built-up virtual DOM tree and renders it to the real DOM, and voila, we have stuff on the screen!

Now, if at this point, you're probably thinking, "wow, React is verbose and looks annoying to write." Well, at this point, I would agree with you! However, what you're going to find shortly is that people usually don't write React apps like this. Instead, they use something called JSX, and that makes it considerably easier to write React apps with. That's for later, though. The critical thing now is that when you write a React app with JSX, under the covers, it produces code similar to this, so I think it makes a lot of sense to understand how React is doing things in the end. Plus, there may be a reason specifically you want to write your apps this way, one of which is when you want to add some React components to an existing app but not go "all-in" with React, so to speak. In such a case, you're likely not going to rewrite the whole thing in JSX. You'll more likely just want to insert some components somewhere onto your existing page. With code like this, you can do precisely that.

But I glossed over a few things here. One of which is *props*, I'm going to get into that fully in the next section, but you can start to get a sense of what they're about in the line:

```
React.createElement("a",
  { href : "https://www.etherient.com" },
  "The home page of Etherient"
)
```

It doesn't take much to figure out that props are how you pass data into an element (or component, as it happens). But there's a bit more to it than that, so let's come back to that in the next section.

One thing that you should realize here is that we really haven't dealt with components at all, we've been dealing with elements. And, hey, components are the name of the game in this section, so what gives? Let's remedy having not seen components specifically yet by rewriting the code a bit, as shown in Listing 4-3.

Listing 4-3. A first foray into components

```
<!DOCTYPE html>
<html>
  <head>
    <meta charset="UTF-8" />
    <title>Intro To React</title>
    <script crossorigin src="https://unpkg.com/react@16/umd/react.
    development.js"></script>
    <script crossorigin src="https://unpkg.com/react-dom@16/umd/react-dom.
    development.js"></script>
    <script>
      function start() {
        class Bookmark extends React.Component {
          render() {
            return (
              React.createElement("li", { },
                React.createElement("h2", { },
                  this.props.title),
                React.createElement("a",
                  { href : this.props.href },
                  this.props.description
                )
              )
            );
          }
        }
        const rootElement =
          React.createElement("div", { },
            React.createElement("h1", { }, "Bookmarks"),
            React.createElement("ul", { },
              React.createElement(
                Bookmark, {
                  title : "Etherient",
                  href : "https://www.etherient.com",
                  description : "The home page of Etherient"
```

```
          }
        ),
        React.createElement(
          Bookmark, {
            title : "Frank's Site",
            href : "https://www.zammetti.com",
            description :
              "The web home of Frank W. Zammetti"
          }
        )
      )
    );
    ReactDOM.render(rootElement,
      document.getElementById("mainContainer")
    );
  }
  </script>
</head>
<body onLoad="start();">
  <div id="mainContainer"></div>
</body>
</html>
```

The Bookmark class is how we define a proper React component, which is why it extends the React.Component class. React components have several characteristics, some of which were touched upon in the previous chapter. Of them, perhaps the most important is a render() method. Without that, it won't be much of a component at all! The render() method, which is the only thing your component is required to contain, is responsible for returning one of several things:

- Another React component

- A React element

- An array of either of those

- A fragment

- A portal (a more advanced topic that won't be covered in this book)

- A string or a number (these are rendered as plain text nodes in the DOM)

- A Boolean or null (results in nothing being rendered)

Of these, the first two are almost always going to be what you return. You would think that arrays or fragments would be common too, but it's more common to return a single component or element that itself has child components, which accomplishes much the same goal.

You can also now see the other side of props, meaning how you use them within a component. The this.props member will be present on any component thanks to React, and React populates it for you when you use the component using whatever you pass as the second argument to React.createElement(). You can then use the data in props as appropriate inside the component. Here, it's just rendering the three props (title, href, and description) as part of the elements returned.

Speaking of using a component, you can see that being done in the rootElement definition. This time, we call React.createElement() but now we pass it the name of the React component as the first argument, React instantiates that component for us, passes the props to it, and whatever that component's render() method returns effectively is inserted at that point in the tree.

Hopefully, you can start to see some of the benefits of this componentized approach. Now, you can avoid having a bunch of redundant React.createElement() calls and instead encapsulate it inside a component and reuse the component wherever you need a Bookmark to appear. There are no real rules about how you break the interface down; I could have created a custom component to encapsulate the <h1> elements and maybe called it a BookmarkGroup component. Whatever makes sense to you is the answer.

Components Need Info: Props

As you saw in the previous section, props, which is short for properties, is how information is passed into components. For the simple HTML elements created earlier, that can be the attributes of those elements that you're familiar with: href for a link or the text inside an <h2> element (the text isn't technically an attribute of the <h2> tag itself, it's actually a text node nested inside the <h2> at the DOM level, but at least in practice it's the same thing). For custom components, though, you get to define whatever props it needs. For the Bookmark component, that's title, href, and description.

What's important to realize about props is three things. First, they are always passed down from a parent component to a child. In the case of the topmost component, you can consider React itself to be the "parent component" conceptually. In any case, the source of the information is always the parent component. Now, where the data that is the value of a prop comes from in the parent can be many things. It could be literal text, as you see in the example code we're dealing with here. It could be the value of a variable inside the parent component. It could be a value that comes from some other object that the parent retrieves. But, from the perspective of the child component, the value comes from the parent always.

Second, props are only given to the child component when it's being created. This is a crucial point because it ties in with the third thing, which is that props are immutable. This will strike you as odd at first because, I mean, how could that be?! What if we wanted to change the description of one of our `Bookmark` components in response to the user editing it somehow? Clearly, that's gonna be a problem if props can't be altered.

But it's true: once set, props cannot be changed.

The way it works is that any time a change must occur to a component, including its props, React will re-render the part of the DOM tree where the component lives. Remember all that stuff about virtual DOM and how React does diffs to determine what to redraw? Well, the level above that is that some data in your code needs to change, data that React recognizes, for it to know it has to do any of that work. We're going to look at something called state next, but where that matters in terms of props is that when state changes, whatever that is, React determines what components need to be re-rendered as a result and do so, passing the props to it again, which may have different values now.

A component isn't just re-rendered, but actually destroyed and re-created from scratch! That means that the component will need to be passed its props from the parent again. If the state impacts those props – because remember, I said the values of props could come from many places, and state is one of them – then the new values are passed to the component when it is re-created. In that way, the `description` of a `Bookmark` could "change" because we will, in fact, wind up with a whole new `Bookmark` component with a new `description` value.

So, yes, props can't be changed once they are passed to the child and the component is created with them, but nothing says the component can't be destroyed and re-created with all-new prop values, and that's precisely what happens under the covers.

Components (Sometimes) Need Memory: State

Effectively, there are two types of data that serve to control components in some way. You've already seen one: props. Now let's look at the other: state.

Props, you know now, are read-only and do not change during the lifetime of a component. If props need to change, then the component is destroyed and then re-created. If you think there must be a more efficient way to deal with data that you know will change, then you'd be correct, and that way is state. Changes to state do not cause React to destroy and re-create a component. Instead, it changes just the tiniest portion of the virtual DOM tree that the change demands, and then the minimum real DOM changes are made.

Let's see a concrete example. Building on the previous code, let's make some changes to our Bookmark class. It will now be what you see in Listing 4-4.

Listing 4-4. The Bookmark class (and, by extension, React component)

```
class Bookmark extends React.Component {
  constructor(props) {
    super(props);
    console.log("Bookmark component created");
    this.title = this.props.title;
  }
  render() {
    return (
      React.createElement("li", { },
        React.createElement("h2", { }, this.title),
        React.createElement("a",
          { href : this.props.href }, this.props.description
        ),
        React.createElement("button", {
          onClick : () => {
            this.title = this.title + "-CHANGED";
            this.setState({});
          }
        }, "Click me")
      )
    );
  }
```

121

The first thing to note is the constructor that I've added. There are two reasons to have a constructor (it is otherwise optional). The first is so that when you try this code out (you are following along and trying the code out, right?!), you will see that when state changes, the constructor does not fire after the two initial times (one per `Bookmark` in the tree), proving that state changes don't result in component re-creation. Note that in a constructor for a `React.Component` instance, you must call the superclass's constructor and pass it the props that will be passed into the constructor. You'll get some nasty JavaScript errors in your browser dev tools console if you fail to do this (ask me how I know!).

The second reason is the line where `title` is set as a member variable, and its initial value is taken from the props that are passed in. This variable becomes the state of this `Bookmark` component. There are no rules about how you store the state inside your component. Many people choose to have a single state variable that is an object that contains all the state for the component, and I frankly tend to do that too. But it can simply be "naked" class members like this too. Whatever makes sense to you, React will accommodate.

Now, down in the call to `React.createElement()` that creates the `<h2>` element, note the change there: rather than getting the value from `this.props` like before, it now comes from `this.title`. That's key, as you're about to see!

A new child element has been added at the end, this one a `<button>` HTML element. Now, the first interesting thing is that the second argument to `React.createElement()`, which you'll recall is the props to pass to the component, can include functions! At the end of the day, this argument is just an object, and what's in it can be virtually anything, so long as it has meaning to your component (or will just be ignored by it, that's a valid possibility too). Here, because we're creating a button and because buttons typically do something when clicked, an `onClick` event handler function is passed in. React knows how to create a `<button>` HTML element, and it knows how to attach that function, so we get a button that does something when clicked, just as we need. The "something" it does when clicked is to change the `title` property of the object.

Now, if that's all it did, then nothing would happen, at least nothing evident on the screen. Yes, the value of the variable would change, but React wouldn't know that anything had happened. You see, React isn't monitoring your state and proactively re-rendering the screen as appropriate. No, you have to inform it that state has changed, and that's precisely what the `setState()` method is for. This method is provided by the base `React.Component` class that our `Bookmark` custom component class extends. It informs React that this component, and its children, may need to be re-rendered (React makes the final determination).

The argument passed to setState() is one of two things: either a function or an object. If it's a function, then it's what is called an updater function. This function receives two arguments: the current state of the object and its props. This function must then return an object that becomes the new state of the component. It's important to understand that this function must not mutate the state object passed in! Instead, it must create a new object and return it. If you change the incoming state object, then nothing will appear to happen (unless you return that same object, but that's a code smell and can sometimes lead to some real nastiness, so don't do that).

Alternatively, and what I've done in the example, is pass setState() an object, an empty object in this case. What this does causes React to perform a shallow merge of the object with the component's current state. In this case, since I've already altered the state variable, that means that the resulting object has the new value, so what's returned is a valid new state object.

Note   In general, it's probably better to always use an updater function. While it involves a little more code and work on your part, it tends to be safer. For a simple example like what we're looking at here, it hardly matters. But as a rule, I suggest always doing it that way. Plus, it's definitely more of a functional approach, which is a popular paradigm these days, so if nothing else, you'll be hangin' with the cool kids this way!

A crucial thing to understand about setState() is that it is more of a request than a demand. What I mean is that React will enqueue setState() calls, and the work it results in, and may batch many requests to optimize DOM updates. So, you aren't so much telling React to update the component right now; you're asking it to do so at some point in the future. Of course, we're not talking about hours or even minutes or seconds later, but the change won't necessarily be immediate. It is asynchronous in other words, and as a result, you can also pass a second argument to setState(), a callback function. This function will be called after the update has occurred. This callback mechanism isn't relevant in such a simple example, but you may find times where you do need it, when you need to trigger some action, but only after the screen has been updated.

In the world of React, there's quite a lot more to state than this (if you've ever heard the term Redux, then that's one such thing: it's another way of dealing with state more globally, but it's a topic I won't be covering in this book). But, at an elementary and fundamental level, this is what state is all about, and you absolutely can use what you've learned in this section alone to deal with state in your React apps.

Note   One other point of terminology: as you've seen, not all components have state. These are, quite obviously, termed "stateless" components. Any component that has state is, equally as obviously, called a "stateful" component.

Making Them Look Good: Style

The final thing I need to touch on is styling in a React app.

Now, at the end of the day, when building an app with React, we're still talking about HTML, JavaScript, and CSS. Components will always render down into some combination of those. So, we can do things very directly if we wish. For example, if we want to make the color of our Bookmark titles red, we could add this to the page:

```
<style>
  h2 {
    color : red;
  }
</style>
```

Since React will ultimately render a plain old HTML <h2> element, that'll get the job done. Of course, we could put this in a separate .css file and import it into the document, just like always with CSS.

Another alternative is to explicitly name a CSS class to use in the component's code.

So, let's alter that style definition a little bit:

```
<style>
  .bookmarkTitle {
    color : red;
  }
</style>
```

Now, in our `Bookmark` code, the call to `React.createElement()` that creates the `<h2>` for the title specifically, let's use that style:

```
React.createElement("h2", { className : "bookmarkTitle" }, this.title)
```

Since class is a reserved word in JavaScript, React makes us use `className` instead. But that will result in the style being applied all the same.

You could also define the style inline with the element, like this:

```
React.createElement("h2", { style : { color : "red" } }, this.title)
```

The style prop must be an object mapping CSS attributes to values. This approach is an important one because it leads to a concept termed CSS-in-JS. If you notice, you're effectively defining your CSS in JavaScript here. Further, there's absolutely no reason you couldn't take that object that defines the styles for the `<h2>` element out of the React `createElement()` call and define it independently:

```
const bookmarkTitle = { color : "red" }
```

Then you just do:

```
React.createElement("h2", { style : this.bookmarkTitle }, this.title)
```

You could put all your style objects for your entire application like those in separate `styles.js` file, and now you've started down the path of skipping CSS, in a sense, and doing it all in JavaScript. Oh, to be sure, you're still dealing with CSS obviously, but in an arguably more flexible way, since the full power of JavaScript is then available to you in defining those styles. Things like calculating values dynamically become a trivial exercise.

However, components are meant to be self-contained entities, remember? Given that, shouldn't that include their style too? But, then, isn't it better code structure to keep the styles at least somewhat separate from the layout code? Most people think so. All that taken together, you might wind up with something that looks like Listing 4-5.

Listing 4-5. The Bookmark component, now with 100% more style

```
class Bookmark extends React.Component {
  constructor(props) {
    super(props);
    console.log("Bookmark component created");
  }
  title = this.props.title;
  titleStyle = { color : "red" }
  render() {
    return (
      React.createElement("li", { },
        React.createElement("h2",
          { style : this.titleStyle }, this.title
        ),
        React.createElement("a",
          { href : this.props.href }, this.props.description
        ),
        React.createElement("button", {
          onClick : () => {
            this.title = this.title + "-CHANGED";
            this.setState({});
          }
        }, "Click me")
      )
    );
  }
}
```

Now, the Bookmark component's style is defined within the Bookmark class, achieving encapsulation, but then within the class, the style information is abstracted from the code that produces the layout in the render() method. This is arguably a cleaner way to write component code.

Whichever approach you choose, whatever meets your needs, the bottom line is that React offers several approaches to styling your components, and thus your user interface.

In the End, Why React?

All of that is fine and dandy, but it doesn't answer a fundamental question: why would anyone want to use React? I think, at least in my mind, a few critical points in React's favor are the following:

- **Simplicity** – As you've seen, React amounts to four fundamental pillars: components, props, state, and style (and virtual DOM as the fifth, in a sense). There isn't much to it at a basic level. It doesn't take much to get started with it, as you saw. It doesn't have a lot of complicated baggage as some frameworks do. The counterargument, of course, is that all that complexity provides additional power, and ultimately that's the judgment call you have to make as a developer.

- **Easy to integrate into existing projects by not being overly opinionated** – You can add React to an existing project little by little if you want, and this is in large part thanks to the fact that React doesn't impose a rigid application architecture on you like other options do. Like with the simplicity argument, there is a negative to this: it's more possible to screw things up with React than with something like, say, Angular, precisely because of that lack of opinionated mindset.

- **A bit of luck!** – React began growing in popularity right around the time something else was happening: Google's Angular framework, another popular front-end development tool, jumped from version 1 to version 2. This was a significant event for Angular users because the version change was not backward-compatible and, frankly, caused many headaches for a lot of people. Many of those people began looking for a more straightforward option that didn't seem as likely to repeat that mistake, and React was gaining a foothold right around that time on its own. So, Google and Angular's misstep aided React, if only indirectly.

- **Backing** – Many people have less than positive feelings about Facebook these days, but one thing you can't deny is that they are a large corporation. When a development tool has sizeable corporate backing, it tends to become a "safe" choice for technologists to suggest on the job. React has had that going for it right from the start.

A Better Way to Write React Code: JSX

JSX, which stands for JavaScript XML, is an extension to the JavaScript language that adds XML syntax to the language. In a sense, it allows us to embed XML inside JavaScript without having to resort to things like string concatenation or even DOM methods. At its core, JSX is interested in allowing us to define tree structures with attributes in a more elegant way than all those JavaScript function calls you saw earlier, which can get verbose and frankly annoying to write in a hurry.

If you think back to our earlier discussion of components, there might be a light bulb above your head right now: React is nothing but trees of components with attributes (props). Wouldn't it be great to write code that uses it more like that too? That's where JSX comes in!

JSX is effectively an extension of JavaScript, but it's not a part of JavaScript, and it's not even *valid* JavaScript on its own. No, it's a bolted-on thing that requires a preprocessing step, the output of which is pure JavaScript. But I'm jumping ahead a bit. We'll get to that in the next section!

The reason JSX came about – aside from the obvious of developers not liking to code their UIs as a series of function calls – is because the React team realized that it's kind of pointless to separate rendering logic from UI logic. That separation is something we've been doing for a long time, but which has started being questioned in recent years. For example, you put your markup in an HTML file, but then you (usually) put your UI logic in a JavaScript file. That keeps things separated a bit. But these things are intrinsically coupled in the final analysis. How events are handled, how the state of your application changes in response to user interactions, how data is prepared for display, all of that is mixed together logically, so does it really make sense to separate them based on technological demarcation lines like HTML vs. JavaScript? Why not combine them?

An argument can be made that no, it doesn't make sense, and that's the argument React makes. Instead, the division in React is on boundaries based on concerns. That's where components come into play: they are separating the various concerns a UI has (a button is concerned with letting the user trigger an action, a grid is concerned with displaying data, etc.). But each component is an encapsulated whole: it contains the logic that knows how to render itself as well as the logic that knows how to deal with the various events that can affect it (and, most often, the style information for what it should look like).

While you absolutely can do all of this without JSX just by adhering to some architectural principles and being disciplined with your code, JSX provides, arguably, a more elegant way to do so. But, especially since most developers are coming from an HTML/JS/CSS background, JSX provides a more natural way into the world of React by allowing them not to have to think in terms of `React.createElement()` but in something more akin to what they're already familiar with: essentially a (weird) form of markup (kinda, sorta – you'll see!).

Yeah, Okay, So What Does It LOOK LIKE?!

So, what does JSX look like? Well, here's a simple example using a `MaterialButton` component (which we'll assume is a real component – because it is, if you add the right add-on library to React – and is available to our code, but this could be any component if course):

```
const button = <MaterialButton color="red"
  onClick="alert('clicked');">
  Click Me
</MaterialButton>;
```

Huh? If you've looked at JavaScript at all (which, remember, I'm assuming you have for our purposes here), that will probably give you cold chills because obviously, that wouldn't be valid JavaScript syntax! You can't set markup as the value of a JavaScript variable like that, and you can't just plop XML into code like that! You'd have to at the least wrap that up on quotes and make it a string, probably doing some concatenations along the way (or maybe multiline strings if you're caught up with ES6, but either way, it's a string).

Earlier, I mentioned a preprocessing step that we have to do with JSX. That step, simply put, is to compile it into standard JavaScript. But, before we even get to that, what do we expect that final JavaScript to look like? The answer is that it's going to look something like this:

```
React.createElement(
  MaterialButton,
  { color : "red",
    onClick : function() { alert('clicked'); }
  },
  "Click Me"
)
```

That should look familiar to you at this point! What's more, if you embed components in JSX...

```
const button = <MaterialButton color="red"
  onClick="alert('clicked');">
  <ButtonLabel text="Click Me" />
</MaterialButton>;
```

...you'll get nested calls as you would expect, given what JSX compiles down to:

```
React.createElement(
  MaterialButton,
  { color : "red",
    onClick : function() { alert('clicked'); }
  },
  React.createElement(ButtonLabel, { text : "Click Me" })
)
```

Okay, so that's JSX in simplest terms. But, clearly, if we load that in a browser, it's gonna spit it back at us unceremoniously because it's not valid JavaScript. How do we get valid JavaScript from JSX? To explain that, we have to take a quick detour and talk about something called Babel.

A Slight Detour into Babel Land

When a new version of JavaScript comes out, it takes time for browsers, and the JavaScript engines they use, to catch up. There is a period of time when there may be some cool new features in the language that you can't use without risking some of your customers not being able to run your code. Even if you're talking about Node rather than a browser, it's true there too: you may have to avoid some language features as you write your code until the engine is updated. Sometimes, a particular browser or engine might never implement a feature you want to use, and certainly trying to keep track of which environment your great new code can run in and which it can't becomes a headache in a hurry.

To give a concrete example, consider this bit of JavaScript:

```
const newArray = [ 44, 55, 66].map((num) => n * 2);
```

That code works in the latest version of Chrome, Firefox, and Opera. But it won't work in Internet Explorer 11 because IE11 doesn't support arrow functions. If your work requires that you support that browser, then you've got a problem if you really want to write your code like that. That's a problem that has existed for a long time, but JavaScript has been evolving quickly over the last decade or so as its usage has increased dramatically, so the problem has only gotten worse over time. Solutions do exist, though: every new feature in the language can be refactored and written using the earlier language features, often with some compromises, but essentially functioning as the new features do. You can do this yourself, or use something called a polyfill that does that work for you while hiding that fact from you.

That's not an ideal solution, though, because it's a lot of work for developers, whether directly (developing and testing the polyfill itself and ensuring it works across all target browsers) or indirectly (waiting for someone else to do it and release it to the world). And, even when it does work, it can often lead to less efficient code. It's also code that you'll probably want to change to the "right" code later when the browser catches up, or you decide not to support it anymore. All of this just means more work.

This is where Babel comes in. Rather than have to go through that effort, Babel allows you to write your code using the new language features you want. What happens next is you run that code through Babel, and Babel takes care of generating the appropriate code that works across all the browsers or JavaScript engines you tell it you want to support. Babel is considered a transpiler, meaning it transforms and compiles at the same time. That means your workflow is altered: there is now a step you must do before you can run your code in a browser, or on Node.

To use Babel, you first have to install it. Before that, though, let's begin a new project. Choose a directory and execute `npm init` at a command prompt, using all the default options when prompted. This sets up a basic project in which NPM will manage dependencies (primarily, that means creating a `package.json` file, and a `node_modules` directory where the dependencies NPM installs for you go). Once that's done, you can install Babel itself:

```
npm install --save-dev @babel/core @babel/cli
```

The `--save-dev` option updates `package.json` file to include Babel as a dependency. That way, when someone else gets the project to work on, they can just do `npm install` and everything, including Babel now, will be installed for them.

Once that's done, you'll be able to run Babel. To do so, issue the command:

```
npx babel
```

The `npx` command is something that is installed by newer versions of NPM. It's an executable, installed alongside the `npm` executable, that is a proxy allowing you to run packages and the CLI tools some packages provide. In the past, you would usually be directed to install Babel globally, which would add the appropriate path entries to your system, allowing you to run it. Now though, the advice usually given is to install Babel local to the project (so that different projects can use different versions of Babel as appropriate) so that it's a part of the `node_modules` directory in your project directory, not a shared global directory. But doing that doesn't give you those same path entries, so running Babel would require a more convoluted command. That's where `npx` comes in: it lets you run those tools without those path entries.

Now, running Babel like this won't do anything yet. That's because, first, you have to tell it what to transpile. So, let's create a file called `test.js` and into it put the code from before:

```
const newArray = [ 44, 55, 66].map((num) => n * 2);
```

Then, execute

```
npx babel test.js
```

What happens? Well, uhh, still nothing, actually! Babel echoes back the code from the file, but nothing is changed, nothing is produced. That's because out of the box, Babel doesn't do anything – it doesn't know how to transform the code. You have to add some plugins to it to give it that knowledge. Plugins are what define the rules for transpiling one language (or version of a language) into another. If you want to see a list of all the plugins available, check out this site: `https://babeljs.io/docs/en/plugins`. For our purposes though, we'll just need one, which we, of course, can install with NPM:

```
npm install --save-dev @babel/plugin-transform-arrow-functions
```

Now, there's still another step, and that's to tell Babel to use that plugin. To do that, we have to create one more file: the `.babelrc` configuration file. Its contents should be

```
{
  "plugins": ["@babel/plugin-transform-arrow-functions"]
}
```

With that in place, Babel now knows to use this plugin when processing our file, which it will do if we execute the npx Babel test.js command again. The output you'll then see should be

```
const newArray = [44, 55, 66].map(function (num) {
  return n * 2;
});
```

Notice how the arrow function was replaced with standard function() syntax? That's Babel doing its thing!

You'll likely want to write that output to a file rather than the console, and to do so is simple enough:

```
npx babel test.js --out-file test_new.js
```

Sure enough, this is a simple example, and the code looks fairly similar before and after transpilation occurs. But, for more complex JavaScript, the difference can be rather drastic.

One final thing, do you think it might be inconvenient to have to install a plugin for every single JavaScript feature you want to be able to transpile? The answer is, hopefully, a clear yes! For this reason, Babel provides the notion of *presets*. These effectively are logical groupings of plugins that can be enabled all in one batch. There are several presets, but the two most used are env and react.

The env preset allows you to do this in your .babelrc file:

```
{ "presets": [
    [ "@babel/preset-env", {
      "targets" : {
        "browsers" : [ "last 3 versions", "safari >= 6" ]
      }
    }]
  ]
}
```

That tells Babel, "I want you to produce code that will work in the last three versions of all browsers, and for Safari, support anything from version 6 on up." Babel will take care of installing the appropriate plugins. Also, if you're working in Node and don't care about browsers, you can do

```
{ "presets" : [
    [ "@babel/preset-env", {
      "targets" : { "node" : "7.00" }
    }]
  ]
}
```

That tells Babel to support Node back to version 7. To make use of this preset, you need to install a single plugin:

```
npm install --save-dev @babel/preset-env
```

Once that's done, and `.babelrc` altered as shown in the preceding text (removing the `@babel/plugin-transform-arrow-functions` plugin), the output will now be

```
"use strict";

var newArray = [44, 55, 66].map(function (num) {
  return n * 2;
});
```

That's the same as before, only now with the `"use strict";` at the top and, critically, not having to explicitly tell it which plugins to use!

Now, to be clear, knowing about Babel is good. However, when you're working with Gatsby, all of this is mostly hidden from you. Gatsby uses Babel under the covers, but you'll be none the wiser as a general rule. You can, if you wish, modify how Babel works when Gatsby uses it but supplying an appropriate configuration file, but that's a topic I'll leave for you if and when you find a need for it. In general, you may never have such a need because Gatsby handles it for you.

But now, let's get back to JSX!

Compile JSX

The previous section described the env preset, but what about the react preset I mentioned there without describing? That's the key to being able to produce plain old JavaScript from our JSX files. To do that, we must make some changes. First, we'll need to install the preset:

```
npm install @babel/preset-react --save-dev
```

You will then need to add a new preset in `.babelrc` to let Babel know how to deal with JSX (and some related React plumbing):

```
{ "presets" : [
    [ "@babel/preset-react" ]
  ]
}
```

Note   You only need the `react` preset, you don't need the env preset, so if you're following along, then you can remove the env dependency from `package.json`. However, it should do no harm to leave it there, so it's entirely up to you.

Now, rename the `test.js` file to `test.jsx` and replace its contents with the JSX from earlier:

```
const button = <MaterialButton color="red"
  onClick="alert('clicked');">
  Click Me
</MaterialButton>;
```

With those tasks complete, you can now run Babel against the `test.jsx` file, just as you did against the `test.js` file before, but now the output should be

```
const button = React.createElement(MaterialButton, {
  color: "red",
  onClick: "alert('clicked');"
}, "Click Me");
```

Just as expected, we get some plain old JavaScript from the JSX. This code may not work as is because we haven't included a `MaterialButton` class, but that's irrelevant at this juncture. The point is how Babel transpiles your JSX file to plain old JavaScript.

And Now, Put It All Together

Now that we know what JSX is, what it looks like, and how to compile it into valid JavaScript, let's put all the pieces together! Here, we'll take the very simple example we've been looking at in this chapter and rewrite it using JSX.

First, let's take the simple project created in the last section and rename `test.jsx` to `main.jsx`. That's our source file that will be compiled into plain JavaScript. But, to do anything with that final product, we'll also need an HTML file. So, create a file named `index.html` and insert the following content into it:

```
<!DOCTYPE html>
<html>
  <head>
    <meta charset="UTF-8" />
    <title>Intro To React</title>
    <script crossorigin src="https://unpkg.com/react@16/umd/react.
    development.js"></script>
    <script crossorigin src="https://unpkg.com/react-dom@16/umd/react-dom.
    development.js"></script>
    <script src="main.js"></script>
  </head>
  <body onLoad="start();">
    <div id="mainContainer"></div>
  </body>
</html>
```

So far, so simple. We have a `main.js` file, which we don't have yet, being imported. So, let's now get that `main.js` file! First, we need some JSX to compile into it. To do that, replace the contents of `main.jsx` with this:

```
function start() {
  class Bookmark extends React.Component {
    constructor(props) {
      super(props);
      console.log("Bookmark component created");
    }
    title = this.props.title;
```

136

```
    titleStyle = { color : "red" }
    render() {
      return (
        <li>
          <h2 style={this.titleStyle}>{this.title}</h2>
          <a href={this.props.href}>
            {this.props.description}
          </a>
          <button onClick={() => {
            this.title = this.title + "-CHANGED";
            this.setState({});
          }}>
          Click me
           </button>
        </li>
      );
    }
}
ReactDOM.render(
  <div>
    <h1>Bookmarks</h1>
    <ul>
      <Bookmark title={"Etherient"}
        href={"https://www.etherient.com"}
        description={"The home page of Etherient"}
      />
      <Bookmark title={"Frank's Site"}
        href={"https://www.zammetti.com"}
        description={"The web home of Frank W. Zammetti"}
      />
    </ul>
  </div>,
  document.getElementById("mainContainer")
);
}
```

Contrast this to what was discused earlier. Here, I've replaced all the `React.createElement()` calls with their JSX equivalents. I've done this in both the custom Bookmark component's definition and the component tree created in the `ReactDOM.render()`. Hopefully, you'll agree that looks a lot cleaner and easier to understand.

With that in place, now we can compile our JSX:

```
npx babel main.jsx --out-file main.js
```

Oh, but if you do that right now, you're going to be greeted by an error message "Support for the experimental syntax 'classProperties' isn't currently enabled." To deal with that, we need to install another Babel plugin to provide support for that language feature:

```
npm install --save-dev @babel/plugin-proposal-class-properties
```

We also need to tell Babel to use it, so an entry is added to `.babelrc`:

```
{
  "presets": [ "@babel/preset-react" ],
  "plugins": [ "@babel/plugin-proposal-class-properties" ]
}
```

Once that's done, the compilation should be successful, and we'll have a `main.js` file ready to be used. The contents of that file should look something like this:

```
function _defineProperty(obj, key, value) { if (key in obj) { Object.
defineProperty(obj, key, { value: value, enumerable: true, configurable:
true, writable: true }); } else { obj[key] = value; } return obj; }
function start() {
  class Bookmark extends React.Component {
    constructor(props) {
      super(props);
      _defineProperty(this, "title", this.props.title);
      _defineProperty(this, "titleStyle", {
        color: "red"
      });
      console.log("Bookmark component created");
    }
```

```
  render() {
    return React.createElement("li", null,
    React.createElement("h2", {
      style: this.titleStyle
    }, this.title), React.createElement("a", {
      href: this.props.href
    }, this.props.description),
      React.createElement("button", {
      onClick: () => {
        this.title = this.title + "-CHANGED";
        this.setState({});
      }
    }, "Click me"));
  }
}
ReactDOM.render(React.createElement("div", null, React.
createElement("h1", null, "Bookmarks"), React.createElement("ul", null,
React.createElement(Bookmark, {
    title: "Etherient",
    href: "https://www.etherient.com",
    description: "The home page of Etherient"
  }), React.createElement(Bookmark, {
    title: "Frank's Site",
    href: "https://www.zammetti.com",
    description: "The web home of Frank W. Zammetti"
  }))), document.getElementById("mainContainer"));
}
```

Note   When you look at this file, you may notice some comments embedded in the output talking about __PURE__ or similar. This depends on the versions that are used for this build. The *actual* code should be the same though, so just ignore those comments.

Well, that's *far* from that code that we actually wrote, isn't it? But, it *does* bear some resemblance to the code you saw earlier where we dealt with React more directly, at a high level anyway, and that's what matters because it proves that our JSX was compiled into plain JavaScript that uses React properly. Now, if you load `index.html` in your browser, you should be greeted with the expected screen, complete with button click event handling.

That, in a nutshell, is JSX!

Prop Expressions?

JSX lets us pass props into our components just as easily – maybe even easier – as we do with the direct `React.createElement()` calls. You saw it earlier when the color of the `MaterialButton` was set. But what about when the value of a prop isn't static like that? That's where prop expressions come into play. Here's an example of passing a prop, in this case, a variable color to the `MaterialButton` component from earlier:

```
const buttonColor = "red";
const button = <MaterialButton color={buttonColor}
  onClick="alert('clicked');">
  Click Me
</MaterialButton>;
```

Now, the `buttonColor` variable's value is passed as the value of the color prop when the `MaterialButton` component is created.

Any valid JavaScript expression can be contained within the braces, so we could do

```
color={buttonColor + "Alt"}
```

You can also pass string literals using expressions. So, `color="red"` is equivalent to `color={"red"}`. There's no real reason to prefer one over the other except perhaps if you want to use expression notation consistently. React and JSX don't really care either way.

Note too that props in JSX syntax will default to `true` if you pass nothing for their value. For example, `<MaterialButton enabled />` is equivalent to `<MaterialButton enabled={true} />`.

You can also use the spread operator for a prop value when you want to pass all the properties of an existing object as props to a component. For example:

```
<MaterialButton color={"red"} enabled={true} />
```

You could write this differently using the spread operator:

```
const props = { color : "red", enabled : true };
<MaterialButton {...props} />
```

This can be handy if you have several prop values that need to be dynamic, and you need to "calculate" the values elsewhere in your code before the component is constructed.

Default Props

Recall from earlier, I said that parent components always pass props down to their children, which then use them however they wish (or not at all – it's entirely their choice!). This works great in most cases, but what happens if a component doesn't pass a particular prop down to the child? There's nothing that enforces a parent passing all props down to its children, so it's something that can happen.

One simple thing you can do is, in the child component, something like this:

```
class Bookmark extends React.Component {
  constructor(props) {
    super(props);
    console.log("Bookmark component created");
  }
  title = this.props.title;
  titleStyle = { color : "red" }
  render() {
    return (
      <li>
        <h2 style={this.titleStyle}>{this.title}</h2>
        <a href={this.props.href}>
          {this.props.description || "Unknown" }
        </a>
        <button onClick={() => {
          this.title = this.title + "-CHANGED";
          this.setState({});
        }}>
```

```
      Click me
      </button>
    </li>
  );
  }
}
```

Take a look at the `<a>` element there. Notice the || in the expression that defines the text of the element? If the parent doesn't pass down a description in the props, then using the or operator like this will result in "Unknown" being the text of the `<a>`. Remember that the value of a prop can be any valid JavaScript expression, so this works just fine.

While that will work, sprinkling or's all over the place doesn't exactly make for clean code, and React recognizes this. So, instead, you can use the `defaultProps` property. This is a special property that React makes available on the component class, and it is where you can define default values for props:

```
class Bookmark extends React.Component {
  constructor(props) {
    super(props);
    console.log("Bookmark component created");
  }
  static defaultProps = { description : "Unknown" };
  title = this.props.title;
  titleStyle = { color : "red" }
  render() {
    return (
      <li>
        <h2 style={this.titleStyle}>{this.title}</h2>
        <a href={this.props.href}>{this.props.description}</a>
        <button onClick={() => {
          this.title = this.title + "-CHANGED";
          this.setState({});
        }}>
        Click me
        </button>
```

```
      </li>
    );
  }
}
```

Here, we go back to just referencing `this.props.description` in the `<a>` definition like before, but now the `defaultProps` definition right after the constructor provides the "Unknown" value when the parent doesn't pass a description down. You can supply default values for all props, or any subset you want to in this way.

It's a handy facility that makes for much cleaner code, so it's usually a good idea to define `defaultProps`. Remember that if you don't do so and a prop isn't passed, its value is going to be undefined. That might be okay in some usages, but not all (e.g., indeed, we wouldn't want to show "undefined" for the text of that `<a>` element).

Typing Props

Having some notion of data types is usually a very good thing in a programming language. JavaScript is famous for not being strongly typed – and gets a lot of flack for it – which has spawned many alternatives (TypeScript being the most well known). When talking about React specifically, though, imagine if you had a prop on a component that expects a number, which maybe it does some calculations with, and then displays the output. What happens if you mistakenly pass a string instead? Well, React and JavaScript underneath it are going to do their best to work with what you give them. In some cases, you might get a valid result displayed. In others, though, the type coercion that will happen under the covers might result in a gibberish answer.

To avoid that, React introduces something called `propTypes`. This is like `defaultProps` in that it's another property of a component class, but this time it's one used to tell React what the types of your props are. If you then pass an incorrect type at runtime, React will output a helpful message to the JavaScript console.

To use it, you must do two things. First, add `propTypes` to the component class:

```
function start() {
  class Bookmark extends React.Component {
    constructor(props) {
      super(props);
      console.log("Bookmark component created");
```

```
    }
    static propTypes = { description : PropTypes.number };
    title = this.props.title;
    titleStyle = { color : "red" }
    render() {
      return (
        <li>
          <h2 style={this.titleStyle}>{this.title}</h2>
          <a href={this.props.href}>
            {this.props.description}
          </a>
          <button onClick={() => {
            this.title = this.title + "-CHANGED";
            this.setState({});
          }}>
          Click me
          </button>
        </li>
      );
    }
  }
  ReactDOM.render(
    <div>
      <h1>Bookmarks</h1>
      <ul>
        <Bookmark title={"Etherient"}
          href={"https://www.etherient.com"}
          description={"The home page of Etherient"}
        />
        <Bookmark title={"Frank's Site"}
          href={"https://www.zammetti.com"}
          description={"The web home of Frank W. Zammetti"}
        />
      </ul>
    </div>,
```

```
    document.getElementById("mainContainer")
  );
}
```

Here, I'm doing something kind of silly just to prove the point: I'm defining the type of the `description` prop as a number. That doesn't make much sense, but it will demonstrate how this works well enough.

But, if you compile that and try to use it, you'll hit an error because `PropTypes` isn't known, and that value is what tells React what type the prop is. So, we need to import that. All you need to do is add a `<script>` tag to the `index.html` file:

```html
<!DOCTYPE html>
<html>
  <head>
    <meta charset="UTF-8" />
    <title>Intro To React</title>
    <script crossorigin src="https://unpkg.com/react@16/umd/react.
    development.js"></script>
    <script crossorigin src="https://unpkg.com/react-dom@16/umd/react-dom.
    development.js"></script>
    <script crossorigin src="https://unpkg.com/prop-types@15.6/prop-types.
    js"></script>
    <script src="main.js"></script>
  </head>
  <body onLoad="start();">
    <div id="mainContainer"></div>
  </body>
</html>
```

`PropTypes` is supplied in a separate module, so that's what we need to import. Once both those things are done, and after you compile the JSX file and open the HTML page in your browser, you'll see the following error in the dev tools console:

```
react.development.js:1818 Warning: Failed prop type: Invalid prop
`description` of type `string` supplied to `Bookmark`, expected `number`.
in Bookmark
```

Perfect! React is aware of the type of the `description` prop and flags it when we pass a string rather than a number. This makes finding some otherwise tricky to ferret out bugs very easy, so it's generally good advice to always supply `propTypes` on your custom components, right alongside `defaultProps`.

There are about two dozen prop types available as of this writing, and you can find a list of them here: `https://reactjs.org/docs/typechecking-with-proptypes.html`. These types are actually functions that are called *validators*. As such, it's quite possible for you to add your own just by appending them on to the `PropTypes` class or, more usually, just passing a function in `propTypes`:

```
static propTypes = { description : descriptionValidator };
```

The `descriptionValidator()` function is passed the collection of props, the name of the prop being validated, and the name of the component. If it then returns `null`, then React assumes everything is okay; otherwise, the function would return an `Error` object (another class provided by the `PropTypes` module) that describes the problem.

Note   One that is worth calling out is `PropTypes.element.isRequired`. This one tells React that your component requires one and only one child component. This one is common enough that I wanted to mention it specifically.

Component Lifecycle

The final topic I want to talk about concerning React is the component lifecycle. You've already seen one: the `render()` method. But, while `render()` is really the final thing we're trying to get to with a component, it's not the whole picture.

Every single React component goes through a series of distinct stages in a well-defined order, which is illustrated in Figure 4-2.

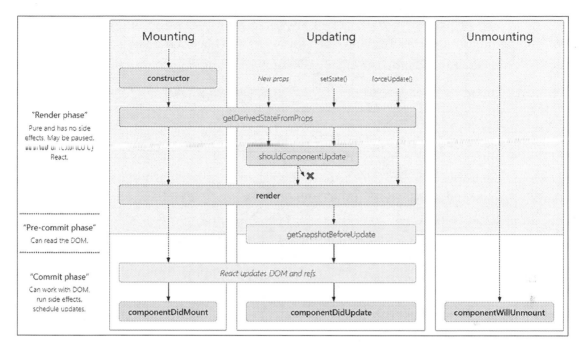

Figure 4-2. *The lifecycle events of a React component*

In sequence, during initial construction (when it's first added to the virtual DOM and actual page DOM), the order will be as follows:

1. The component class's constructor is called. That should be pretty obvious: it's a JavaScript class after all, and if they define a constructor, then that always gets called first (and if they don't specify a constructor, then an automatically added one will be called).

2. The getDerivedStateFromProps() method is called. This is responsible for returning an object to update the state, or null if there is nothing to update. This is called during the initial construction of the component, called "mounting" because it's when the component is constructed, of course, but is also when it is added, or "mounted," to the virtual DOM, as well as during subsequent updates.

3. The render() method is called. You already know about this one!

4. The `componentDidMount()` method is called immediately after the component is inserted into the virtual DOM. This is where you can do initialization that required actual DOM nodes.

During an update (when the component exists and may need to be changed), the sequence will be as follows:

1. The `getDerivedStateFromProps()` method is called.

2. The `shouldComponentUpdate()` method is called. The results of this tell React whether the component's output is affected by the current change in state or props. By default, the method automatically supplied will result in re-rendering on every state change, and unless you have good reason to do otherwise, you should rely on this functionality.

3. The `render()` method is called.

4. The `getSnapshotBeforeUpdate()` method is called. The job of this method is to capture some information from the DOM, like perhaps scroll position, right before the render output is committed to the DOM, potentially changing it. Like `shouldComponentUpdate()`, most of the time, you should just let the default version of this method do its thing.

5. Finally, the `componentDidUpdate()` method is called. Things like network requests for data you need to display are often done here. But you can ignore this if you don't need it.

You can override any of these, or none of them (except for `render()`, of course, which you have to override) as your needs dictate.

Note   There are a small handful of other available methods, but they are now considered legacy, and developers are discouraged from using them, so I'm not describing them here. I wanted to mention this though, in case you see code using them, you will be aware that it's probably valid code, but is no longer code you should follow. It's also code that, it's a good bet, will be broken by a future react update when support for those lifecycle events are removed from React entirely.

Summary

In this chapter, you took further steps into the world of React than in the preceding chapter. You got a brief tour of where it all started, why it came into being, and who's responsible. We talked a bit about what it offers, why that's valuable, and why it's become so popular. Then, you saw some basic React code and got familiar with the four main pillars of React: components, props, state, and style.

You also got a look at concepts, including JSX, the component lifecycle, PropTypes, and default props. Going along with JSX, you got a brief introduction to Babel (even though you might never interact with it directly when working with Gatsby). This places all the necessary tools for working with React in your toolbox, preparing you for the application code to come.

In the next chapter, we'll take all you've learned in the first three chapters and start building a real application so you can get some real experience working with Gatsby and building a JAMstack application beyond the simple one generated in the last chapter.

CHAPTER 5

Building JAMboard

Now that you're all but a JAMstack expert, know a fair bit about React, have played with Gatsby, and have seen one static site built, let's put it all together and make the leap to building a more "proper" application, an app that *does something*!

With this chapter and the next, we'll put an app together, using Gatsby to give us a jumpstart. In the process, we'll get to see something called Netlify, and we'll finally get a look at some APIs (though those two things come in the *next* chapter because before then, we have to get the basic app built and working on our own machine first).

So, let's jump right in and talk about what it is, exactly, that we're building!

What We're Building

The app we're going to build is called JAMboard, and it's a shared whiteboard, so to speak, where people can collaboratively mark up documents. The documents will be in Markdown form and will be deployed as part of the app itself. In contrast, the process of marking up the documents – which means highlighting sections of text in the document and attaching comments to it – will be dynamic, meaning they will not be part of the build. So, to make a new document available for markup means rebuilding and redeploying the site, but actually marking them up does not.

For this chapter, the collaborative part will be eschewed as we'll save comments to browser local storage. It's in the next chapter where we'll add the collaborative elements. But, it makes little sense to get into that aspect of the app without getting the app itself built, so that's where we'll start.

The app will consist of two pages: a home page, which contains a list of documents that can be marked up, and the "main" page, where the document is displayed and can be marked up. Much of the code will be on the latter page, but without the former, it wouldn't be of much use since you wouldn't be able to get to a document to mark up!

© Frank Zammetti 2020
F. Zammetti, *Practical JAMstack*, https://doi.org/10.1007/978-1-4842-6177-4_5

Figure 5-1 shows the document list page. And yes, I know it looks a little kitschy, but I've added some elements that are purely for embellishment so that I could demonstrate some concepts to you, including more GraphQL usage and how to work with images. It's the document list at the bottom that provides the functionality we need.

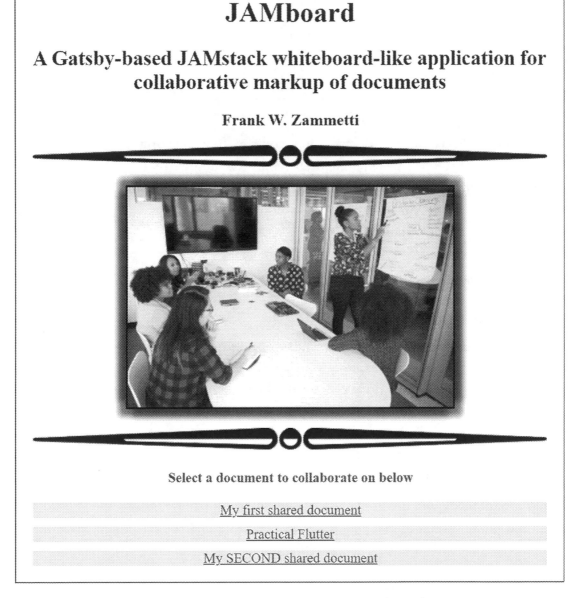

Figure 5-1. *Be it so humble, there's no place like home (page)/document list*

The real meat of JAMboard is found on the page that the user will see once they select a document from the document list, which I call the whiteboard page, and which Figure 5-2 shows. The interface is simple and is divided into three sections. Up top is the control bar, and in it, you have a button to return to the document list screen. There's also a button for adding a marker. A marker is a thing that marks a bit of text as having comments attached. The way it will work is the user will select some text, click that button, and that text will become a link. When that link is clicked, the third button, Add Comment, will be enabled. Any comments that might exist for the marker (if it wasn't just created, obviously) will be shown in the comment section at the bottom. In-between the control bar and the comment section is the main display area where the document itself is displayed. This area, and the comments section, can scroll independently as needed.

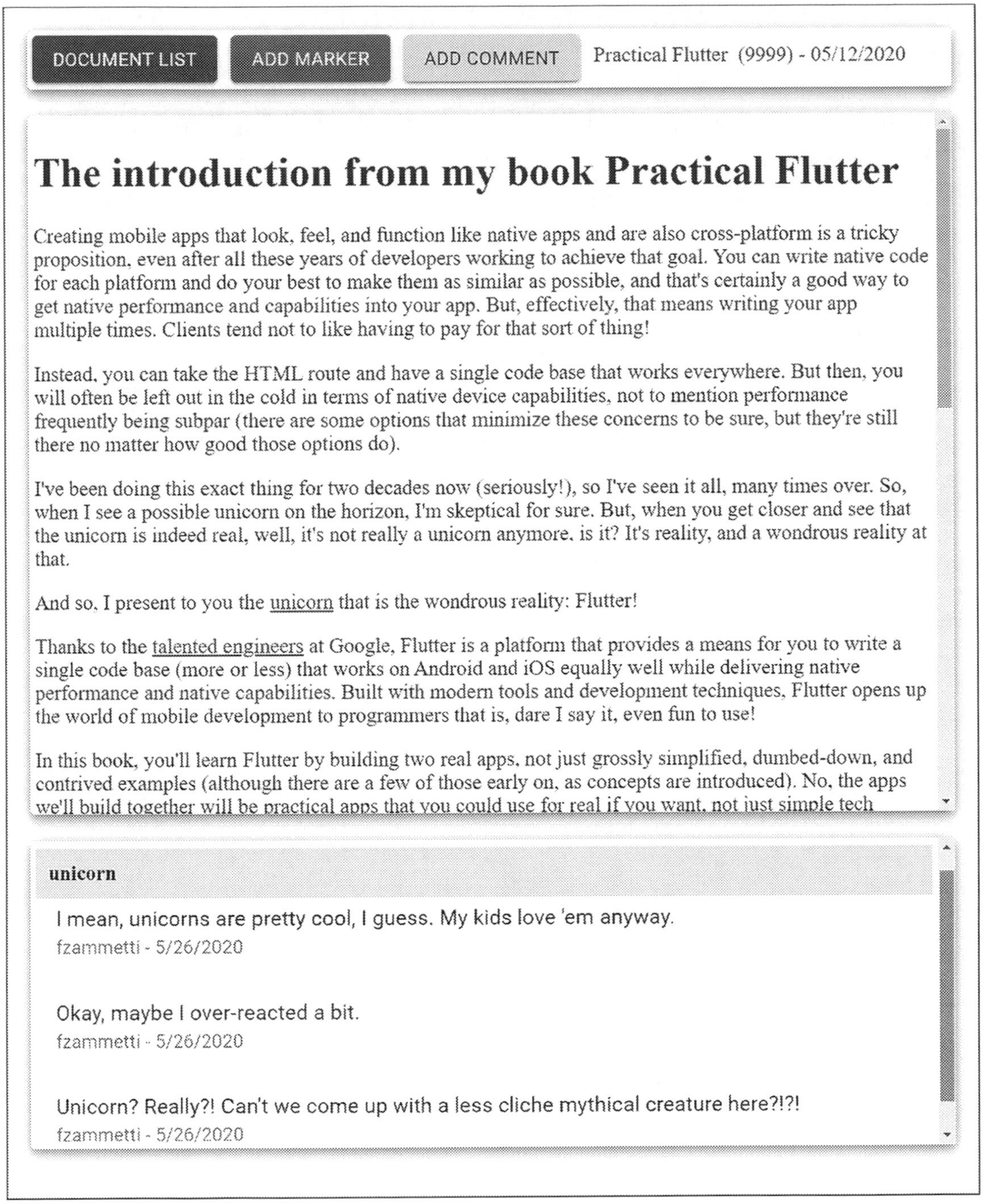

DOCUMENT LIST   ADD MARKER   ADD COMMENT   Practical Flutter (9999) - 05/12/2020

The introduction from my book Practical Flutter

Creating mobile apps that look, feel, and function like native apps and are also cross-platform is a tricky proposition, even after all these years of developers working to achieve that goal. You can write native code for each platform and do your best to make them as similar as possible, and that's certainly a good way to get native performance and capabilities into your app. But, effectively, that means writing your app multiple times. Clients tend not to like having to pay for that sort of thing!

Instead, you can take the HTML route and have a single code base that works everywhere. But then, you will often be left out in the cold in terms of native device capabilities, not to mention performance frequently being subpar (there are some options that minimize these concerns to be sure, but they're still there no matter how good those options do).

I've been doing this exact thing for two decades now (seriously!), so I've seen it all, many times over. So, when I see a possible unicorn on the horizon, I'm skeptical for sure. But, when you get closer and see that the unicorn is indeed real, well, it's not really a unicorn anymore, is it? It's reality, and a wondrous reality at that.

And so, I present to you the unicorn that is the wondrous reality: Flutter!

Thanks to the talented engineers at Google, Flutter is a platform that provides a means for you to write a single code base (more or less) that works on Android and iOS equally well while delivering native performance and native capabilities. Built with modern tools and development techniques, Flutter opens up the world of mobile development to programmers that is, dare I say it, even fun to use!

In this book, you'll learn Flutter by building two real apps, not just grossly simplified, dumbed-down, and contrived examples (although there are a few of those early on, as concepts are introduced). No, the apps we'll build together will be practical apps that you could use for real if you want, not just simple tech

unicorn

I mean, unicorns are pretty cool, I guess. My kids love 'em anyway.
fzammetti - 5/26/2020

Okay, maybe I over-reacted a bit.
fzammetti - 5/26/2020

Unicorn? Really?! Can't we come up with a less cliche mythical creature here?!?!
fzammetti - 5/26/2020

Figure 5-2. *The whiteboard page*

Here, you can see two markers, one on the word "unicorn" near the bottom and then another on "talented engineers," as denoted by them being links. And, you can see that I've clicked the "unicorn" maker, and the comments associated with it are displayed at the bottom (I have weird conversations with myself sometimes, apparently!). You can scroll that section and the comments scrolls behind the header at the top with the marker text in it.

As I mentioned earlier, any markers created, and comments added, are stored in browser local storage for now, which means that for this chapter, only a single user can mark up a document. In the next chapter, we'll bring a server, an API, and a database into the mix to make it truly collaborative. Splitting it up like this across two chapters allows us to focus on each part separately, which I think makes for a better learning experience.

So, let's not waste any more time, you have a good idea what we're building, let's get to coding!

Bootstrapping the App with Gatsby

The first thing we want to do is create a Gatsby app to serve as the foundation of JAMboard. That's easy enough to do:

```
gatsby new JAMboard
```

We'll use the default started for this since, in this case, there is no starter that is like what we're building. What we'll wind up doing is taking the project produced by the default starter and then removing everything we don't need, which leaves us a configuration that has all the basics but nothing else we don't need.

At this point, you should have a complete, working Gatsby project. Feel free to fire it up if you like with `gatsby develop`, but at this point, we're ready to start removing what we don't need, so we have a clean slate with just the necessary foundation to build on.

Trimming the Fat

The first step is simply to delete some stuff:

- Delete the entire `.git` directory. You'll get a new one once the code is checked into your own repo (in the next chapter).

- Delete the entire src/components directory. It, and its contents, won't be needed by JAMboard.

- Delete all files under src in all remaining subdirectories except for index.js and 404.js in the src/pages directory (but leave the directories, which should just be images and pages now). These are the only two pages in this project (oh, missed being a single-page app, or SPA, by *that* much!).

That leaves extraordinarily little, really, but it leaves what we truly need. It also leaves you with a nonfunctional app! It won't even build now. Let's start to fix that.

gatsby-config.json

The first problem is that we need to clean up the gatsby-config.json file to remove some things we no longer need. To make it simple, here's the content it should have, anything else can be removed:

```
module.exports = {
  siteMetadata: {
    title: "JAMboard",
    description: "A Gatsby-based JAMstack whiteboard-like application for
    collaborative markup of documents",
    author: "Frank W. Zammetti"
  },
  plugins: [
    {
      resolve: "gatsby-source-filesystem",
      options: {
        name: "images",
        path: `${__dirname}/src/images`,
      },
    },
    "gatsby-transformer-sharp",
    "gatsby-plugin-sharp"
  ]
}
```

Even though we don't have any images at this point, we will later, so we'll leave the plugins for dealing with them in place. Everything else can come out (and the siteMetadata can be changed to be appropriate for JAMboard).

The app still won't build at this point, though, so let's keep going with the cleanup.

index.js

The index.js page needs to be trimmed down too. By default, it will be referencing content in the src/components directory, but we deleted that earlier, so it's causing build problems now. For the moment, just put this in it to deal with that:

```
import React from "react"

const IndexPage = () => (
  <div>I am the Index page</div>
)

export default IndexPage
```

Try to build again (or, if you had already executed gatsby develop, then it will have tried again already automatically), and you'll see that it still doesn't work. There is still one more piece to the fix-up puzzle!

404.js

The 404.js page also needs to be trimmed down. Now, just make it this:

```
import React from "react";

const NotFoundPage = () => (
  <div>
    <h1>NOT FOUND</h1>
    <p>
      You just hit a route that doesn&#39;t exist.  Sorry!
    </p>
  </div>
)

export default NotFoundPage;
```

At this point, you should get a clean build (warnings excepted), and you should be able to access the site, though it only displays "I am the Index page," but that's as it should be.

Note   Although it's not needed to get the site working, please also create two new directories under the src directory named documents and templates. We'll need them in short order so they may as well get in there now (they'll do no harm).

The Home/Document List Page

Now it's time to start building JAMboard for real. The first step will be to build a new IndexPage component in the `index.js` file to be the home/document list page you saw in the screenshot earlier. It begins with some imports:

```
import React from "react";
import { graphql } from "gatsby"
import Img from "gatsby-image";
import "./index.css";
import Button from "@material-ui/core/Button";
import Dialog from "@material-ui/core/Dialog";
import DialogActions from "@material-ui/core/DialogActions";
import DialogContent from "@material-ui/core/DialogContent";
import DialogTitle from "@material-ui/core/DialogTitle";
import TextField from "@material-ui/core/TextField";
```

Obviously, we need React. And, since we know that the list of documents must be dynamic, that implies a GraphQL query, so we import that as well. We have some images to display, so we need the Img component.

Then, we have another file that we need to create, `index.css`, being imported. This is what the name implies: styles for this page. This is a plain old CSS file, and there are only four classes in it, so not even a complicated one! But, I think it makes more sense to look at those as they are used in context, so let's set that aside for the moment.

The remaining few imports, which are various React components from something called Material-UI, require a quick detour to explain, so let's take that now!

A Quick Detour: The Material-UI Toolkit

Around 2014, Google realized that most of the web app products were going in different directions in terms of look, feel, and function. Android, too, was a completely different beast visually, and in fact, Android is where the eventual solution began. They determined that this wasn't a sustainable direction to go, and they needed to come up with something to unify their products.

As a result, the Material Design language was created (`https://material.io`). Although it's not terribly important for our work here, I think a very brief description of Material Design itself is in order.

Material Design is a set of design principles that are informed by how people interact with real objects in the physical world. Primarily influenced by print media, Material Design begins with concepts like sheets of paper and their digital equivalents. When you read a book, you, of course, turn pages. That motion is encapsulated in Material Design, just as the underlying pattern of the sheet of paper itself is.

Material Design is concerned with how layers of content can slide over each other, for example, and those slides, those animations, are vital elements. Everything is intended to be reactive to touch (remember that this all started with Android, at least in its initial implementation, so touch was automatically a crucial part of Material Design).

As I said, knowing this doesn't make a huge difference in our work here, but a little context never hurt anybody!

Now, what does matter is the Material-UI library itself (`https://material-ui.com`). Simply put, this is a library of React components built on top of Google's Material Design language. Being a React library means you simply add it to your project with NPM like any other library, import the appropriate parts of it, and use it in your code. For example, if you want to put a button on the screen:

```
import React from "react";
import Button from "@material-ui/core/Button";
const App = () => (
  <Button variant="contained" color="primary">
    Hello World
  </Button>
);
```

It's a simple example, but it demonstrates all the key ideas. First, React was naturally imported and so too was the `Button` component from Material-UI. Then, it's merely a matter of dropping a `<Button>` tag into the code, with appropriate props attached and some text to show on the button, and we have ourselves a Material-UI button.

The Material-UI library offers a wealth of components with which to build a user interface. It has all the usual suspects like buttons, check boxes, radio buttons, drop-down lists, grids, lists, progress bars, alert dialogs, menus, and a lot more. The website referenced in the preceding text does a great job of presenting it all. You'll find a list of components with numerous simple examples for each and then links for the API of each that details the properties and options available.

It really is an easy-to-use library that also makes your apps look and function great with minimal effort on your part. You'll only see a small portion of what it has to offer in this book, so I highly encourage you to spend some time on the Material-UI website exploring all it has to offer. I think you'll be very impressed, and it will, I bet, quickly become your favorite collection of widgets for building UIs with React (FYI, it perennially ranks among the most popular React libraries, so it's not just me singing its praises!).

Of course, in order to use this library in our project, we'll need to add it first:

```
npm install --save @material-ui/core
```

Once that's done, all the imports work as expected, as does all the code that makes use of Material-UI.

Another Quick Detour: Adding Markdown Support

As mentioned earlier, the documents that users can mark up are included in the project as Markdown files. For Gatsby to be able to handle those, we have to add a dependency and some configuration to `gatsby-config.json`. Let's start with the latter first. Add the following to `gatsby-config.json`'s `plugins` array:

```
{
  resolve: "gatsby-source-filesystem",
  options: {
    name: "documents",
    path: `${__dirname}/src/documents`
  }
},
"gatsby-transformer-remark"
```

This is telling Gatsby to read the files in the `src/documents` directory and create internal nodes for them. This is termed "sourcing" the files in Gatsby-speak. This is just like how images are handled by the `gatsby-source-filesystem` plugin entry that you left in `gatsby-config.json` earlier.

However, that's only part of the equation: we then need a transformer plugin that extends Gatsby with the capability to ingest those Markdown files, parse them, and store them internally. That gives us the ability to query these documents later to use them, and that's where the `gatsby-transformer-remark` plugin comes into play.

For this to work, we need to add a dependency to `package.json` for this plugin with an NPM command:

```
npm install --save gatsby-transformer-remark
```

Now, Gatsby knows how to read any Markdown files in the `src/documents` directory and make them available for GraphQL queries later, which you can bet is exactly what we're going to do with them!

Back to the Code!

Now that you have a rough idea of what Material-UI is, you know what those imports were all about. On this home/document list page, Material-UI is used to present a pop-up dialog window that prompts the user for a username if they don't already have one stored. For that, we'll need the Material-UI `Dialog`, `DialogTitle`, `DialogContent`, `DialogActions`, `TextField`, and `Button` components.

Don't get hung up on what those are right now – that will become clear very soon – but most of them are probably obvious if you think about any pop-up dialog you've ever seen. Before we even get to the actual dialog code, though, we must start building the `IndexPage` component that this file exports.

Building the Component

After the exports is the start of an `IndexPage` React component:

```
export default class IndexPage extends React.Component {

constructor(inProps) {

  super(inProps);
```

161

```
  const username = localStorage.getItem("username");
  this.state = {
    dialogVisible :
      (username === null || username.trim() === ""),
    username : localStorage.getItem("username")
  };

  this.data = inProps.data;

}
```

The constructor has a couple of chores to accomplish. First, we have to pass the incoming props to the superclass constructor, as you learned in the previous chapter. Next, we look for a `username` key in local storage. Every user must have a username, but since we're not creating a high-security system here, it's just stored on the user's machine. Next, a state object for the component is constructed and attached to the instance. The `dialogVisible` property is what triggers the dialog where the user enters their username if one isn't present already (we'll come back to this shortly). If there's no username, then `dialogVisible` will be `true,` and the dialog will appear. The username itself is stored in state as well.

After that, we need to store the data that Gatsby automagically injects into the component's props. This is the result of a GraphQL query that we'll look at near the end, but it's where we'll find the `siteMetadata` from the `gatsby-config.json` file, which we'll use to build the screen, as well as the list of Markdown documents.

Rendering the Component

That takes care of the basics of setting up the component, so now we can begin to render its content:

```
render() {

  return (
    <div className="outerContainer">
```

As you know, the render() method must return a single element, and it's a plain old <div> here. It has the first of those four styles I mentioned from the styles.css file that was imported earlier attached to it, outerContainer:

```
.outerContainer {
  margin : auto;
  width : 600px;
  text-align : center;
}
```

This gives us a 600-pixel wide box, horizontally centered, with its contents also horizontally centered.

Prompting for Username

As I mentioned, when the dialogVisible property of the state object is true by way of the constructor code, that means the user needs to enter a username. In this case, a Material-UI Dialog component is used to get that entry. Recall that React will re-render the page as necessary when state changes, so the way you hide and show dialogs like this is to mutate a state property, dialogVisible in this case, and reference it in the content the render() method returns. In this way, the dialog can be hidden and shown.

Let's look at that dialog now to see how it's built and how that state property is used:

```
<Dialog open={this.state.dialogVisible} maxWidth="sm"
  fullWidth={true} disableBackdropClick={true}
  disableEscapeKeyDown={true}>
  <DialogTitle>
    You need a username to use JAMboard
  </DialogTitle>
  <DialogContent>
    <TextField label="Enter username here" fullWidth
      variant="outlined" required={true} defaultValue=""
      onChange={ (inEvent) =>
        this.setState({
          username: inEvent.target.value
        })
      } />
```

163

```
    </DialogContent>
    <DialogActions>
      <Button onClick={this.handleDialogSave.bind(this)}
        color="primary" variant="outlined">Save</Button>
    </DialogActions>
  </Dialog>
```

Okay, so, it all starts with a `Dialog` component, which you can see in action (well, so to speak!) in Figure 5-3. This is a container for the other parts of the dialog. As you can see, the `open` prop, which you can read as "is this dialog visible or not," gets its value from the state object's `dialogVisible` property. The `maxWidth` prop determines the maximum width the dialog can be. The dialog will grow according to the size of the browser window, but the value of `sm` means "make is small, relatively-speaking." The `fullWidth` prop ensures that the dialog will stretch to `maxWidth` and those two combined ensures that the `TextField` will flex with the size of the dialog (which itself flexes with the size of the browser window). Finally, the `disableBackdropClick` and `disableEscapeKeyDown` result in the dialog not being dismissible any way other than clicking the Save button (usually, pressing ESC or clicking outside the dialog causes it to go away, but we *need* them to enter their username, so we don't want that to be the case here).

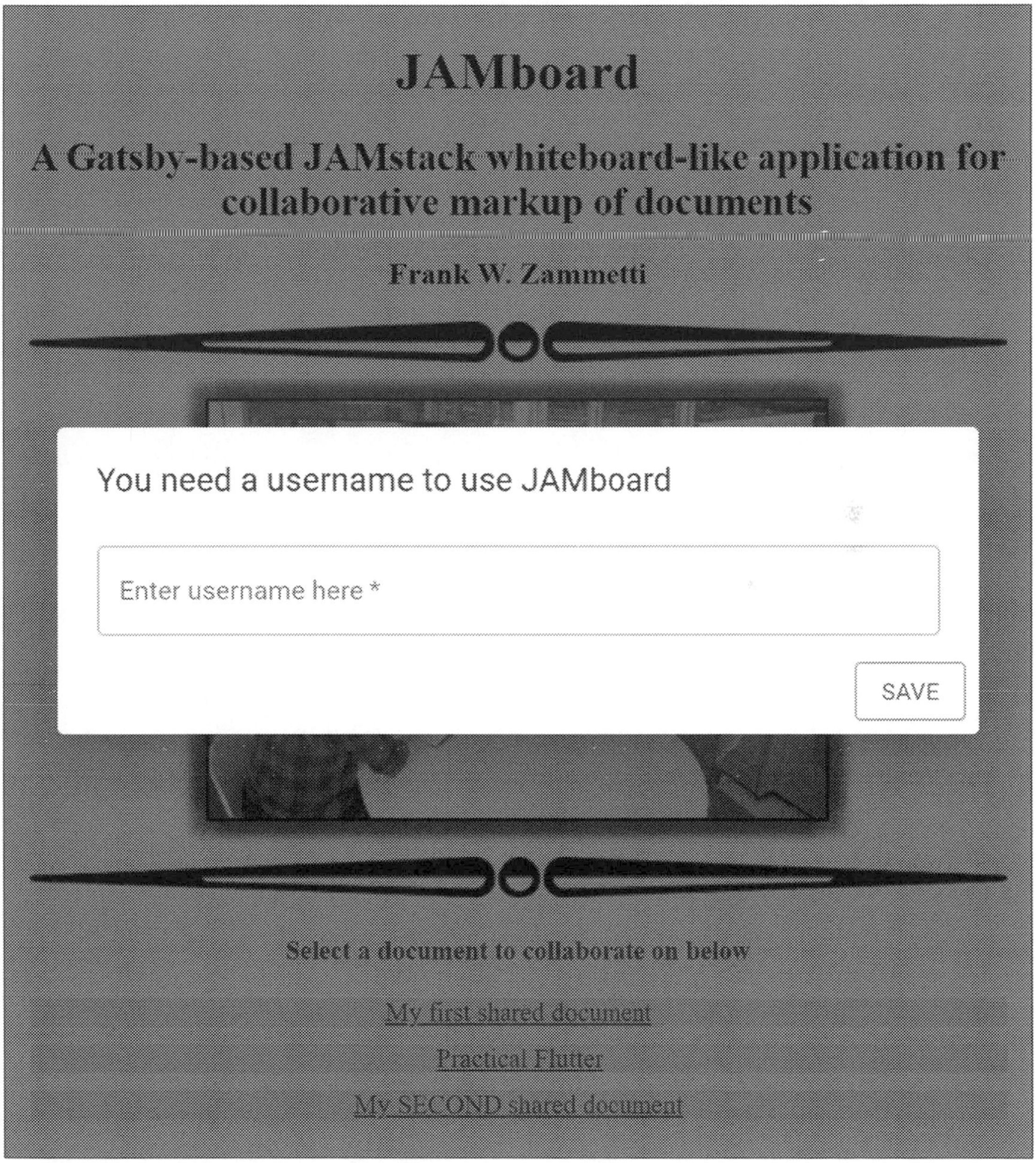

Figure 5-3. *Prompting for username*

Inside the `Dialog` is, firstly, a `DialogTitle` component. As its name implies, this provides a place for a title on the dialog. After that comes the `DialogContent` component, which is where whatever main content you want to show in the dialog is placed. In this case, all we need is a single `TextField` component, which provides the user a place to enter their username.

A `TextField` can optionally have a `label`, as I set here to provide some directions. The `fullWidth` prop tells the `TextField` to stretch horizontally to fill its container, which makes it stretch to fill the dialog (minus some built-in padding). The `variant` prop allows us to change the style of the `TextField`. You can make it a plain line with the `standard` variant, or a filled-in box with the `filled` variant. Here, the `outlined` variant gives it a more traditional box look. Setting `required` to `true` results in an asterisk being shown to indicate the field is required. The `defaultValue` is just that: what value the field should have to begin with, and obviously, an empty string makes sense. Finally, we must add an `onChange` event handler prop. Otherwise, nothing will happen. Without it, you can type in the field, but nothing is done with the value. That part is up to us to implement. Here, the value of the `username` property of the state object is updated with the current value of the field as provided by the `target.property` field of the incoming event object.

Finally, we have a `DialogActions` component that sits at the bottom of the dialog and contains any actionable elements we want, which usually means buttons, hence the `Button` you see in it. Let's skip the `onClick` prop for just a moment. The `color` prop lets us style the button a bit. The value `primary` gives us a blue button, while `secondary` would be a red one. Like the `TextField`, the `Button` component offers a `variant` prop (which, incidentally, is something you'll find on many Material-UI components). For this dialog, I've opted for a more traditional-looking button, so it's `outlined` again.

Now, about that `onClick` prop... this is what's executed when the button is clicked obviously, and that results in the `handleDialogSave()` method of the `IndexPage` component being executed. Before we look at that code, note that whatever function is executed in response to a click executes in the context of the `Button` component itself. That's a problem for us because we're going to need to update state to hide the dialog, which you'll recall can only be done from code inside the component. Although `handleDialogSave()` is lexically inside the `IndexPage` component, at runtime, the `this` reference in it will point to the `Button` component, and we have a problem, Houston! The simple solution is to bind the function to the `IndexPage` component, as you can see done here.

Now, onto the actual code of that handleDialogSave() method:

```
handleDialogSave() {

  if (this.state.username !== null &&
    this.state.username.trim() !== ""
  ) {

    this.state.dialogVisible = false;
    this.setState((inState, inProps) => {
      return this.state;
    });

    localStorage.setItem("username", this.state.username);

  }

}
```

First, realize that the user could click Save without having entered a username. So, we check for that and only do something if they entered something. That way, the dialog remains until they enter something. Once they do, we change the dialogVisible property of the state object to false and call setState(), passing it the state object. React dutifully repaints the screen, resulting in the dialog now being hidden. Finally, the username is saved to local storage, and we've accomplished the goal of getting a username from the user.

Showing Site Metadata

Following the dialog markup, we start to build out the IndexPage component and what the user will see on the screen all the time:

```
<h1>{this.data.site.siteMetadata.title}</h1>
<h2>{this.data.site.siteMetadata.description}</h2>
<h3>{this.data.site.siteMetadata.author}</h3>
<Img fixed={this.data.divider.childImageSharp.fixed} />
<Img fixed={this.data.splash.childImageSharp.fixed} />
<br />
```

```
<Img fixed={this.data.divider.childImageSharp.fixed} />
<div className="documentListLabel" >
  Select a document to collaborate on below
</div>
```

If you compare this markup to the screenshot of this screen earlier, it should make a lot of sense. Recall that in the constructor, we captured the data that Gatsby injects into the props for the IndexPage component, so that's available to us now to display the site's title, description, and author (hey, I gotta get my props in, right? – and I don't mean React props!) from the siteMetadata in the gatsby-config.json file.

The Img component allows us to display the images that, as you'll in a few sections from now, are part of the returned query data, just by referencing them in that data, as we do any of the data that comes from gatsby-config.json. Note that as you saw in Chapter 3, Gatsby can create images of various sizes for us automatically and fluidly use them as appropriate for the browser viewport. But, in this case, I just wanted some plain old, boring fixed-width images, so the fixed prop is used to indicate that. The divider and splash images are still processed by Gatsby's gatsby-plugin-sharp and gatsby-transformer-sharp plugins even though they're fixed, so that's why we have to drill down into the data a bit to get at them.

Near the bottom, we have the list of documents, the header for it at least, in a plain of <div>. This <div> has the documentListLabel class from index.css applied and is this:

```
.documentListLabel {
  color : #0000ff;
  font-weight : bold;
  margin-top : 20px;
  margin-bottom : 20px;
}
```

As you can see, it's just enough to make the text bolder and put some space above and below it to make it aesthetically pleasing.

Now, let's get into producing the actual list of documents.

The Document List

The list of documents is relatively easy to produce given that Gatsby has queried them and so they are in our data object. But, we have to dynamically generate potentially several elements, `<div>`s in this case, so we're going to need a loop of some sort. Here, I've used the `map()` method of the `this.data.allMarkdownRemark.edges` array, which simply states is the list of documents Gatsby found in our documents directory. This all gets wrapped in braces to make JSX happy:

```
{this.data.allMarkdownRemark.edges.map(
  (inItem, inIndex) => { return (
    <div key={inIndex} className="documentDiv">
      <a href={inItem.node.frontmatter.slug}
        onMouseOver={(inEvent) =>
        inEvent.target.parentNode.style.backgroundColor=
        "#ff0000"
        }
        onFocus={() => {}} onBlur={() => {}}
        onMouseOut={(inEvent) =>
        inEvent.target.parentNode.style.backgroundColor=
        "#eaeaea"
        } >
        {inItem.node.frontmatter.title}
      </a>
    </div>
  );}
)}
```

The outcome is a `<div>` per document with an `<a>` inside it. Each element that is produced in this manner should have a unique key prop; otherwise, React will give you a warning (though not an error, it should be noted). Hence, the index in the array is used, which is a good choice. The `<div>` has the `documentDiv` style applied, which is from `styles.css` and is this:

```
.documentDiv {
  width : 600px;
  margin-bottom : 10px;
  background-color : #eaeaea;
}
```

This is what gives the items in this list a gray background color and ensures spacing between documents.

Within each `<div>`, we obviously need the document's title, and that must be clickable so we can navigate to that document. The `href` of the link comes from the data for the current document we're working with in the `map()` function. We can drill down into its `node.frontmatter` property, and within it, we find the values in the document.

We should probably stop here and take a look at one of these documents, since we haven't done that yet, and it's kind of important! Here's one you might see:

```
---
slug: "/documents/practical_flutter"
date: "2020-05-12"
title: "Practical Flutter"
id: "9999"
---
#   The introduction from my book Practical Flutter

Creating mobile apps that look, feel, and function…
```

I've cut this short, hence the ellipses at the end, to save some space. But this gives you the important stuff. First, at the top, between the `---` markers, is what's called the "frontmatter." This can mostly be any details you want and it results in key/value pairs being made available to you via GraphQL query. Let's skip the `slug` element for just a moment. The `date`, `title`, and `id` elements I'd hope are pretty obvious, and their values can be whatever you like. The only real requirement, or else JAMboard won't work right, is that `id` must be unique (and also, the date must be in YYYY-MM-DD format, though even if it's not I think you'll find things still generally work, though the date values you see may wind up being nonsensical).

After the front matter comes the document contents itself, and you are free to use any Markdown styling you like here. For example, the `#` in front of the first line makes this a big, bold bit of text. The `gatsby-transformer-remark` plugin we added earlier converts this Markdown content to HTML for us, ready to be used as such.

Now, back to that slug element. As I'm sure you've guessed, that's the path to this document. This is what the value of the href of that <a> tag will be so that it will navigate to the document. In the next section, you'll learn how we can create a template for displaying these documents and telling Gatsby how to use that template, but that's jumping ahead a bit. Back to the list!

When the user hovers over the link, I want the background to turn red and the text to turn yellow. This is accomplished with two things. First, another style from index.css:

```
a:hover {
  color : #ffff00;
}
```

That takes care of making the text yellow on hover. For the background, though, since I wanted the *whole* bar to change, not just the text, we need an onMouseOver event handler. All it must do is get the parent node of the <a> node, which is the <div> with the gray background, and change its color to red. To then undo that when the mouse moves off the link, the onMouseOut event handler kicks in and changes the bar back to gray (the text is handled by virtue of reverting to the default style for a hyperlink).

Note   Oh, and that empty onFocus event handler? That's literally just to get rid of a Gatsby build warning, something I'm a bit of a stickler for (you'll find that there are still two warnings produced when building this app, but those can't be avoided as far as I can tell, so I grudgingly have to live with them, though I'm sure even they could be gotten rid of by modifying a Gatsby config file somehow).

Finally, the text of the link is taken from the title element of the document's frontmatter in the data. All of this is done for each document Gatsby found, and we get a list of <div>s, one per document, just like we want.

Now, I've mentioned that Gatsby finds those documents, parse them, and add them to its internal data store, making all this possible, but I've glossed over exactly how that happens. You know that part of the equation is the plugins added earlier to gatsby-config.json to handle Markdown. Still, there's another piece of the puzzle – two really, if you count the query that gets us all this data to work with – so let's take a look at those pieces next, starting with something entirely new!

A Quick Detour: gatsby-node.js

In the "The Whiteboard Page" section, we'll look at creating a template, which is what Gatsby uses to render our documents. But, even before we can do that, we have to extend Gatsby a bit more in order for it to construct pages that marry that template with the parsed Markdown data we added the plugins for earlier. This is done in another Gatsby configuration file: gatsby-node.js.

Gatsby exposes a powerful Node API for doing things such as dynamically creating pages. The code you write to use this API is executed at build time. The way it works is that each thing you export from this file is executed by Gatsby during the build process. The API exposes various lifecycle "hooks" such as createPages (used to dynamically create pages – which is what we're going to use here), createNode (called any time a new node is created during file parsing and data querying), onPostBuild (called after all other parts of the build process are done), and createSchemaCustomization (allows you to customize Gatsby's GraphQL schema by creating type definitions and field extensions or adding third-party schemas), just to name a few.

As I mentioned, we're going to use createPages for our work here, so we drop some code into gatsby-node.js like so:

```
exports.createPages = ({ actions, graphql }) => {

  const { createPage } = actions;

  const documentTemplate = require.resolve(
    `./src/templates/documentTemplate.js`
  );
```

Most importantly, here, we're bringing in the documentTemplate.js file, which we'll be looking at in the next major section and is the template for displaying the document, along with all the code that makes all the markup of it by user's work. Once that's done, we need to run a GraphQL query to get our documents:

```
return graphql(`
  {
    allMarkdownRemark(
      sort: { order: DESC, fields: [frontmatter___date] }
      limit: 1000
    ) {
```

```
    edges {
      node {
        frontmatter {
          slug
        }
      }
    }
  }
}
`).then(result => {
```

Here, you can see how you can do some new things with GraphQL, including sorting – on the date field in the frontmatter here in descending order, so the newest are at the top – and limiting how many documents are parsed to 1000. Any documents beyond the 1000th will be ignored (which is the only reason I bothered sorting here: that way, we know the *oldest* documents will fall off if any are going to fall off at all, not the newest). Then, the query digs down through the edges and nodes collections, as produced by Gatsby when it sourced and transformed the document files, and eventually pull out the slug value from the frontmatter.

Next, we have some error handling inside the then() function:

```
if (result.errors) {
  return Promise.reject(result.errors);
}
```

Gatsby will abort the build at that point should the Promise be rejected. But, assuming that doesn't happen, it's then time to create some pages:

```
return result.data.allMarkdownRemark.edges.forEach(
  ({ node }) => {
  createPage({
    path: node.frontmatter.slug,
    component: documentTemplate,
    context: {
      slug: node.frontmatter.slug
    }
  })
})
```

For each document Gatsby sourced and transformed, and which we queried for earlier, an internal node is created. With that node passed to our anonymous `forEach()` function, we can call the `createPage()` function that the Gatsby Node API provides, passing it the `path` (which is the `slug` value), the component that is the template (`documentTemplate`, as was imported earlier), and the `context`, which is just the `slug` again. This all causes Gatsby to create a page that renders the Markdown document in whatever way `documentTemplate` implements, and then adds it to the internal data store, as well as its navigation model, allowing other pages of the site to navigate to it easily. As we're JAMstack'ing it here, the resultant page is, of course, static. It's entirely built and won't require processing at runtime to create – that work is already done by virtue of this code.

Querying for Data

The final step to making the home page/document list work is to query for the data that is used throughout the code. This is a page-level query, so Gatsby automagically delivers its results to the React component that renders this page. You've already seen it all used, so you know that you should expect to see two images, some `siteMetadata` and, of course, a list of documents. Here's the query - see if it meets your expectations of what it should generally be:

```
export const pageQuery = graphql`
  query {
    splash: file(relativePath: { eq: "splash.png" }) {
      childImageSharp {
        fixed(width: 420, height: 296) {
          ...GatsbyImageSharpFixed
        }
      }
    }
    divider: file(relativePath: { eq: "divider.png" }) {
      childImageSharp {
        fixed(width: 600, height: 25) {
          ...GatsbyImageSharpFixed
        }
      }
    }
```

```
site {
  siteMetadata {
    title
    description
    author
  }
}
allMarkdownRemark(sort: {
  order: DESC, fields: [frontmatter___date]
}) {
  edges {
    node {
      id
      frontmatter {
        title
        slug
      }
    }
  }
}
}
```

The two images, `splash` and `divider`, reference files that will have already been parsed by Gatsby thanks to the plugins in `gatsby-config.json`. The `childImageSharp` is where those images wind up since that plugin processes them. But, again, we're just dealing with fixed-width images here, so that's what we request. The `width` and `height` are specified as query parameters (we could request alternate sizes here if we wanted to).

For the static text at the top of the page, that's in the `siteMetadata`, which is parsed into the site collection and comes from the `gatsby-config.json` file.

Finally, the list of documents winds up in the `allMarkdownRemark` collection by virtue of the plugins that sourced and transformed them. Once again, sorting is implemented so that the list shows the newest documents at the top. The only information we need from the `frontmatter` this time is the `title`, since that's what we'll display in the list, and the `slug`, since that's what we need to construct a link to the document, as you're about to see in the next section where we discuss that template component from earlier.

Note   As you can see here, a GraphQL query can contain multiple pieces of data, and not just data with a parent-child relationship. Here, we have four unique elements at the same level: splash, divider, site, and allMarkdownRemark. This is something that can be confusing at first, especially if you're used to completely hierarchical data structures (which this still in fact is, but what I mean is it's not a hierarchical structure that you can only build downward through a tree, which is the case with most types of hierarchical data). You've got to remember that essentially, a GraphQL query is defining the structure of the JSON object you want back, which, of course, can have many properties at the same level. This is what makes GraphQL so efficient: you don't need to make four different queries to get all this data, which is what your mind will probably tell you is required outside of GraphQL. No, you can simply define the structure you want, all in one go, and the query processing engine that interprets it effectively does that work for you and give you back the structure you requested.

The Whiteboard Page

Now we come to what is for sure the meat of JAMboard, the place where most of the good stuff is, and that's the template I mentioned in the last section. The file we're talking about is the documentTemplate.js file found in the src/templates directory. In it, you'll find all the code related to a React component named – wait for it – Template! This constitutes what I call the Whiteboard page because it's the place where users collaborate to mark up documents.

But, before we get to that, we have one of those little detours I like to take now and again, something that will set up the code in that component a bit: StorageManager.

Another Quick Detour: StorageManager

As I've mentioned, this initial version of JAMboard stores markers and comments on the user's machine in local storage. In the next chapter, we're going to expand that so that they are saved on a server, available to all users, thus making it a truly shared environment for collaboration.

To make that switch easier, I've abstracted the code that stores and retrieves markers into a separate StorageManager class in the aptly named StorageManager.js file in the src directory. It's a simple bit of code right now, beginning with a function for getting all markers for the current document from local storage:

```
export function getAllMarkerKeysFromStorage(inDocumentID) {

  const markerKeys = [ ];
  for (let i = 0; i < localStorage.length; i++) {
    const key = localStorage.key(i);
    if (key.startsWith(inDocumentID)) {
      markerKeys.push(key);
    }
  }
  return markerKeys;

}
```

All we need to retrieve here are the keys of all the markers, not the markers themselves. The keys are in the form "<document_id>-<current_datetime>". That makes them unique enough for our purpose here. So, we get an array of all elements in local storage and then construct an array of any keys that begins with the specified document ID. That's all there is to it.

Next up is getting a specified marker, and that's even easier:

```
export function getMarkerFromStorage(inKey) {

  return JSON.parse(localStorage.getItem(inKey));

}
```

Yes, it's just one line of code! We know that an invalid key can't be requested (since it's the user clicking on a link that triggers a request), so there's not even a need for error checking.

Similarly, writing a marker out is just as easy:

```
export function saveMarkerToStorage(inKey, inMarker) {

  localStorage.setItem(inKey, JSON.stringify(inMarker));
}
```

Note that when comments are added, we're still writing the entire marker object out, and comments are just an element in a `comments` array within it, so this one function is all we need. It's not necessarily the most efficient data structure, but it'll get the job done just fine for this first pass.

Back to the Code!

All right, with that out of the way, let's get into the component itself, starting with the imports:

```
import React from "react"
import { graphql } from "gatsby"
import Button from "@material-ui/core/Button";
import Dialog from "@material-ui/core/Dialog";
import DialogActions from "@material-ui/core/DialogActions";
import DialogContent from "@material-ui/core/DialogContent";
import DialogTitle from "@material-ui/core/DialogTitle";
import Grid from "@material-ui/core/Grid";
import List from "@material-ui/core/List";
import ListItem from "@material-ui/core/ListItem";
import ListItemText from "@material-ui/core/ListItemText";
import Paper from "@material-ui/core/Paper";
import TextField from "@material-ui/core/TextField";
import * as StorageManager from "../StorageManager.js";
```

React and GraphQL, as always, are imported and then some Material-UI goodness. We'll use our friend the `Dialog`, and its subcomponents, to give users a place to enter comments. Also, we're going to use a `Grid` component for the overall layout, and we'll get to that soon. For the comments section, we need a scrollable list. Now, certainly, it would be straightforward to do that with a plain old `<div>` with the `overflow` style property set to `auto` or `scroll`. Still, I decided to do it with the `List` component – and its relatives `ListItem` and `ListItemText` – just to give you a little more exposure to Material-UI. Similarly, the `Paper` component is what gives each of the three sections a 3D "card" look, as it's often called. Finally, all the methods of `StorageManager` are naturally imported.

After that comes our first real code, though it ain't much:

```
let mr = null;
let fm = null;
```

As you'll see, the data that Gatsby produces when it parses the document this template is rendering (and remember, it's by virtue of the user clicking a link that we're getting to this page, which has already been rendered at build time with the associated document as data and associated with the URL of the link) needs to be available to all the code here, and these variables hold references to that and make the code more concise (mr is short for MarkdownRemark, and fm is short for *FrontMatter*, if that wasn't obvious).

After that comes another variable we'll need throughout the code:

```
let currentMarkerKey = null;
```

When the user clicks one of the markers in the document, assuming there are any, the key of that marker must be stored and available to the rest of the code.

Finally, we have one more variable, this one with a bit more content:

```
let state = { addCommentButtonDisabled : true,
  addCommentDialogVisiblc : false, newComment : "",
  comments : [ ]
};
```

The object referenced by state is the React state of the Template component. As in the case of the IndexPage component, we have a dialog to hide and show, so there's a property for that. Also, the Add Comment button should only be enabled when a marker has been clicked, so we have a flag property for that too. When the user is typing a comment, we need to store it in state, just like when they entered their username on the dialog on IndexPage, so we find that here too. Finally, remember that for React to re-render our page, or part of it, at least, state has to change. So, imagine the user clicking a marker. We need to show its comments at that point, so we need something in state to change. That something is the comments property, which will be populated with the comments for the clicked marker and trigger a repaint.

> **Note**   Recall that for IndexPage, the state was a member of the component.
> That's the bit more "proper" way to do it in React-think. At least, it's more typical.
> However, in this case, code outside the component's code needs access to state
> too. React is flexible, and you can usually do things multiple ways, so in this case,
> to make the access by that code more straightforward, I decided to put state
> outside the component. Realize that it's still locally scoped to this module, so it's
> not like this is global-scope pollution, which is generally considered bad. True, it's
> polluting global scope of the *module*, but that's not really an issue since modules
> are separate from one another anyway. How you organize your code is ultimately
> up to you, and React will usually accommodate you. Still, I wanted to describe the
> rational and difference here, at least.

Building the Component

Right, it's time to build us a component! The `Template` component that we told Gatsby to use to render our Markdown documents by way of some `gatsby-node.js` configuration begins simply enough:

```
export default class Template extends React.Component {

constructor(inProps) {

  super(inProps);

  mr = inProps.data.markdownRemark;
  fm = mr.frontmatter;

  window.showComments = window.showComments.bind(this);
  addComment = addComment.bind(this);
  handleDialogClose = handleDialogClose.bind(this);

}
```

Gatsby executes the page query that you'll see is at the end of all of this code, and injects it into the props passed into the constructor as the `data` property. So, after the props are passed to the super constructor as per React rules, the first thing to do is to pull the parsed `markdownRemark` data out of it, and then the `frontmatter` data from that, and assign them to those mr and fm variables declared earlier. Then, three functions exist outside this component (you're going to see several functions used in the component, and we'll look at them after the component itself, since that's where they are in the source file), but which need to execute within the context of it. So, all three get a bind() call made on them to take care of that. Note that the showComments() function is a bit different in that it needs to be accessible to code outside of this module. Usually, any function declared here wouldn't be, and usually, that's not a problem, but it is, in this case, for reasons you'll see before long. So, I've appended it to the window object so that it'll be callable from anywhere.

After that comes something new:

```
componentDidMount = () => loadMarkers();
```

The componentDidMount function is one of the lifecycle functions that React provides. This is called after the component's output has been written to the DOM. If you think about the basic flow here, when the page loads, this component is instantiated and its render() method called. Whatever output it returns is written to the DOM (by way of the virtual DOM). At that point, the markers – which are stored in local storage remember – haven't been loaded, and the text not turned into links. They *couldn't* be yet because the text doesn't actually exist in the DOM until that point. But, if we specify a function for the componentDidMount property of our component, React calls it once the component is rendered, which is a logical time to go get the markers from local storage and turn the text, which is now present on the page, into links, and that's precisely what the loadMarkers() function does, as you'll see later.

Rendering the Component

Every React component needs a render() method, and that's what's next:

```
render() {
  return (
    <div style={{
      display:"flex", flexDirection:"column", height:"96vh"
    }}>
```

First up, we have the single element that you know render() must return. In this case, it's just a <div> that uses a CSS flexbox layout. Since we know we want three horizontal sections, that means we want a column flexDirection (it's always seemed backward to me that when you want rows, the direction is column, and vice versa, but it is what it is, as the saying goes!). I've set the height to 96% of the viewport's height, leaving a little empty space at the bottom. That ensures that no matter how you resize the browser window, the layout should always fit. It's just a cheap and simple way to accomplish that at the cost of a little bit of vertical space (because sometimes 4% just isn't worth fighting with CSS about frankly!).

Next up is the definition of the dialog for entering comments:

```
<Dialog open={state.addCommentDialogVisible}
  onClose={handleDialogClose} maxWidth="lg"
  fullWidth={true}>
  <DialogTitle>Add Comment</DialogTitle>
  <DialogContent>
    <TextField label="Enter comment here" fullWidth
      variant="outlined"
      onChange={(inEvent) =>
        state.newComment = inEvent.target.value} />
  </DialogContent>
  <DialogActions>
    <Button onClick={handleDialogClose}
      color="secondary">Cancel</Button>
    <Button onClick={handleDialogSave}
      color="primary">Save</Button>
  </DialogActions>
</Dialog>
```

You should pretty much understand this already given your previous exposure to the Material-UI Dialog component and its cohorts. The handleDialogClose() function that is called when the dialog is closed any way other than clicking the Save button (which the user can do with this dialog, in contrast to the one for username that couldn't be dismissed without entering a username), as well as the handleDialogSave() function attached to the Save button itself, we'll look at a bit later.

Note that this time, I decided to have different styling for the buttons, not for any particular reason other than to show you it's possible to do so. You can see the result of this in Figure 5-4.

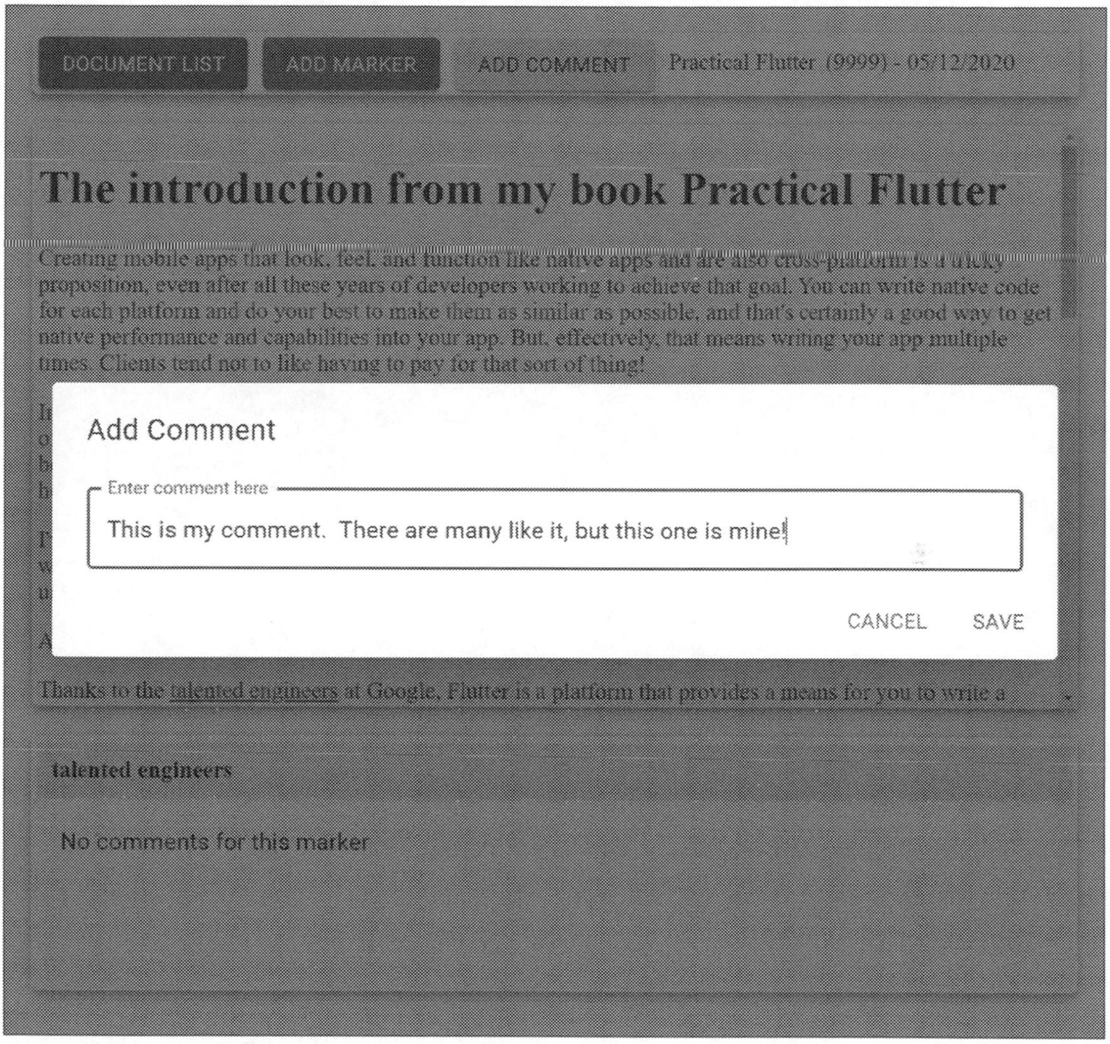

Figure 5-4. *The Add Comment dialog*

Since the dialog is nothing new, let's move on to the control bar area at the top:

```
<Paper elevation={5}
  style={{ margin:"10px", padding:"4px", height:"46px" }}>
  <Grid container>
    <Grid item>
      <Button variant="contained" color="primary"
        style={{ marginRight:"10px" }}
```

```
      onClick={() => window.location = "/"}>
      Document List
    </Button>
    <Button variant="contained" color="secondary"
      style={{ marginRight:"10px" }} onClick={addMarker}>
      Add Marker
    </Button>
    <Button variant="contained"
      style={{ marginRight:"10px" }}
      onClick={addComment}
      disabled={state.addCommentButtonDisabled}>
      Add Comment
    </Button>
    {fm.title} ({fm.id}) - {fm.date}
  </Grid>
 </Grid>
</Paper>
```

The Paper component from Material-UI is meant to mimic the appearance of a piece of paper. It's not much more than a stylized <div> with a drop shadow (by default, at least – you can turn it off if you like), and you can define that shadow with the elevation prop, as I've done here. In addition, I'm putting some margin around it to space it out from the edges of the screen and the next Paper component below where the document itself goes. I've also put some padding inside to keep its contents off the edges just because that looks better, and I've given it a static height, so it'll be the only one of the three sections that won't flex with the browser window.

Inside it, I've used a Material-UI Grid component to lay out the contents. This is a component that, internally, uses CSS flexbox to lay out its children, so it's suitable for flexible layouts and comes with built-in support for breakpoints so you can implement fluid layouts easily with it (although that's not necessary here). So, yes, to answer the question that I bet you're asking: I could have done this with a plain <div> and some CSS just as well, but I figured why not use some more Material-UI to show what it can do?

The Grid component comes in two variants: a *container* and an *item*. This one has a container prop on it with no value. Then, as a child of that Grid is another Grid, this one with the item prop. With prop names alone like this (container on the outer Grid, item on the inner), it defaults to a value of true, which indicates that the outer Grid serves as a *container* and the inner serves as an *item*. Container means just that: it contains children that should be laid out using Flexbox. Item means that its width is set as a percentage of its container and that it has padding automatically to separate it from other items.

Now, in this case, I have, in fact, *not* defined a width for this item. That's okay: it defaults to 100% and so expand to fill its parent. Then, inside of this Grid item are three Button components. The first brings the user back to the home/document list page. The second allows them to add a marker. The third, which is disabled until a marker is clicked, allows them to add a comment to the marker. The handler functions attached to these will be looked at later.

After those buttons is some text: the title of the document, its ID, and the date it was created. The result, since this item stretches across the screen, is that all of that text together uses up whatever space is left after the two buttons.

Next up is the section for the document's content:

```
<Paper elevation={5} style={{
  margin:"10px", padding:"4px", height:"70vh", overflow:"auto"
}}>
  <Grid container>
    <Grid item>
      <div dangerouslySetInnerHTML={{ __html : mr.html }} />
    </Grid>
  </Grid>
</Paper>
```

It's another Paper component, and here I've set it to use 70% of the viewport's vertical space. I've also set overflow to auto so that it will scroll independently to allow for large documents. Finally, it may be surprising for you to see how the content is actually rendered; it's just a <div> with the strange-looking dangerouslySetInnerHTML prop set to an object with a single __html property – the value of which is the html property from the MarkdownRemark object from the query's data by way of that mr variable. That's all it takes!

Tip   The reason that prop is named that way is that this can be a vector for cross-site scripting (XSS) attacks and is *intended* to scare you a bit! There are other ways to render this HTML that allows for sanitizing of the data, but I've used the way that much of the Gatsby documentation itself shows because it's about the easiest way. And, in this case, it's probably not a significant security concern because presumably, you're going to control who can push new documents into your source repository, build the site with it, and deploy it. Since user input isn't the source of the content being rendered, the XSS risk *should* be low (and certainly, within the context of a book like this, NSA-level security isn't really the goal anyway). But, I wanted to point this out because if you were writing this as a production-level application, you would almost certainly want to look at alternate approaches. One such option is the `hast-to-hyperscript` module (`https://github.com/syntax-tree/hast-to-hyperscript`). This works in conjunction with the fact that in addition to `mr.html`, there is also an `mr.htmlAst` property available (if you also add it to the query later) that provides the document's content as an Abstract Syntax Tree (AST) which that module can ingest and give back HTML from, fully sanitized, which you can then safely insert.

The final thing to render is the comment section at the bottom, and it's where most of the action is:

```
<Paper elevation={5} style={{
  margin:"10px", padding:"4px", height:"30vh", overflow:"auto" }}>
  <div style={{ fontWeight : "bold", position : "sticky",
    top : "2px", padding : "10px",
    backgroundColor : "#eaeaea", zIndex : 99
  }}>
    { currentMarkerKey === null ? "" :
      StorageManager.getMarkerFromStorage(
        currentMarkerKey
      ).markerText
    }
  </div>
```

```
<Grid container>
  <Grid item xs>
    <List>
      { currentMarkerKey !== null &&
        state.comments.length === 0 ?
          <ListItem key={0}>
            <ListItemText
              primary="No comments for this marker" />
          </ListItem>
        :
        state.comments.map((inItem, inIndex) => { return (
          <ListItem key={inIndex}>
            <ListItemText primary={inItem.comment}
              secondary={
                `${inItem.author} - ${inItem.dateTime}`
              } />
          </ListItem>
        )})
      }
    </List>
  </Grid>
</Grid>
</Paper>
```

To start, the entire section is contained within a Paper component again, this one taking up the remaining 30% of the viewport (remember that the 70% for the middle Paper and the 30% for this one are effectively 70% and 30%, respectively, of whatever space is left after the control bar, which is statically sized, and all the margin and padding are factored in). After that, we have a <div> that shows the text of the selected marker as a header bar. I set the position to sticky and bump the zIndex up so that if there are enough comments for this section to scroll, they scroll behind the header, and the header remains at the top. The content of the <div> is blank when no document is selected, as signified by currentMarkerKey being null and which is the case until the first marker is clicked. Otherwise, the marker is retrieved from local storage, and the value of the markerText property is shown.

After that, we have another Material-UI `Grid` component to contain the actual comments. Then, as a child of that `Grid`, there is a single `Grid` marked as an `item`. And then, as a child of that, is a `List` component. A `List` component is for displaying a continuous, vertical index of text and/or images. They are composed of `ListItem` components, and together, they provide scrolling mechanisms automatically. So, again, this is a situation where you could accomplish the same thing with plain old HTML and CSS. Still, the `List` component makes it a bit nicer. It provides more flexibility, including things like iconography, selectable list items, check boxes, and switches on items, headings to group items, and more.

Now, we have to build one or more `ListItem` components, and it's done in much the same way as the document list was that you looked at earlier. But, first, we look to see if a marker has been selected, and if so, whether it has any comments. If either is false, then the text "No comments for this marker" is displayed by creating a single `ListItem` component with a key of zero (to keep React from warning us that list items should always have a key). Then, inside that, we place a `ListItemText` component. The `ListItem` component is what every item in the `List` must be in. It provides many things, such as the ability to add action buttons for an item, the ability to display divider lines on items, and the ability to disable or select items. The `ListItemText` component simply allows us to display text and provides options like single or multiline text and insetting of text.

Now, if there *is* a marker selected and if it *does* have comments, then it's basically the same: render a `ListItem` with a `ListItemText` inside of it. However, for the `ListItemText`, we take advantage of some of its features and set its `primary` prop to the comment itself and its `secondary` prop to the author (username) and the date it was written. The primary text is more prominent and bolder, while the secondary text is smaller and slightly duller.

With the comments section complete, this component itself is complete! Now, we can look at the functions involved in making all of this work, beginning with the one you saw called earlier: `loadMarkers()`.

Loading Markers

So, when the page loads, the component renders, and we have our document visible, it's time to see if there are markers associated with this document and turn them into links if so. The `loadMarkers()` function does that for us:

```
function loadMarkers() {
```

```
  const markerKeys =
    StorageManager.getAllMarkerKeysFromStorage(fm.id);
  markerKeys.forEach(function(inKey) {
    linkifyMarker(inKey);
  });

}
```

The getAllMarkerKeysFromStorage() on the StorageManager object that we looked at earlier does that for us. We just need to feed it the document's ID. Then, for each marker returned, if there were any, the linkifyMarker() function is called.

Note   I'm going to tackle the next few functions in logical order rather than the order they appear in the source code so that things, hopefully, have more context and make more sense to you.

"Linkifying" a Marker

To "linkify" a marker, we need to find the text that was highlighted by the user in the document and then surround it with an <a> tag. Let's walk through how that's done:

```
function linkifyMarker(inKey) {

  let marker = StorageManager.getMarkerFromStorage(inKey);
```

First, we go grab the marker object from local storage based on its ID. Next, it's time to go find the text that was selected by the user to create the marker in the document:

```
const textNodes = [];
let node = document.body.childNodes[0];
while (node != null) {
  if (node.nodeType === 3) { textNodes.push(node); }
  if (node.hasChildNodes()) {
    node = node.firstChild;
  } else {
    while (
      node.nextSibling == null && node !== document.body
```

```
    ) {
      node = node.parentNode;
    }
    node = node.nextSibling;
  }
}
```

This first block of code boils down to one simple task: get a flat array of all text nodes on the page. We're traversing a tree – the DOM – of course, which can be done either iteratively with a looping construct or recursively. I opted for the former since the code is, I think, more straightforward than a recursive version would be (debatable, I admit). We only care about nodes in the DOM with a `nodeType` of 3, which are text nodes. Everything else is ignored.

Next, with that array populated, we need to find the text node that contains the selected text, or its parent, to put it another way:

```
let parentNode = null;
for (let i = 0; i < textNodes.length; i++) {
  if (textNodes[i].data === marker.parentNodeData) {
    parentNode = textNodes[i];
    break;
  }
}
```

What gets saved when a marker is created is

- The start location of the selected text inside the parent text node

- The end location of the selected text inside the parent text node

- The textual content of the parent node

- The text that was selected as a marker

- An array of comments associated with the marker (empty at creation time, of course)

The issue here, and what this bit of code is for, is that we can't save something like an ID for the text node, because we don't know if the node has an ID (and in almost any case in this application, it won't). We also can't store the node itself because it can't be properly serialized to a string for saving into local storage. But, we need to be able to identify it later because of the Range API, which we'll get into next, but in short, it's what allows us to select text and replace it with a link and what allows us to see what the user selected later. The only real possibility here is to store the text in the text node itself and then look through all the text nodes until we find the matching text node based on its content (which, yes, means that if someone changes the text of a document, the markers will be broken, so there's an assumption that a document is immutable after deployment). Each node has a `data` property that is that text, and later you'll see that it gets stored in the marker as `parentNodeData`. So, we can then iterate the `textNodes` array until we find the parent node of the selected text.

Once we do that, it's time to turn it into a link:

```
const range = document.createRange();
range.setStart(parentNode, marker.startOffset);
range.setEnd(parentNode, marker.endOffset);
```

The Range API is a JavaScript API provided by modern browsers that allows us to both select text on the page and see what text is selected by the user. We can ask the browser for a new Range object by calling `document.createRange()`. A Range object needs to know the parent node of the selected text and the start and end offset inside that parent of the selected text. So, the `setStart()` and `setEnd()` methods of the Range object are called, supplying that information from the marker object. If you paused the code here at runtime with a debugger, you would find that the text that was initially selected by the user is again selected.

Then, we create the link for the text:

```
const link = document.createElement("a");
link.setAttribute("href", "#");
link.setAttribute("onClick",
  `window.showComments("${inKey}");`
);
range.surroundContents(link);
```

That's basic DOM code to create an `<a>` element, setting its `href` to # so that the browser won't navigate anywhere when it's clicked. Instead, the `onClick` event handler is attached and the `window.showComments()` function is called, passed the key of the marker. Now you can see why `showComments()` had to be attached to the `window` object: it wouldn't have been accessible to this `onClick` handler if it was inside the `Template` component or even outside it but in the `Template.js` module because this link is created on the page outside both of those things.

The final line called the surroundContents() method on the Range object. This takes in a node and surrounds the text with it. And, just like that, we have a new link on the page that, when clicked, shows the comments for this marker (the showComments() function is coming up next).

There's just one final thing we need to do:

```
document.getSelection().removeAllRanges();
```

The text that we selected earlier is still selected, and there's no reason for it to be at this point. You can ask the browser for any currently selected text employing the document.getSelection() function, and its return value offers a removeAllRanges() function to clear any selected text, so we're good to go after that.

Showing Marker Comments

Now, when a marker's link is clicked, we need to show any comments it may have, and that's where showComments() comes in:

```
window.showComments = function(inKey) {

  currentMarkerKey = inKey;
```

First, we record the key of the marker in the module-scoped currentMarkerKey variable since that information is needed in other places at other times. Next, we get the marker:

```
const marker = StorageManager.getMarkerFromStorage(inKey);
```

Next, we must update state so that React will repaint the screen with any comments this marker may have. First things first though, we must clear the comments array in the state object in case they were looking at another marker earlier:

```
state.comments.length = 0;
```

That's the quickest and easiest way to do it in this situation because the first thing you may think to do is this:

```
state.comments.length = [ ];
```

But, if you do that, despite it being prevalent, React won't see our changes because a new array isn't treated as a change, paradoxically! So, we have to clear the existing array, which setting its length to zero does quickly.

Next, we enable the Add Comment button since that button is only available after a marker has been clicked:

```
state.addCommentButtonDisabled = false;
```

Next, we need to add all the comments from the marker into the `state` object's `comments` array that we just cleared:

```
marker.comments.forEach(
  inValue => state.comments.push(inValue)
);
```

One last thing we need to do it reverse the order of the array because, at this moment, the newest items are on the bottom, which means the user won't see it immediately, which would be weird:

```
state.comments.reverse();
```

With that done, we just need to tell React about the state change:

```
this.setState((inState, inProps) => { return state; });
```

And voila, we have comments on the screen (or the message saying there aren't any).

Adding a Marker

Okay, great, you now know how existing markers are loaded, how they are linkified, and how their comments are shown. What about adding a new marker? That's fairly easy and is handled by the `addMarker()` function, called when the Add Marker button is clicked:

```
function addMarker() {

  let range = null;
  if (window.getSelection().rangeCount !== 0) {
    range = window.getSelection().getRangeAt(0);
  }
  if (!range) { return; }
```

First, we ask the browser for the currently selected range, and if there is one, we get a Range object from the call to `window.getSelection.getRangeAt(0)`. Note that more than one piece of text can be selected at a time, and this API allows you to get them through an index (treating it like an array in other words), but I'm making a simplifying assumption here that only one ever will be when they click this button. If they *do* select more than one, then all but the first will simply be ignored. If we get no Range object, then that means no text is selected, and we just return.

After that, we construct a marker object:

```
const marker = {
  startOffset : range.startOffset,
  endOffset : range.endOffset,
  parentNodeData : range.startContainer.data,
  markerText : range.toString(),
  comments : [ ]
};
```

We talked about what gets saved in a marker earlier, but now you can see how that information is pulled from the Range object itself. Interestingly, calling `toString()` on the Range object gives us the text that was selected. That seems a little weird to me, but it's what the API designers decided on, so we'll go with it!

Next, we construct a unique key for the marker based on the document's ID (pulled from the frontmatter in the `fm` variable) and the current time, and save it to local storage:

```
const key = `${fm.id}-${new Date().getTime()}`;
StorageManager.saveMarkerToStorage(key, marker);
```

As when we linkified the text earlier when markers were loaded, we want to clear any current selection(s) now too:

```
document.getSelection().removeAllRanges();
```

And, also like when loading markers, we want to linkify what they selected immediately, and fortunately, we have a function explicitly for that:

```
linkifyMarker(key);
```

And that's all it takes to add a new marker.

Adding a Comment

When the user clicks the Add Comment button – assuming it was enabled by them clicking a marker first – the addComment() function is called:

```
function addComment() {

  state.addCommentDialogVisible = true;
  state.newComment = "";
  this.setState((inState, inProps) => { return state; });

}
```

Well, uhh, that's not much, is it? Nope, all we really need to do is show the dialog for adding a comment and ensure there's no comment text currently in state and then tell React to update state. Pretty simple, right!

Closing the Dialog

When the comment add dialog is closed either by clicking outside of it or the user pressing the ESC key, the handleDialogClose() function is triggered:

```
function handleDialogClose() {

  state.addCommentDialogVisible = false;
  this.setState((inState, inProps) => { return state; });

}
```

All it has to do is hide the dialog. Anything the user may have entered is ignored, so that's all there is to it.

Saving the Comment

When the user clicks the Save button on the comment add dialog, the handleDialogSave() function is called:

```
function handleDialogSave() {
  handleDialogClose();
```

First, since the dialog should, of course, close in this case, we'll make use of the handleDialogClose() function, so we don't duplicate code.

Next, we have to see if they actually entered anything:

```
if (state.newComment === null ||
  state.newComment.trim() === ""
) {
  return;
}
```

If not, then we're done at this point. However, if something *was* entered, then we have to add it to the selected marker:

```
const marker = StorageManager.getMarkerFromStorage(
  currentMarkerKey
);
marker.comments.push({
  author : localStorage.getItem("username"),
  dateTime : new Date().toLocaleDateString(),
  comment : state.newComment
});
StorageManager.saveMarkerToStorage(currentMarkerKey, marker);
```

The marker is retrieved from local storage by virtue of having its key stored in that currentMarkerKey you saw earlier. Then, we just push a new object into the comments array that contains three pieces of information: the author, which is the username pulled from local storage; the current dateTime (as a string – and note that an assumption is made here that the user's machine's date format is set to MM-DD-YYYY, which is a safe assumption in most places, but this is a flaw that you may want to correct as a learning exercise); and the comment itself, which we find in state.newComment since as the user typed, that gets updated (as per the onChange handler attached to the TextField component in the dialog). The marker object is then saved to local storage thanks to the saveMarkerToStorage() method of the StorageManager object.

Finally, we need to update the display to show the new comment. Once again, rather than duplicating code, we can use the existing showComments() function:

```
window.showComments(currentMarkerKey);
```

And with that, all the code for the Template is almost complete! There's just one last piece to the puzzle, and that's the page query that makes all the data we've used throughout available.

Querying for Data

Finally, we come to the page query that provides all the data you've seen used throughout this code:

```
export const pageQuery = graphql`
  query($slug: String!) {
    markdownRemark(frontmatter: { slug: { eq: $slug } }) {
      html
      frontmatter {
        id
        date(formatString: "MM/DD/YYYY")
        slug
        title
      }
    }
  }
`
```

First, there are some parameters passed to the query element. The $slug parameter is injected by Gatsby and will be the value of the slug from the document's front matter that is being generated with this template. The exclamation point indicates it's a required element, so Gatsby knows to provide it. Then, when we start drilling down into the markdownRemark data collection, the slug value is used to get the appropriate data from the data layer. The parameter passed to MarkdownRemark() is saying that we want the data where the frontmatter's slug value equals (eq) the $slug value passed in to the query (because, remember, that's what ties the page generated by processing a document through a Template to the link the user clicks to get to it).

After that, it should be relatively straightforward because it's just getting the html that Gatsby parsed from the Markdown document, along with some values from the frontmatter. As you know, the results from this query are injected into your component's props, and ready for your code to use.

And with that, our journey through the JAMboard application is complete, at least as far as it being a purely client-side application goes. This is the foundation we need to make it a genuinely collaborative application in the next chapter.

Suggested Exercises

When possible, I like to offer things you can do on the side to a project to help you learn a little more. I do indeed have a few suggestions for this one:

- As mentioned earlier, there is an assumption made that there is only one bit of text selected at any time. It might be helpful if, upon selection of a second bit, all others were cleared so that you *know* there's only one by the time `addMarker()` is called.

- Also, as mentioned, I made a simplifying assumption that all users have their system's date format set to MM-DD-YYYY. Obviously, that's not always true. So, how about adding some code that creates the `dateTime` value when saving a comment from `Date` object components so you can ensure it's always in that form regardless of system settings?

- While in a single-user situation like this, the uniqueness of marker IDs is guaranteed when based on time like it is now. Still, if this were a multiuser environment (which it will be after the next chapter!), that wouldn't be the case. It would still be somewhat unlikely to have an ID collision, but it would be possible in theory. So, how about making that ID based on document ID combined with a GUID (Globally Unique ID) instead of time? There are ways to generate those in JavaScript, and that would avoid that issue entirely, but you'll need to research a bit (hint: maybe there's some existing module you could add as a dependency?).

Summary

In this chapter, we built the bulk of the JAMboard app. In the process, you got some more expanded experience working with Gatsby and GraphQL, and you got a look at the Material-UI toolkit for React, plus of course, some more React experience.

The app is at this point working, but it isn't collaborative – you're the only one that can use it! So, in the next chapter, we'll introduce some new concepts, including something called Netlify and a database called FaunaDB. You'll also finally get a look at some APIs to interact with them and make this an authentic, shared whiteboard experience.

CHAPTER 6

The "A" in JAMstack

Okay, with Chapter 5 complete, we have ourselves a nice little app for marking up documents. However, it's purported to be a "shared" environment for document markup, but that's not the case right now. So, let's remedy that!

In this chapter, we'll get into the third letter of JAM in JAMstack that we haven't touched on much yet: the A, for API. We'll see how to host this app on a provider with a bit more to offer than GitHub Pages – APIs for one thing – and we'll enhance JAMboard to be a real shared workspace. Let's set the table by talking about two new service providers that we're going to make use of to make all of this happen, beginning with a service called Netlify.

Of Amazing Hosting Providers: Netlify

In Chapter 2, you saw how GitHub Pages can provide you a cheap and easy web hosting solution. But, it's certainly limited. You can't do much but host a purely static website. I mean, that's good, given that this book is all about static websites! But, what if you need things like a server-side database behind an API of some sort? You could do the website part with GitHub Pages, but that database and API functionality would need to be hosted elsewhere since GitHub Pages doesn't offer that sort of functionality (as of this writing- GitHub is expanding rapidly!).

Thankfully, while there are several other options you could choose, one arguably stands out above the rest: Netlify.

Netlify began, at least in a sense, around 2013 when a Danish entrepreneur named Mathias Biilmann took a look around at what developers were doing and noticed that new, modern tools were being used to build static sites and were centered around Git-based workflows. At the time, Mathias was running a startup in San Francisco named MakerLoop. But, when he noticed what was happening, he began a new venture with childhood friend Christian Bach in 2015: Netlify.

© Frank Zammetti 2020
F. Zammetti, *Practical JAMstack*, https://doi.org/10.1007/978-1-4842-6177-4_6

Before long – just about two years later in December of 2018 – MakerLoop was rebranded as Netlify as, I suspect, they realized this was the way forward for them.

But, what *is* Netlify? Simply put, it's a web hosting company that specializes in cloud-based deployments and serverless back ends. In other words, they host your sites, which tend to be static, without providing you a dedicated server infrastructure like more traditional hosts. In that regard, Netlify is a lot like GitHub Pages, but Netlify offers so much more.

Netlify is ridiculously simple to use in virtually every way, and it's all done through an excellent, clean web interface. Let me tell you, I've dealt with a lot of different hosting companies over the years, and one thing I can say for sure is that Netlify is one of the best experiences I've ever had in just how easy and logical everything is. I wouldn't say it's exactly perfect – I sometimes find myself hopping between a few too many pages for my liking – but it's all laid out very well, and you never lose your place, and that's big.

One of the most impressive things Netlify provides is CI/CD, or continuous integration/continuous deployment. This is done by linking to a GitHub repo (Netlify also supports GitLab and Bitbucket). Every time a change is checked in, your site is rebuild and redeployed automatically. To be sure, Netlify doesn't require this – you can manually upload your code each time, manually trigger your builds and deploys each time – but the real power comes when you take advantage of that CI/CD pipeline.

Netlify also offers some common services, such as form submission handling. You don't need to write any back-end code yourself, Netlify can accept your form submissions and then presents a dashboard where you can view the collected information. That's great for many use cases that don't require a ton of processing of the form data, just collection of it.

Netlify offers a one-click rollback of deployments, so it's always easy to get things back to a previous state if anything goes wrong. Netlify also provides the ability to do preview builds so you can check your work before it goes live.

Netlify also offers SSL for all hosted sites, so security is baked right into the platform. Netlify also offers rewrite and redirect functionality so you can provide custom error pages and "pretty" URLs in your site.

Netlify provides resource optimization functions such as automatic optimization of images, CSS, and JS. Of course, Netlify works perfectly with most static site generators, Gatsby, among them.

Netlify also offers integration with Amazon's AWS, specifically its lambda functions. These are functions, written in JavaScript, that your website can call on to do all sorts of complex tasks.

Ah-ha! That sounds a lot like an API, doesn't it? If you're thinking that we might wind up using these Netlify functions, as they're known, to enhance JAMboard, then congratulations, your crystal ball is working well today! We're going to wind up writing three separate functions, one for each of the functions in the `StorageManager` module. The `StorageManager` module on the client will then call the associated functions in the cloud, and those functions will read the data from a database and return it. In other words, these functions, and the calls to them, will do the same job as `StorageManager` does now with local storage, but with a remote database in its place. You'll find that these functions are nothing but JavaScript source files that Netlify automatically deploys to Amazon AWS as lambda functions for you automatically and makes them available through a URL in your application. You don't even need an AWS account. It's blissfully all transparent to you.

But, I'm jumping the gun here!

Before we get to any of that, first things first: you need to sign up for a Netlify account. Here's the best part: it's free! Netlify offers a rather robust free tier that provides more than enough capabilities for JAMboard and really will allow you to host quite a few sites of your own later at no cost. True, if they wind up being the next Facebook, you're gonna wind up having to fork over some cash, but when you've got Zuckerberg money coming in, I hardly think you'll mind!

Head over to `www.netlify.com` and look for the "Sign up" link somewhere in the upper-right-hand corner. Click that, and select how you want to sign in. I strongly recommend using the GitHub option, assuming you set up a GitHub account earlier in this book as discussed, or had one already. Even if you don't use an existing account, you don't have to enter much of anything to sign up, really just an email address. Then you'll verify your account via an email, and that's it, you're off to the races!

When you go back to Netlify and log in, you'll wind up on your account dashboard page, which should look something like Figure 6-1.

Naturally, you won't see any sites there, but I've already deployed a few. Since you should, at this point, have a GitHub repo for the vanity site from Chapter 2, go ahead and deploy it! See that big, green "New site from Git" button? Click it! You'll then need to pick a Git provider, GitHub, in this case. Netlify will then authorize access to your GitHub account, and after that, you should see a list of your repositories.

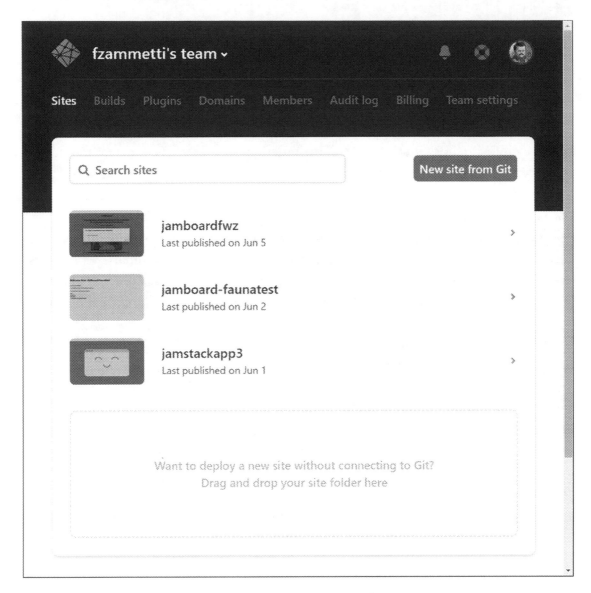

Figure 6-1. *The Netlify account dashboard, Sites tab*

Well, actually, you may well not see that, so let's fix that.

There's a link at the bottom of the Netlify page though that says, "Can't see your repo here? Configure the Netlify app on GitHub." Click that, and Netlify will be installed into your GitHub account. You'll have to run through some simple configuration, most importantly is selecting which repositories you want to give Netlify access to. Just to make life simple, select the "All repositories" option (you can always change this later).

Once you do that, you'll wind up back at Netlify, and now you should see your repositories, including the vanity site. Go ahead and select it. You'll then wind up at a page that asks you some basic questions, including who the owner of your site is (uhh, you!), what branch you want to deploy (master by default), and some basic build commands, which you can just leave blank because there's no build required for the vanity site. Once you do that, click the "Deploy site" button, and you'll wind on a page that looks like Figure 6-2.

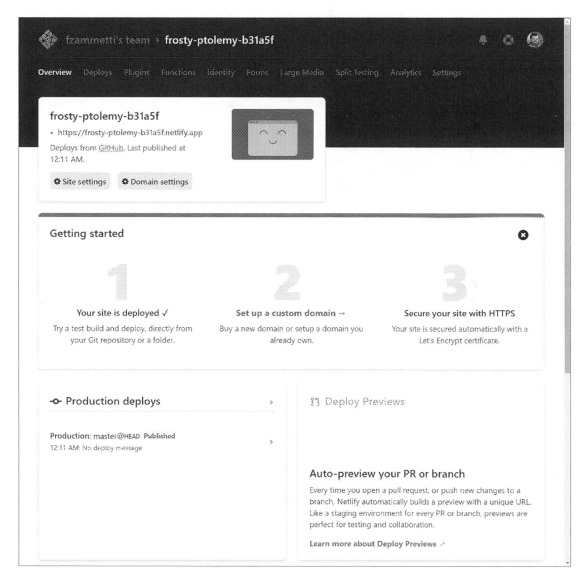

Figure 6-2. *The site is deployed!*

It should only take a few seconds, and the page will show you a status indicating the site is being deployed, and before long, it'll be published (you can see the status there in the "Production deploys" section). At this point, the site is live! You can click the link up next to the smiley face (frosty-ptolemy-b31a5f in the screenshot, but whatever name is generated in your case) to see it.

Of course, that's probably not the name you want, so you can head over to the "Site settings" via the button there and hit the "Change site name" button you'll find there. Assuming the name you choose is available, you'll wind up with a more reasonable URL. For example, if the name is changed to `jamvanity`, the URL will be `jamvanity.netlify.app`. It'll always be a subdomain of Netlify, though Netlify does offer the ability to use a custom domain you own too.

Now, click the Deploys link at the top. You should see one build, which is the initial one that was just done. Stay on that page, and then make a change to some file in the Git repo (you can do this through the GitHub site itself, or locally and then push the change). You'll find that Netlify almost immediately sees the change, starts a build, and publishes the change. Since there really is no build for this site at this point, the change will be very nearly instantaneous, a few seconds at most. That's the power of the CI/CD integration between Netlify and GitHub.

At this point, you have all the essential information about Netlify you need for our purposes in this chapter. The other thing we'll need to get into, as I mentioned earlier, is Netlify functions. But that will come a little later. Before that, though, let's talk about another service provider, one that will provide a place to store our document markup data: FaunaDB.

A Database for All Seasons: FaunaDB

Now, when it comes to thinking about a remote database, for all that Netlify offers, this isn't one of them. We need to look elsewhere. One provider of such a service that you'll find – which just so happens to work beautifully with a Netlify-hosted site like JAMboard will be – is FaunaDB.

FaunaDB is what's known as a NoSQL database. That's a slightly catty way of saying it's not a traditional relational database where you have tables that you query with SQL (Structured Query Language – get it? NoSQL?). Instead, in a NoSQL database, you deal with documents. In most such databases, these documents take the form of JSON data (though that's not, strictly speaking, required).

A key difference between a NoSQL database like FaunaDB and a relational database is that there are no rigidly defined data structures. In the same database, you might find a document like this:

```
{ firstName : "James", lastName : "Kirk" }
```

And, right alongside it, you might find another like this:

```
{ middleName : "Tiberius" }
```

The fact that they have different structures doesn't matter to the database. Your application will care, of course, and you'll have to code for the differences, but as far as the database is concerned, it's all good!

FaunaDB specifically is a global, serverless database. It's designed especially for JAMstack apps, though it's in no way exclusive to them. You can think about this similarly to how you think about a CDN: your data is "out there," available from anywhere. This provides you ubiquitous, low-latency access to your application data. Also, FaunaDB offers built-in authorization to secure your data. It also offers native GraphQL queries to your data. It is 100% ACID (Atomicity, Consistency, Isolation, and Durability), which means that your reads and writes to a FaunaDB can be trusted (read: will persist and be read consistently).

Note   This section is only scratching the surface of what FaunaDB offers, just enough to make JAMboard work. This is undoubtedly true of Netlify in the previous section as well. I strongly encourage you to spend some time exploring the website of both these service providers, browsing their documentation, to get a feel for what else they can do. Even if you never use them beyond this book, it's good to be informed!

All of this is made accessible to your application through some fairly simple APIs, as you'll see just a few sections from now. And, just like Netlify, FaunaDB is free, at least up to a fairly generous point. The free tier is more than sufficient to get through this project and will allow for a fair bit more after that before you have to consider jumping up to a paid plan.

To start with FaunaDB, head over to fauna.com and sign up for an account. Assuming you've already signed up for your Netlify account, you can go ahead and authenticate with that account. You'll be asked by Netlify to authorize the access, after which you'll be good to go (and, of course, you can sign up for an account completely separate based on your email address if you prefer, just like you could with Netlify itself). You'll find yourself on a dashboard page after that, as you see in Figure 6-3.

Figure 6-3. *My FaunaDB dashboard*

As with Netlify, I've already created some databases, but you won't have any to start. To remedy that, click the New Database link at the top there. Give the database a name, leave everything else as it is by default, and click the Save button. For the sake of our purposes here, name it "jamboard."

In a FaunaDB database, you have one or more collections. As the screen you'll see after creating the database says, collections are akin to tables in a relational database. So, go ahead and create a collection, naming it "markers" by clicking the New Collection button. Once again, leave everything but the name at its defaults, and click the Save button.

Once you do that, you will land on a screen like in Figure 6-4.

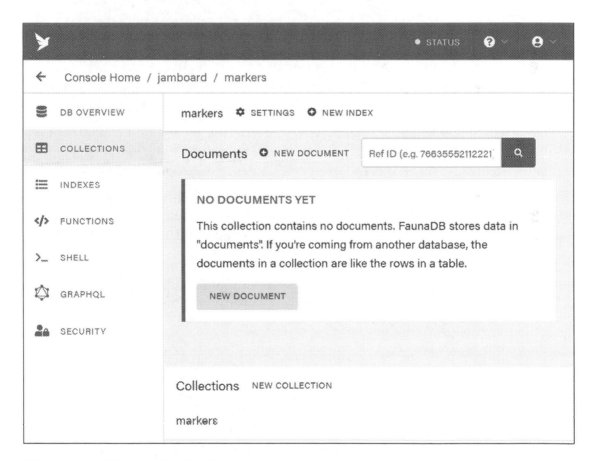

Figure 6-4. *Your collection is ready for use!*

Now, just click the New Document button, and you'll find yourself in an editor where you can create a document. You'll see that to start, the editor has {} in it. This denotes that you are entering JSON. You can enter one of the documents I showed earlier, or create whatever one you like, then hit Save. That's it! You've got yourself a document! Do that a few times and note that each document has a unique ID, or reference (usually written ref for short), and that is shown at the top of the page. If you now click the Collections line on the sidebar, you'll see a list of documents in the collection. You'll be able to examine them, delete them, and edit them. Play with them a bit to see what you can do, but when you're done, delete them all so that this database and collection are ready for JAMboard later.

Now, one last concept you need to be aware of is that of indexes. As with a relational database, indexes allow you to query your data based on attributes within the data. You can define indexes, for example, for the `firstName` property of documents, to enable you to quickly find all documents with a `firstName` property of "James."

For our purposes in JAMboard, we won't really need to query data like this, but we *will* need to retrieve all documents, and that still requires an index. The simplest index that FaunaDB provides is called a "collection" index. Simply put, a collection index includes all the documents in the collection. So, you'll need to create one. To do so, make sure you're on the markers collection page, and you should see a "New Index" link up top. Click it, and give the index the name "markers," leave everything else alone (the Source Collection should default to "markers" while everything else is blank, and the Serialized check box is checked), and click the Save button. That's it; the JAMboard FaunaDB is ready to rock and roll!

The last piece of the puzzle is to get the necessary code into the JAMboard code base to be able to interact with FaunaDB from our code. That's as easy as adding the `faunadb` package to the `package.json` file by executing

```
npm install --save faunadb
```

Interestingly, the code that will access FaunaDB is code that will wind up running in the cloud, not on a user's machine in a browser. But, to be able to do that, Netlify will have to build our application, which must include this dependency; otherwise, that cloud code won't work. We'll get to that a bit later, but with this section, the groundwork has been laid, and we can get into some code!

First: Some Necessary Code Changes

Before we can think about writing and integrating any functions that will run in the cloud and that JAMboard can make use of, we have to deal with some problems that are present in the code as it exists in Chapter 5, which of course is the starting point for what we're doing in this chapter.

Thus far, you've only been using `gatsby develop` when dealing with Gatsby. As a development setup, that's great: changes are instant. A big reason that can be so is that Gatsby isn't minifying your files, isn't packaging them up like you would for a production deployment. To do that, you run the `gatsby build` comment. However, if you go back and try that on the Chapter 5 code, you'll run into some problems pretty quickly, and if we don't deal with those, then we're not going to get very far in this chapter, so let's deal with them now.

Where Did My Window Go?!

The problems are a result of how Gatsby builds your code. It uses something called Server-Side Rendering, or SSR. SSR is basically what it sounds like: the "server" is rendering the page, acting like a web browser, but obviously not displaying anything. The term server here doesn't necessarily mean a remote machine. No, it can be your own machine, as is the case when you ask Gatsby to do a build. Remember that Gatsby is a *static* site generator. But how do you go from your source files, and data queries, to final static HTML that can be served to clients? SSR is the answer. Gatsby (and the tools it makes use of) acts almost as if it were a web browser, loading all the resources specified in your source file, querying your data, marrying it all together, and creates final HTML documents that a real browser can display.

In the phrase "*almost* as if it were a web browser," the word "almost" is the operative word because it's obviously not a web browser, and there are indeed some significant differences. Running `gatsby` build on the Chapter 5 code presents the first one, as Figure 6-5 shows.

```
Administrator: C:\Windows\System32\cmd.exe

C:\temp\etc>gatsby build
success open and validate gatsby-configs - 0.031s
success load plugins - 1.411s
success onPreInit - 0.005s
success delete html and css files from previous builds - 0.026s
success initialize cache - 0.016s
success copy gatsby files - 0.163s
success onPreBootstrap - 0.021s
success createSchemaCustomization - 0.010s
success source and transform nodes - 0.061s
success building schema - 0.450s
success createPages - 0.037s
success createPagesStatefully - 0.067s
success onPreExtractQueries - 0.002s
success update schema - 0.029s
success extract queries from components - 0.440s
success write out requires - 0.010s
success write out redirect data - 0.003s
success onPostBootstrap - 0.002s

    bootstrap finished - 8.299s

success Building production JavaScript and CSS bundles - 8.741s
success run queries - 8.893s - 2/2 0.22/s
failed Building static HTML for pages - 1.728s

  ERROR #95313

"window" is not available during server side rendering.

See our docs page for more info on this error: https://gatsby.dev/debug-html


  272 |   * @param inKey The key of the marker.
  273 |   */
  274 | window.showComments = function(inKey) {
      |
  275 |
  276 |     console.log("showComments()", inKey);
  277 |


WebpackError: ReferenceError: window is not defined

- documentTemplate.js:274 Module../src/templates/documentTemplate.js
  src/templates/documentTemplate.js:274:1

- Button.js:73 Module._compile
  node_modules/@material-ui/core/esm/Button/Button.js:73:1

- Button.js:93 Object.Module._extensions..js
  node_modules/@material-ui/core/esm/Button/Button.js:93:1

- Backdrop.js:15 Module.load
  node_modules/@material-ui/core/esm/Backdrop/Backdrop.js:15:1

- extends.js:9 Function.Module._load
  node_modules/@babel/runtime/helpers/extends.js:9:1
```

Figure 6-5.   *Oops, somebody closed the window on us!*

The window object is only present on a real browser, so remember when we attached the showComments() method to window, so it was available outside the Template component code?

Yeah, well, that doesn't work with SSR.

The fix for this is seemingly simple: just put showComments() in global scope. However, that's a little harder than it may seem because, with React, you're working in modules, so it's not apparent how to do this.

As it happens, React offers a solution: the global object. In simple terms, you use it in place of window. So, there are a few changes in the documentTemplate.js file to make. In the constructor, instead of

```
window.showComments = window.showComments.bind(this);
```

...we instead write

```
global.showComments = global.showComments.bind(this);
```

Then, in the linkifyMarker() function (and also in the handleDialogSave() function), replace

```
link.setAttribute("onClick", `window.showComments("${inKey}");`);
```

...with

```
link.setAttribute("onClick", `showComments("${inKey}");`);
```

Remember that the global object represents global scope, so here, we don't need to write global.showComments() because, like window in code running in a browser, it's implied. But, we do need to use it in the declaration

```
global.showComments = async function(inKey) {
```

...because if we left it off here, since we're in a module, the function would be global to the module, not global to the browser (and the pseudo-browser using during SSR).

With those changes made, that error goes away. But, we immediately run into another, similar problem.

Ugh, What's the Problem with Local Storage Now?!

Now, rerunning gatsby build, we get a new error, as seen in Figure 6-6.

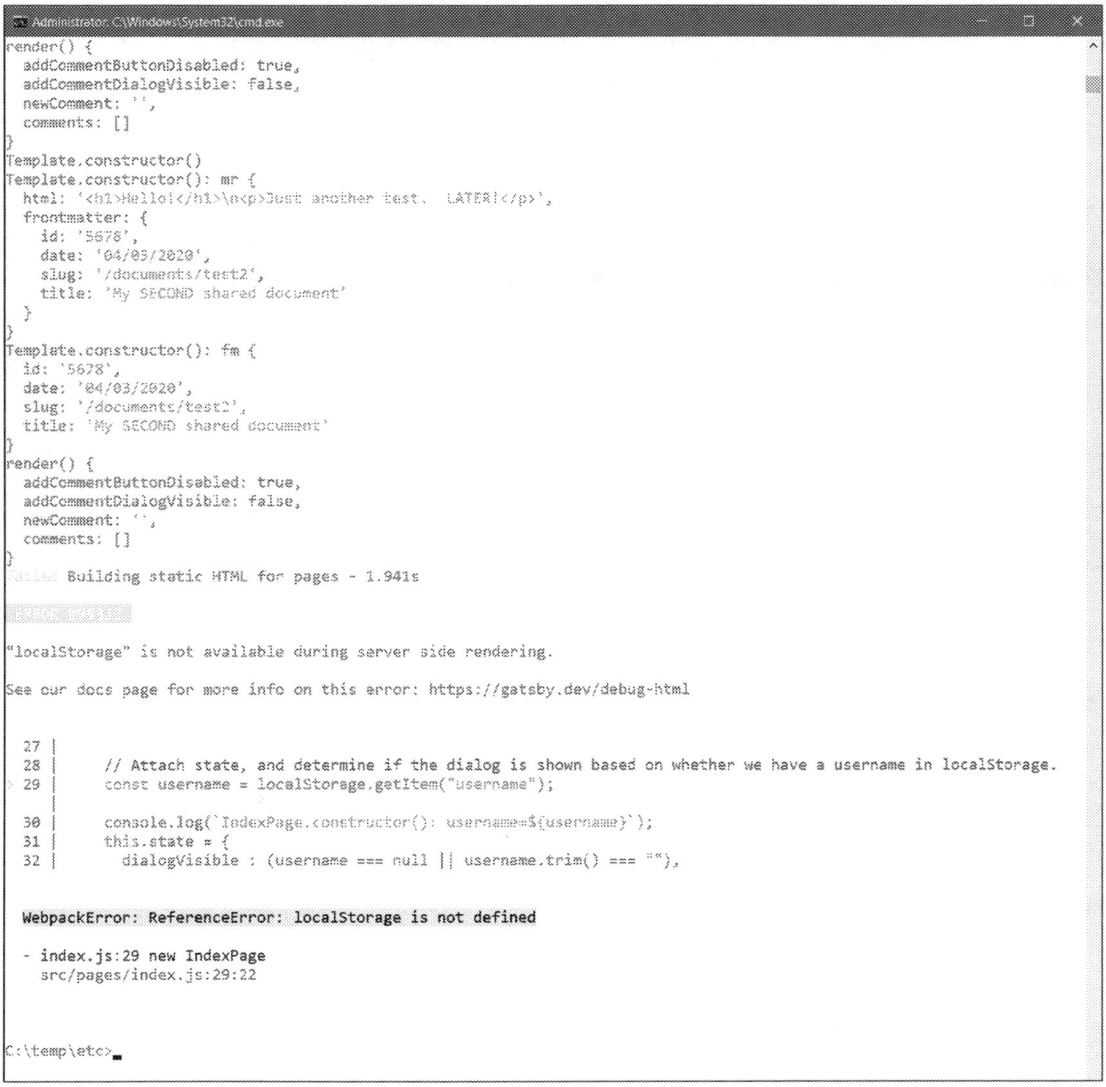

Figure 6-6. *Now you're tellin' me we can't use local storage?! ARGH!*

Yep, this time, local storage is reported as not available. It's the same problem: SSR isn't a real browser, so some things aren't available, and local storage is another.

However, this time, things get trickier. You see, when SSR is used to build the static site, some of our code is actually executed, including instantiating the `IndexPage` component. That's a problem because local storage is accessed in the constructor:

```
const username = localStorage.getItem("username");
console.log(`IndexPage.constructor(): username=${username}`);
this.state = {
  dialogVisible :
    (username === null || username.trim() === ""),
  username : username
};
```

We can't do that during SSR. Now, to be clear, we absolutely *can* use local storage in our code generally. It ultimately *will* be running in a web browser, of course, and web browsers have local storage, so we're fine in general terms. We just can't use it in any code that will be executed during SSR.

So, how do we fix this? Well, first, that block of code there from the constructor needs to be changed to

```
this.state = { dialogVisible : false, username : null };
```

That, in and of itself, will resolve the build error. Local storage is no longer being accessed during SSR. But, we actually *do* need to consult local storage at startup to look for a username. In order to do that, we have to use a React lifecycle event function: `componentDidMount`:

```
componentDidMount = () => {
  const username = localStorage.getItem("username");
  const s = { ...this.state };
  s.dialogVisible =
    (username === null || username.trim() === "");
  this.setState((inState, inProps) => { return s; });
};
```

This is added into the `IndexPage` component (after the constructor), and this code will only be executed when the component is rendered and added to the DOM, which won't actually happen until the page loads in the browser (it can't happen before: there is no DOM before the static HTML page is loaded into the browser – remember, a static site can still use JavaScript to build dynamic content on the client, which is what React is all about). Therefore, it's safe to use local storage from here. Now, of course, we can't just set the value in the component's state, we have to use `setState()` to mutate it, so there's a touch more code than initially, but the result is the same: the dialog is shown prompting for a username if none is found; otherwise, it's stored in state.

And, with those changes in place, `gatsby build` is now successful. This means that at this point, you can deploy the app to Netlify successfully, and everything should work as expected, like when you run it locally with `gatsby develop` (a little faster even, given you're now running optimized, production-quality code). Before now, these build errors would stop you from doing so because the build would fail at Netlify just as it does on your own machine. Now though, you just need to check the changes into your GitHub repository that Netlify is monitoring, and you should see a successful build in the Netlify console. You can actually watch the build in real time by selecting the site in your Netlify console, then go to the Deploys tab, look for the build that's currently building – it should be the first one – and click it to see the deploy log. You'll see all the build action as it happens (or, as it happened, if you get there after it's done).

Of course, JAMboard is still client side only at this point, but at least it's deployable and working. Now, let's write some functions and hook in FaunaDB and make it a real shared environment.

Readying StorageManager for Remote Storage

Now that the necessary changes have been made to allow Netlify to build JAMboard, it's time to make the changes that will connect it to the FaunaDB database that you set up earlier. This requires touching one file in particular: `StorageManager.js`. Some changes will be forced upon us by these changes, but they are minor. Let's get the `StorageManager` module's code ready first and then deal with those.

But first, we have a critical question to answer: how exactly is our client code going to talk to the remote code – whatever "remote" means in this context (hint: Netlify functions)? Hmm, I'd say that question is worth…

A Quick Detour: Axios

AJAX is a technique that came to life, so to speak, in the mind of one Jesse James Garrett in an essay he wrote in February 2005. There, he coined the term AJAX, which stands for Asynchronous JavaScript and XML. The interesting thing about AJAX, though, is that it doesn't have to be asynchronous (but virtually always is), doesn't have to involve JavaScript (but virtually always does), and doesn't need to use XML at all (but probably doesn't 99+% of the time).

AJAX is, at its core, an exceedingly simple and, by no stretch of the imagination, original concept: it is not necessary to refresh the entire contents of a web page for each user interaction, or each "event," if you will. When the user clicks a button, it is no longer necessary to ask the server to render an entirely new page, as is the case with the "classic" Web. Instead, you can define regions on the page to be updated and have much more fine-grained control over user event handling as a result, not to mention the potential for much better performance. No longer are you limited to merely submitting a form to a server for processing or navigating to an entirely new page when a link is clicked.

The interesting thing about AJAX is that it was in no way, shape, or form new, even when Mr. Garrett coined the term. A bit over a decade ago, when AJAX was still somewhat new to most developers, I liked to say that you could always tell who had done AJAX before and who hadn't because those who had are mad that it was a big deal and they didn't get credit for "inventing" it themselves!

Nowadays, the term AJAX isn't used as much as before. People tend to talk about "out-of-band requests" or simply "asynchronous requests" or, indeed, simply "server requests" because it's pretty much the de facto way of communicating with a server on the Web when you aren't refreshing the entire page.

At its core, AJAX works because of something invented originally by Microsoft: the XMLHttpRequest object. This is a JavaScript object that allows you to write code like this:

```
let req;
let which;
function retrieveURL(url) {
  if (window.XMLHttpRequest) {
    req = new XMLHttpRequest();
    req.onreadystatechange = processStateChange;
    try {
      req.open("GET", url, true);
```

```
      } catch (e) {
        alert(e);
      }
      req.send(null);
    } else if (window.ActiveXObject) {
      req = new ActiveXObject("Microsoft.XMLHTTP");
      if (req) {
        req.onreadystatechange = processStateChange;
        req.open("GET", url, true);
        req.send();
      }
    }
  }
}
function processStateChange() {
  if (req.readyState == 4) {
    if (req.status == 200) {
      document.getElementById("urlContent").innerHTML =
        req.responseText;
    } else {
      alert("Problem: " + req.statusText);
    }
  }
}
```

Even if this is your first time seeing such code, I bet you can understand it without much trouble. In short, you create an XMLHttpRequest object (branching based on whether the object exists or not, because, for a while, not all browsers exposed the object in the same way). You then hook a callback function up to it that will be called whenever the state of the object changes (e.g., when it connects to the server or when the response comes back – the object has an entire lifecycle you can hook into). You give it the URL to connect to, optionally tell it about any data you're sending (in this case, there is none), and finally, send the request. The callback function will be called, multiple times, in fact, based on the lifecycle events provided. We only care about the readyState 4, which is what occurs when a response comes back. Then, assuming we got an HTTP 200 back, we take the responseText, which is what the server sent, and insert it into a DOM node, presumably a <div>, or do whatever else we want with it. That's it, that's all there is to it.

Nowadays, you wouldn't even write that kind of code most likely, and instead, you'd use the newer Fetch API. Although not quite ubiquitous across all browsers, it's now supported by the vast majority, so now you can write code like this:

```
const response = await fetch(url);
```

Yep, that's much better, isn't it?

However, aside from the browser having to support this API, it also must support async/await, as you can see. If you want to reach the widest audience possible, but you don't want to write all the `XMLHttpRequest` code as in the preceding text, you'll probably want to use a capable library that abstracts all of this away from you (and, most likely, provides many other benefits). For JAMboard, and the functions we need to call from it, that's exactly what we're going to do!

Rather than doing "naked" AJAX like the preceding code, we'll instead use a popular library for it: Axios (`https://github.com/axios/axios`). In simplest terms, Axios is a Promise-based HTTP client that works in both browsers and Node. It uses XMLHttpRequest under the covers in a browser and uses the Node http library when used in a Node-based app. Being Promise-based means that you can use async/await with it (or the more "classical" Promise approach), which makes for a very nice API.

Axios offers some more advanced capabilities, including the ability to hook into the request and response cycle to make modifications broadly (think cross-cutting concerns in aspect-oriented programming, or AOP, for things like logging and security). And, it offers the ability to transform request and response data in various ways automatically and the ability to cancel requests, if necessary. This makes using it to call API functions a breeze.

Using Axios also means security because it includes protection against client-side XSRF, or cross-site request forgery. This is a trick nefarious sorts can use to transmit requests to the server, masquerading as you, a legitimate user. That's bad news, obviously, and Axios can keep your application safe from it without doing anything special on your part.

Axios has broad browser support and is as easy to use as

```
const response = await axios.get("your_server_url");
```

Or if you don't want to use async/await (what's wrong with you?!), you can use the Promise version instead:

```
axios.get("your_server_url").then(function(response) {
  // Do something with the response.
});
```

Do you need to POST some data to the server? No problem:

```
axios.post("your_server_url",
  { firstName : "Burt", lastName : "Reynolds" }
);
```

Axios will automatically serialize that object into JSON for transmission to the target endpoint (naturally, you can pass an object reference there; it doesn't need to be an object literal like that). It will also automatically deserialize a JSON response so that you have a nice JavaScript object to play with. That all means a lot less boilerplate code for you to write when dealing with functions that are almost certainly JSON-based.

You can use any other HTTP method there too: DELETE, HEAD, OPTIONS, PUT, PATCH, whatever you need, it's all there for you. This makes Axios great for REST-based (Representational State Transfer) APIs.

You can optionally pass a configuration object to any of the request methods after the URL (or even in place of the URL if the object itself contains the URL), which allows you to modify the request in many ways. The options available are numerous, so I won't go through them all, but a few of particular interest are the following:

- **transformRequest** – You provide a function here, and this will allow you to modify the response before it's passed to the response handler function (or returned to the variable specified in an await call). You can do the same for the request with the transformResponse property.

- **params** – You can provide a list of URL parameters to append to the URL with this.

- **timeout** – By default, Axios waits forever for a response (well, at least until the browser itself times out). With this option, you can specify how long to wait.

- **proxy** – Does your network require you to go through a proxy? If so, you can specify that information with this property.

- **onDownloadProgress** – This is a function to be called periodically while a response is downloading, allowing you the ability to show a progress bar or spinner or similar UI element (you can do this with onUploadProgress in the opposite direction too).

Axios is a very robust but extremely simple-to-use library that, for me, is the obvious choice for our remote communication needs in JAMboard.

Oh, by the way, because Axios is available in the NPM registry, all we have to do to get our project ready for it is

```
npm install --save axios
```

Once that's done, we're prepared to start using Axios.

Back to the Code!

Okay, now you've got some understanding of Axios, it's time to write some code with it. Each of the three existing functions in the StorageManager module needs to be altered to make remote calls (to the functions we'll build in the next section; that's the simple goal here).

getAllMarkerKeysFromStorage()

First up is the getAllMarkerKeysFromStorage() function. As is the case with all three of these functions, what it returns is the same; it's just that rather than getting the data from local storage, it's instead the result of a remote call.

```
export async function getAllMarkerKeysFromStorage(inDocumentID) {

  global.maskScreen(true);
  try {
    const res = await axios.get(
      "/.netlify/functions/getAllMarkerKeysFromStorage",
      { params : { documentID : inDocumentID } }
```

```
    );
    global.maskScreen(false);
    return res.data;
  } catch (inError) {
    global.maskScreen(false);
    return [ ];
  }

}
```

Let's ignore that `global.maskScreen(true);` line for the moment; we'll come back to that after we're done with these functions. All we need to do here is use Axios to do an HTTP GET request to a remove function. Now, we're going to get into the functions that are on the other side of these calls, but the critical thing to understand here is that when you write these functions, they're just JavaScript source files in your project. Netlify sees them and automatically deploys them to Amazon AWS as lambda functions. Those are callable via HTTP by nature. But, Netlify takes it a step further and makes them available via URLs in your application's URL structure. It creates a path under your app in the form `./Netlify/functions/xxx` where `xxx` is the filename of the function. It's really that simple! Once the app gets deployed, so too do the functions, and they are available to be called.

To get markers, we have to send in the ID of the document, just like before, so that's passed as a query string parameter to the function. Once again, we'll skip over the `maskScreen()` call inside the try block, but ultimately, the `data` property of the response object referenced by the `res` variable is returned to the caller. Axios will have already transformed the response, assumed to be JSON (which it will be!), into an object, so the code calling this `getAllMarkerKeysFromStorage()` function gets what it always has and is none the wiser that the data is now coming from a remote source. Of course, if any errors occur during the call, an empty array is returned. This isn't the most robust error handling to be sure, but it keeps our code from blowing up. It would probably be nice instead to show a message to the user saying the remote system couldn't be reached (take that as a hint for a suggested exercise!).

getMarkerFromStorage()

Next, we have the getMarkerFromStorage() method for getting all the data for a requested marker:

```
export async function getMarkerFromStorage(inKey) {

  global.maskScreen(true);
  try {
    const res = await axios.get(
      "/.netlify/functions/getMarkerFromStorage",
      { params : { key : inKey } }
    );
    global.maskScreen(false);
    return res.data.data;
  } catch (inError) {
    global.maskScreen(false);
    throw inError;
  }

}
```

Once again, it's a simple Axios call to the appropriate function URL. Note that the term "key" here is an application-level meaning. That is to say that FaunaDB doesn't have keys; it has references. But, from the perspective of our application code, because we started this with local storage, which *does* have keys, we still call it the same here since conceptually it's the same thing.

Note that this time, if we have an error, it's thrown back to the caller, which *will* blow up the app. That's because in contrast to getAllMarkerKeysFromStorage() where there's a reasonable return value we can force in this case, that's not really true here. If we returned an empty object – which would make some sense given that the caller expects an object from this function – it wouldn't work because that object wouldn't have all the data the caller expects. Sure, we could mock up such an object for the caller, but then we're effectively inventing a marker, which doesn't make sense. No, in this case, just allowing the error to bubble up and "error out" the app is a better choice. But, again, it would be a good exercise for you to implement some better error handling here, and figuring out what form that takes exactly is part of the exercise!

saveMarkerToStorage()

Finally, we have the saveMarkerToStorage() function to deal with, and it's just as easy as the first two, although this time there are some changes necessary:

```
export async function saveMarkerToStorage(inKey, inMarker, inIsUpdate) {

  global.maskScreen(true);
  try {
    await axios.post(
      "/.netlify/functions/saveMarkerToStorage", {
      key : inKey, marker : inMarker, isUpdate : inIsUpdate
    });
  } catch (inError) {
    console.log("saveMarkerToStorage(): inError", inError);
  }
  global.maskScreen(false);

}
```

The problem we face here is something with FaunaDB. Look back at the code for this function in the last chapter. It simply saves the marker to local storage using the supplied key. If the marker doesn't exist, no problem, it's created. If it *does* exist, again, no problem: it's overwritten. The problem is that if we try to tell FaunaDB to save a marker that already exists – if we try to use the same ref, in FaunaDB-speak – it won't allow it. We're going to need to use some different code when creating a marker vs. updating one when a comment is added, and the function we'll be writing before long will need to know which operation is being done. So, not only does this function still need the key passed in, but now it also requires the marker being updated and a flag to tell it whether this is an update or not. All that information is sent to the saveMarkerToStorage function via an HTTP POST request (since the marker itself can be large and have a lot of data potentially, it can't just be a query string parameter). Otherwise, though, the flow is the same. If an error occurs, we just log it because there's not too much else we could do (and one last time: feel free to enhance this as a learning exercise).

A UI Change: Masking the Screen

Okay, the final thing to talk about here are those calls to `maskScreen()` that I skipped over before. The name, I'm sure, gives it away, but the thinking here is what do you do when you make a remote call that can take some time to complete? It's a question you have to ask with any user interface design because the user could still be clicking things and trying to do something, and it's possible what they do impacts that remote call. There are several strategies for dealing with this, but one of the simplest is just to mask the screen so the user can't interact with it for the duration of the remote call. That's what I've chosen to do here.

To make that work, there's a couple of pieces, and the first begins with a new property that needs to be added to the state object of the `Template` component:

```
spinnerVisible : false
```

Material-UI provides a progress indicator, several, in fact. The one I'm going to use is a circular form of progress spinner. You have seen them many times on various sites: those animated circles of one variety or another to indicate activity. As with any React component, hiding and showing it requires a change to state, and that's where this new `spinnerVisible` property comes in.

Now, as you've already seen, we're going to have a `maskScreen()` function attached to the `global` object (so that the code in `StorageManager` can call it). But, since we know it's going to have to mutate state of the `Template` component, and only code that's attached to that component can do so, we need to add a line to the `Template` component's constructor:

```
global.maskScreen = global.maskScreen.bind(this);
```

With that done, there are only two things left to do. First, we have to add a few lines to the `render()` method of the `Template` component:

```
<Backdrop style={{ color : "#ffffff", zIndex : "999" }} open={state.
spinnerVisiblc}>
  <CircularProgress color="inherit" />
</Backdrop>
```

The Backdrop component comes from Material-UI (so there's also an import for this at the top of the documentTemplate.js file now) that is the actual mask of the screen. It's just a gray overlay that covers the screen (hence the zIndex set to a high value like that) and keeps the user from interacting with anything below it. Then, over that, is another Material-UI component that an import is added for: CircularProgress. That's the circular spinner thing I mentioned. Its color prop is set to inherit, which means it'll take its color from its parent, so it'll be white in this case (#ffffff).

The last piece of the puzzle should be obvious: the maskScreen() function itself:

```
global.maskScreen = function(inMask) {

  state.spinnerVisible = inMask;
  this.setState((inState, inProps) => { return state; });

}
```

Yep, just two lines! The mask can be hidden or shown with this function by passing true to show it or false to hide it, and it's a simple matter of altering that spinnerVisible state object property and telling React about it.

Let's Add Some API: Netlify Functions

Okay, finally, we come to the point where we can actually write the functions I've been talking about off and on throughout!

Well, almost.

To be able to do that, we first will need to take care of three things, beginning with adding a new configuration file to the mix, this one specific to Netlify. The netlify.toml file, which goes in the root of the project, can be thought of as the file-based equivalent of the Netlify project configuration pages on your project dashboard. Most of what you can do in one can be done in the other (there may be some exceptions, things can only be done in one place or the other, but *mostly* they are equivalent, and I purposely left one thing to do in the console to give you some hands-on experience with that). You already know, whether you realize it or not, that netlify.toml is optional: you have (presumably) already deployed the vanity site to Netlify, and that project didn't have this file, yet it worked fine. That's because the file is optional.

Anything you don't include in this file will use whatever is set up in the console, and if you don't make any changes in the console, then it uses its default value, whatever that may be.

Note   If you aren't familiar with TOML, it's a file format for configuration files. It is intended to be easy to read and write due to obvious semantics that aim to be "minimal" (it's literally an acronym for Tom's Obvious, Minimal Language, referring to its creator, Tom Preston-Werner). In short, it is designed to map unambiguously to a dictionary. If you're familiar with YAML, then you'll have no trouble navigating TOML (you'll have no trouble if you're not familiar with YAML either, believe me!). If you want more details, have a look here: `https://github.com/toml-lang/toml`.

For our purposes, we need just three things:

```
[build]
  command = "npm run build"
  functions = "src/functions"
  publish = "public"
```

Anything in the `[build]` section applies to all build contexts unless overridden in a specific context. We only have one build context for this project, though, so that doesn't much matter in practice here.

The `command` element is simply what command will be used to build our project. This will reference the `build` command in our `package.json`.

The `functions` element tells Netlify what the path to the deployed serverless lambda functions will be. Remember earlier you saw requests made to `./Netlify/functions/xxx`? Well, this is what determines the `functions` part of that path.

Finally, the `publish` element tells Netlify what directory, relative to the root of your repo, contains the deploy-ready assets that result from the Gatsby build.

With this file in place, we have two more things to deal with before we can write, deploy, and use functions.

Addressing Another Problem: FaunaDB Key Requirements

First, we have a bit of an issue in that keys in FaunaDB cannot be anything but numeric values. That's a problem because, as you'll recall, the keys for the marker objects that are currently stored in local storage are in the form "documentID-markerID". That works for local storage, but not FaunaDB, and it's the dashes that are the issue.

Thankfully, the fix is straightforward: in the `addMarker()` function in the `documentTemplate.js` module, we have

```
const key = `${fm.id}-${new Date().getTime()}`;
```

We just need to change it to

```
const key = `${fm.id}${new Date().getTime()}`;
```

Everything else works the same because when we get the list of keys from storage to determine which markers are for the selected document, we're using `startsWith()` to determine which marker keys start with the specified document ID, and that'll still be true even with the dash (although we'll be doing that in a remote function now, it's the same basic idea).

One Last Quick Detour: FaunaDB Authentication

There's yet one more piece to the puzzle that we need to complete before we can write code to make use of FaunaDB, and that's dealing with authentication. Fortunately, it too is an easy problem to deal with:

- Head over to the FaunaDB console.

- Select your jamboard database.

- Click the Security link on the side.

- Click the big, green button labeled "New Key".

- Hit the "Save" button, using all the defaults.

At the end of all that, you'll be presented with a secret key. This is the authentication token that FaunaDB will expect all incoming requests to include, so it knows the call is valid. This key also directs FaunaDB to the appropriate database, so each database will need its own key (and you can have multiple keys with different capabilities too if you want – some for read-only operations, some for updates, etc.).

The next step is to tell Netlify about this key. While this can be included in your `netlify.toml` file, I'm instead going to direct you to enter it manually in the Netlify console just to give you some hands-on experience doing that. Head over to the Netlify console, select the app, and then

- Click the "Site Settings" button at the top

- Click the Build and Deploy link on the left

- Click the "Environment" link underneath it

- Click the "Edit Variables" button

- Click the "New variable" button

- Enter the name FAUNADB_SERVER_SECRET and the secret key you got from FaunaDB

- Click the "Save" button

With the next deployment, that variable will be available to the functions and hence the calls they make to FaunaDB.

Back to the Code!

Okay, it's been a long road, getting from there to here, as the theme song for probably the least popular of the Star Trek shows says... which I hope isn't a bad omen, but I digress... now, we can start writing those Netlify functions!

All three of these source files go in the `src/functions` directory, and Netlify will manage deploying them to Amazon AWS as lambda functions there and presenting the URLs for our application code to use. Each of these mimics the names of functions in StorageManager, since StorageManager will call them in place of the code that previously used local storage.

Because these ultimately wind up as AWS Lambda functions, that means they have a simple structure:

```
export.handler = function (event, context, callback) { }
```

That is the entirety of the API for these, at least as far as we care about here. All you do is write the code inside that function that does whatever work is involved. In the end, you call a function that lambda passes in as the callback argument, and to it, you provide an error object and a response object (the error object would be `null` for any nonerror response, logically). That's really all there is to these functions. Neat, isn't it?

Hang on, here we go!

getAllMarkerKeysFromStorage.js

First up is the function to fetch all the keys of all the markers in the collection:

```
const faunadb = require("faunadb");
const query = faunadb.query;
```

To use FaunaDB, we make use of its module, which you'll recall we added to `package.json` for the project so that it will be deployed alongside our function. To make the code a little cleaner, we'll pull the `query` object out of it and have a shorter reference for it in the `query` variable.

```
exports.handler =
  async function(inEvent, inContext, inCallback) {
```

There it is, the function signature I mentioned earlier. One difference, though, is that because we're calling a remote system (FaunaDB itself), there's an asynchronous component to this. There are a few different ways you could code this, but as it happens, AWS Lambda is fine with you making this handler function `async`, so we'll do that, and use `await` inside of it.

```
  const documentID = inEvent.queryStringParameters.documentID;
```

All the query string parameters to the request, if any, are presented in the event object that is passed in, so we can pull out the `documentID` very easily.

```
  const client = new faunadb.Client({
    secret: process.env.FAUNADB_SERVER_SECRET
  });
```

Next, we need to instantiate a FaunaDB client object, which is what we'll interact with to work with FaunaDB. Note that the secret parameter in the object passed to this constructor is the secret key we got from the FaunaDB console and that you added as an environment variable in Netlify. This is how FaunaDB will know which database this request is for and will authenticate your requests.

Caution   One thing I found out the hard way is that you must instantiate the client inside the handler function, not before it. The code will appear to work, but you will most likely encounter hung socket errors after a few requests that will make you bang your head against the wall for a while. That's because AWS will keep the previous instance around and keeps the connection open to FaunaDB, which seems like it would be more efficient, but it leads to this problem. Instantiating it every time, as is what happens when you do it inside the handler, may be slightly less efficient, but is 100% more working!

```
await client.query(
  query.Paginate(query.Match(query.Ref("indexes/markers")))
)
```

The FaunaDB module uses a highly hierarchical API, so you wind up with a bunch of nested function calls like this. First, we're writing a query, so it makes sense that we start with a call to the query() function of the client. The Paginate() function of a query allows for pagination through result sets, and though we won't use that capability here, we still need to go through it. Then, the Match() function, as its name implies, allows us to find matches against the data in the database. In this case, we're looking for an object with a Ref value of indexes/markers, which you should recognize as the collection of indexes against our markers collection. This will return to you a response object that contains an awful lot of stuff, but all of it can be ignored, saved for one: a list of refs, one per index – which in our case means one per document in the markers collection. So next, we need to find just the ones for the requested document:

```
.then(async inResponse => {
  const docRefs = inResponse.data;
  let keys = docRefs.filter(
    inRef => inRef.id.startsWith(documentID)
  );
  keys = keys.map(inRef => inRef.id);
  inCallback(null,
    { statusCode : 200, body : JSON.stringify(keys) }
  );
})
```

First, we need that list of refs, and that's available in the response's `data` property. Next, we have to find the ones just for the requested object. We're dealing with an array, so we can use `filter()` to get down to what we need. Remember that in FaunaDB, you're dealing with document IDs, but to JAMboard, those are keys. Same thing, different name. Those values are in each `Ref`'s `id` property, so we can use `startsWith()` on those to find the applicable documents.

At that point, we'll have an array of `Ref` objects, and just those for the requested document. But, we actually need to return an array of keys. So, the array's `map()` function is used to return just the `id` property of each `Ref,` and we have what we need! All that's left is calling that callback function I mentioned. We didn't have an error, so the first argument is `null`, and then the second object supplies an HTTP status code and the body of the response, which is just a JSON version of the array of keys.

All that's left is to deal with errors:

```
.catch(inError => {
  return { statusCode : 400,
    body : JSON.stringify(inError) };
});

};
```

The client may or may not handle this well, of course, but at least it'll show up on the browser somewhere for debugging purposes. As with the error handling before, this could be much more robust, and this might present you a good opportunity to gain experience by enhancing it here as well.

getMarkerFromStorage.js

The second of the three functions is the one for getting a specific marker from the database. It's quite simple, really:

```
const faunadb = require("faunadb");
const query = faunadb.query;

exports.handler =
  async function(inEvent, inContext, inCallback) {
```

```
const key = inEvent.queryStringParameters.key;
const client = new faunadb.Client({
  secret: process.env.FAUNADB_SERVER_SECRET
});
```

To this point, this is the same almost boilerplate code as in the getAllMarkerKeysFromStorage function. It's the next bit that's different:

```
await client.query(
  query.Get(query.Ref(query.Collection("markers"), key))
)
.then((inDoc) => {
  inCallback(null, { statusCode : 200,
    body : JSON.stringify(inDoc) });
})
```

As before, we call client.query() to kick things off. This time, since we know we're getting one item only, Pagination isn't needed, and we can instead use the Get() method. Also, this time, we aren't doing a query, so we don't need to Match() anything. Instead, we can get a specific Ref directly using the Ref() method. We pass to this a reference to a named collection that is retrieved using the collection() method, along with the specific key we want, pulled from the query string again.

We get a single document back in the then() function, and it's just a simple matter of serializing it to JSON and constructing a proper response.

As before, we deal with error:

```
.catch(inError => {
  return { statusCode : 400,
    body : JSON.stringify(inError) };
});

};
```

And that's all there is to this function!

saveMarkerToStorage.js

While the previous two functions were about retrieving data, the final one –
saveMarkerToStorage – is about writing data to the database. It begins in exactly the
same way:

```
const faunadb = require("faunadb");
const query = faunadb.query;

exports.handler =
  async function(inEvent, inContext, inCallback) {

  const incomingData = JSON.parse(inEvent.body);
  const client = new faunadb.Client({
    secret: process.env.FAUNADB_SERVER_SECRET
  });
```

Well, there's one difference, isn't there? A marker's data can be large depending
on how many comments there are, so passing it in the query string isn't really feasible.
Instead, it comes in as a POST request body. Fortunately, AWS Lambda makes it just as
easy to get as query string parameters: it's available as the body property of the passed-in
event object. We just JSON.parse() it to get an object to work with.

Now, I mentioned this earlier, but there's a bit of a problem here in that unlike with
local storage, there is a difference in how we save an update vs. when creating a new
marker. So, we first have to determine which we're doing:

```
const whichMethod =
  incomingData.isUpdate ? "Update" : "Create";
```

All the client tells this function is whether this is an update. When the isUpdate of
the object send in the body is true, it's an update; when it's false, it's a create.

What's the point of setting whichMethod to Update or Create based on that? Well,
here's the point:

```
await client.query(
  query[whichMethod](
    query.Ref(
      query.Collection("markers"), incomingData.key
    ),
```

```
    { data : incomingData.marker }
  )
)
```

The only difference in terms of the code we write when saving to FaunaDB is whether we call `query.Update()` or `query.Create()`. After that, it's the same. So, rather than write some branching logic to determine that, I dynamically call the correct method based on the value of `whichMethod`. It just makes the code a bit clearer in my eyes.

Caution   I actually love this form of code, but you always have to remember that if you write something like this, never use input from the user directly to determine which method to execute. You'll be opening up a big, gaping security hole if you do. Here, only the `Update()` or `Create()` can ever possibly be called, so we're safe.

Whichever gets called, it's just a matter of providing the `Ref` via the `query.Ref()` method, providing the target collection via the `query.Collection()` method, the key (ID in FaunaDB-land) that was passed in, and of course, the object to store.

After that, we construct a response that includes the saved document for good measure (it's not used in JAMboard, but it's good form as far as API design goes):

```
.then((inSavedDoc) => {
  inCallback(null, { statusCode : 200,
    body : JSON.stringify(inSavedDoc) });
})
```

And lastly, deal with errors:

```
.catch(inError => {
  return { statusCode : 400,
    body : JSON.stringify(inError) };
});

};
```

That takes care of the functions and almost completes the JAMboard code. We just have a few problems to deal with now before it will properly build, deploy, and work as expected.

Finally: Addressing Remaining Problems

Two final problems have to be dealt with before all of this code will work, and it stems from the use of await in StorageManager. To make a long story short, on the first problem: because StorageManager uses async/await when making Axios calls, that means that anywhere that calls StorageManager functions must now be in an async function and the calls must use await'ed. The only source file where this comes into play is documentTemplate.js. The following functions must now be marked async:

- **loadMarkers()** – Because it awaits StorageManager. getAllMarkerKeysFromStorage())

- **addMarker()** – Because it awaits both StorageManager. saveMarkerToStorage() and linkifyMarker()

- **linkifyMarker()** – Because it awaits StorageManager. getMarkerFromStorage()

- **showComments()** – Because it awaits StorageManager. getMarkerFromStorage()

- **handleDialogSave()** – Because it awaits both StorageManager. saveMarkerToStorage() and showComments()

The calls to the StorageManager functions – as well as to the functions that themselves call StorageManager functions – must now use await.

The other problem is in the render() method of the Template component – specifically, this chunk of code for displaying the marker's text in the header of the comments section:

```
<div style={{ fontWeight : "bold", position : "sticky",
  top : "2px", padding : "10px", backgroundColor : "#eaeaea",
  zIndex : 99 }}>
  { currentMarkerKey === null ? "" :
    StorageManager.getMarkerFromStorage(
      currentMarkerKey
    ).markerText }
</div>
```

The problem here is that the call to getMarkerFromStorage() there to get the current marker's text, if any, has an await in it, but render() isn't marked async. Making render() async is, strictly speaking, doable, but React is built with the expectation that it's not, so things may not work as expected. Instead of that bit of logic there, instead do

```
<div style={{ fontWeight : "bold", position : "sticky",
  top : "2px", padding : "10px", backgroundColor : "#cacaca",
  zIndex : 99 }}>
  { currentMarkerText }
</div>
```

The currentMarkerText variable is a new one that is introduced at module scope at the top of this source file, and its value will be set whenever a marker is selected. Since selecting a marker is done asynchronously, that works fine and avoids the problem because the component's state will be updated during that process, which will include re-rendering this <div> with the marker's text, as expected. There's no longer a concern about needing to do something asynchronously inside render() because it happens elsewhere and at a different time now. Problem solved!

Note   Naturally, the download bundle for this book includes the complete and fully modified version of all of this code. I don't expect you to go making these changes yourself! The point to all of this, though, was to explain the delta between the code in Chapter 5 and the code in this chapter and what changes were required to make it work with Netlify, FaunaDB, and everything that goes into both.

Suggested Exercises

That completes our look at the code changes needed to make the final version of JAMboard complete!

For this project, I purposely left two important things on the table specifically to offer as suggested exercises, two things that I think will challenge you and make for excellent learning opportunities. These are in addition to the previous suggestions about error handling, but those are kind of minor in comparison to the following.

The first suggestion relates to when you think about what happens if two people try to add comments to a marker at the same time. As it stands, whichever one occurs later will overwrite the first because the marker is sent completely on each update. Assume two users load a document at the same time. They grab all the markers at startup, so they are "in sync" with each other at that point. Now, if user A submits a new comment for a marker, it will be saved as expected, no problem so far. But then, when user B submits a comment for that same marker, user A's comment will effectively be removed because user B's marker data doesn't include user A's comment. So, suggestion number one is to change it so that adding a comment calls a new function that takes in just the comment and the marker key, and the function pulls the marker out of the collection and adds the comment. That should take care of that problem.

The second task is really the second half of that scenario and is when you think about simultaneous work. If user A enters a comment, or creates a new marker, and user B is working on the document at the same time, how will they know about user A's comment? User B's screen won't update in response to what user A does unless and until they refresh the page. That's not good for a shared work environment. So, the second task is to deal with that.

There is more than one way to do this, but one way is that on every marker, you add a timestamp, and the same for every comment. Then, add another new function that is called every few seconds from clients (a "polling" approach). It accepts a timestamp from the client and then looks at all the markers, and the comments within them, and returns any that are newer than the timestamp (to make things a little simpler, just return the entire marker regardless of whether the entire marker is new or whether it just has a new comment). Then, the client has to linkify any new markers and, for markers that had new comments, ensure the screen updates if the user happens to be viewing that marker.

I think both of those, if you pursue them, will really solidify a lot of the concepts from this chapter, and the previous one. Of course, there's also the point I've made a few times about error handling to tackle too.

Have fun with these!

Summary

In this chapter, you learned about a new way to host JAMstack apps: Netlify. You learned about the functions it provides to create an API, and you saw how they can be used to interact with a FaunaDB database. You learned a bit about Axios, and you saw how all of this put together allows us to create a genuine shared document markup application.

In the next chapter, we'll go a completely different direction and see how JAMstack concepts can be used to create another application that couldn't be more different: a *game*!

CHAPTER 7

JAMstack for Fun and... Well, Just FUN!

In the immortal words of one Homer J. Simpson, "All work and no play makes Homer something, something." Well, Homer, I agree! We can't sit around making business applications all day; we gotta sneak some fun in there every so often!

In my capacity as a team lead, I've been asked several times by junior developers what they can do to improve their skills. My answer has always been the same: make games! It sounds weird, but the truth is that games force us to overcome challenges in ways you can't anticipate. Games require us to use all our skills in novel ways, from data structure and algorithms to time and space complexity, from data flow to object design.

Games are a learning exercise, and they also by their nature are *fun* to make! After all, games are meant to be fun to play, so shouldn't they be fun to make too? I think so!

With those thoughts in mind, the final project we're going to tackle in this book is a game. It will give you a somewhat different perspective on Gatsby, React, and JAMstack and will introduce a few new things in the process. It'll be a good learning experience while also being enjoyable to do.

So, let's figure out what this game of ours is going to be and then get into actually putting it together!

A Short Time Ago, in a Galaxy Right Around the Corner…

Okay, here's the story: you're the lowest-ranking astronaut on a ship whose job it is to steal energy orbs from alien civilizations (because isn't that always how it is?!). Yeah, you know the drill: you're a disposable red shirt!

© Frank Zammetti 2020
F. Zammetti, *Practical JAMstack*, https://doi.org/10.1007/978-1-4842-6177-4_7

Of course, the aliens who own these energy orbs are not too happy about this, so you'd better run for your life!

There's just one catch: you have to navigate a series of stone pathways suspended over lava (yikes) which, for some reason, seems to be a common defense strategy by all energy orb-possessing alien species. Why that may be is a discussion for another day because there are two far more pressing concerns. First, if you and the orb you're carrying at any given moment fall into the lava, not only will you most certainly be dead (no giant eagles to save you here!) but second, you'll also create a rupture in the spacetime continuum that will destroy the universe (and to be clear: *that's bad*!).

Finish a planet, and you'll move on to the next and do it all over again – at least until you die… or are promoted into a better position (presumably – that possibility is covered in the inevitable sequel – #SixSeasonsAndAMovie!).

To play, you use the left, right, and up arrow keys to jump left, right, and straight up, respectively. Get to the end, and you'll get beamed up to your ship, safe and sound, ready for the next heist… err, retrieval!

It's not a complicated game to be sure – it's certainly not going to compete with the Halo's and FIFA's of the world – but it'll get the job done for our purposes here, which is to learn and gain experience with JAMstack.

And, of course, to have some fun!

So, what does this game, which I'm calling JAMJumper, look like? Figure 7-1 provides that answer, and hopefully, it's not much different than what you imagined reading the description.

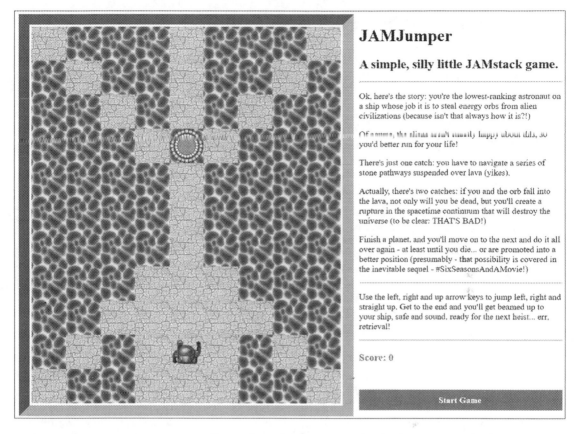

Figure 7-1. *JAMJumper, in all its glory (trust me, it looks better in color)*

As you can see, there's not much to it. The main game area is on the left, a title, and instructions on the right. Your score is below that and, of course, a button to start the game with. Once you click the button, the stone walkway begins to scroll (along with the fire in a nice parallax manner), and you can jump as needed to stay on the stone pathway until you reach the end (here, the endpoint, a teleport pad, is visible). You get some points as you go automatically, plus a bonus when you reach the end. There are several levels to navigate, and if you finish them all, there's another score bonus. The player will just try to survive to get the maximum possible score; that's the end goal.

As Captain Kirk Says: "Fire Phaser!"

Okay, now that you know what we're building, how are we going to accomplish it? Well, we'll use Gatsby for this, and we'll also be hosting it on Netlify. But that will come in the next chapter. Before we get to that, we have to talk about building HTML5 games in general and one particular library for doing so: Phaser.

While it is 100% possible to build a web-based game with plain old HTML, CSS, and JavaScript, like so many things in web development, there's great value in choosing a library, toolbar, or framework to help. Game development is no different, and, in that arena, few things stand out above Phaser.

Phaser is a game framework that is 100% free and open source that is specifically geared to writing 2D games. It is extremely fast, allowing your games to perform exceptionally well on most devices. Honestly, it can be rather shocking how good Phaser games run!

Phaser, the website for which can be found at `https://phaser.io`, does all its magic using WebGL when the browser supports it (which is most of them these days) and falls back on Canvas otherwise. In other words, Phaser isn't using the DOM (except at a basic level). That's a big part of why it's so fast: it's really just pushing pixels around at a low level (relative to a web page and the DOM anyway). In fact, in many cases, maybe even most, this will all be hardware-accelerated, so the performance can be remarkably close to native. The only real bottleneck is JavaScript itself, but that too can be surprisingly fast when the DOM isn't really involved.

Phaser provides a great deal of functionality that games require including things like sprites (including animation), a physics engine (which includes collision detection), a particle engine for real-time particle effects, tweening (for animations of all sorts), audio, input control, primitives drawing (geometric shapes and such), tiles, text, and more. It's all cross-platform, pretty easy to use, and very well performing. Phaser is an extremely robust platform on which to create games (though note that there's nothing that says you have to build games with it – you could make just about any app you wanted with it, though it clearly is geared toward games).

As you may have guessed, we won't be going into excruciating details on Phaser here. Ultimately, this isn't a book about game development, so that wouldn't make sense. No, you'll get a good look at the basics as we progress into the code, but there will be a lot of Phaser surface area not touched. If game development is an interest of yours, then spend some time looking at the Phaser website to see all it offers, including some examples of games built with it that I think you'll find extremely impressive.

Before we get into the code, though, and see the basics of Phaser, we need to create a basic project to build on, so let's do that now.

Note   I'm expecting at this point that you'll pause here and play the game a little bit (just execute gatsby develop and then access it at localhost:8000, like always) to get a little familiarity with what it is and how it plays. That will give you context for the rest of this chapter that I think you'll need to understand what I'm talking about throughout.

Starting from "Hello, World!"

Once again, we'll use Gatsby for this project, but also once again, we won't be using a comprehensive template. At the time of this writing, no Gatsby template includes Phaser, and in fact, none I could find is even geared toward making a game. So, instead, we're going to start with the gatsby-starter-hello-world starter:

```
gatsby new JAMJumper https://github.com/gatsbyjs/gatsby-starter-hello-world
```

This is even more minimal than the starter we used in previous chapters. In fact, you'll find (assuming the starter hasn't changed since this writing) that there is only a lone source file, index.js, and it's just the following:

```
import React from "react"
export default function Home() {
  return <div>Hello world!</div>
}
```

If you then look in gatsby-config.js, it's just as minimal:

```
module.exports = {
  plugins: [],
}
```

Yep, it doesn't get any more basic than that! There are no other Gatsby config files by default with this starter. The only bit of cleanup to do is to delete the favicon.ico in the static directory because we won't need it, and we'll be using something else for the same basic purpose in the next chapter. However, leave the static directory itself because that we *will* use – more on what that is later!

Finally, the only dependencies in `package.json` are `gatsby`, `react`, and `react-dom`, the bare necessities for a Gatsby project. This is perfect for our needs! We can begin adding on to this as needed without having to clean anything up like for past projects, and the first thing we'll need to add is Phaser itself:

```
npm install --save phaser
```

With that, we're ready to start building JAMJumper!

The Starting Gate: index.js

Of course, the `index.js` file created by the hello-world starter has to be replaced altogether. For this project, we are going to accomplish what we just barely missed accomplishing with the last project: this *will* be an actual SPA! Of course, in this case, that's not saying all that much given that there's only ever one screen that the user will see. Still, by the letter of the definition, that's what JAMJumper is.

As usual, we begin with some imports:

```
import React from "react";
import * as gameCore from "../gameCore.js";
import { graphql } from "gatsby";
```

The only one you haven't seen before is `gameCore.js`. That's where the majority of the code for this project is and what we'll be dissecting that right after we're done with `index.js`. But, we still need to create a React component for this single page, and that's what we do next:

```
export default class IndexPage extends React.Component {
```

That looks pretty boring by now, I hope! So, we'll move on to the constructor for the `IndexPage` component:

```
constructor(inProps) {
  super(inProps);
  global.levelData = inProps.data.allLevelsJson.edges;
}
```

As always, we call super() to ensure React has everything it needs to be happy. As you'll see a bit later, every level in the game is defined by some data that is in a JSON file, one per level. There are actually two ways we could deal with these, and I'm going to show you both. This is the first way: they will be read in by Gatsby and made a part of the data model for the site, which means we can write a query to access them. The query, since it's a page query, will be at the end, but here is where the query results are used. As you'll recall, Gatsby automagically includes the query results in the props passed to the constructor. In this app, unlike the previous one, that data is *not* used by the component itself, or any of its children. Instead, it's going to be used by the code in that gameCore.js file I mentioned. So, we have to make the data available to that code. There are a couple of ways that can be done, but I felt that the simplest is just to add it to the global object that React provides us as a global namespace. In a small project like this, I'm not worried about global-scope pollution or any of those sorts of concerns.

And don't worry, I haven't forgotten: I'll show you the second way to deal with the JSON level data files when we get to the gameCore.js code. Before that, we have to add a componentDidMount() method to this component:

```
componentDidMount = () => {
  gameCore.init();
};
```

Here's the basic idea: if you were writing as plain HTML/JS/CSS app with Phaser, you would need to initialize some things (which you'll see later) when the DOM is ready. If you try to do it before, it won't work. The same is true here, but with React, you learned in the last chapter that componentDidMount() must be used for that task. That's true here too. The init() function in gameCore.js is what kicks everything off, what gets Phaser involved, and starts the game up, but none of that can happen until the DOM is done being built by React; hence, componentDidMount() comes into play again.

After that, it's time to render our component:

```
render() {

  const pStyle =
    { paddingTop : "10px", paddingBottom : "10px" };
  const hrStyle =
    { marginTop : "10px", marginBottom : "10px" };
```

Even before rendering the component, I know that there are a couple of styles that are going to be used several times, so I define them here. Making them objects like this means that I can write

```
<hr style={hrStyle} />
```

The hrStyle object will populate the style prop for the <hr> element exactly like you'd expect. It's just another syntactic way of doing styles.

Next, the component's return value is begun:

```
return (
  <div style={{ display : "grid",
    gridTemplateColumns : "624px 380px", gap : "10px" }}>
    <div id="gameContainer"
      style={{ border : "20px inset #c0c0c0",
        padding : "4px 0px 0px 4px" }} />
```

For JAMJumper, there's nothing fancy here. There's no Material-UI, no React components except for the one that is parent to everything else. All we'll be returning is plain old HTML. The topmost element, a <div>, is what provides the overall structure to the page, which is a two-column layout where one column is 624 pixels wide and is where the gameplay area is, and the second is 380 pixels wide and is where our instructions, score, and one control button is.

The gameplay area, which is where Phaser will render the game content later, is the first child <div>. I give it a thick, inset border to try and sort of mimic an arcade machine look.

After that is another <div>, this one representing the second column:

```
<div>

  <h1>JAMJumper</h1>

  <h2>A simple, silly little JAMstack game.</h2>

  <hr style={{hrStyle}} />
```

As you can see, it's just basic HTML now, and you can see the first instance of those styles defined earlier being used.

The explanation of the game begins next:

```
<p style={{pStyle}}> Okay, here's the story: you're the lowest-ranking
astronaut on a ship whose job it is to steal energy orbs from alien
civilizations (because isn't that always how it is?!)</p>
```

There are several more paragraphs like this, but just to spare a few trees, I'm going to refrain from listing them here. Let's pick up after that with the divider below the description and the instructions:

```
<hr style={{hrStyle}} />
```

```
<p style={{pStyle}}>Use the left, right and up arrow keys to jump left,
right and straight up.  Get to
the end and you'll get beamed up to your ship, safe and sound, ready for
the next heist... err, retrieval!</p>
```

```
<hr style={{ ...hrStyle, marginBottom : "20px" }} />
```

Well, there's something a little bit interesting! In this case, I want to use the hrStyle object, but I need to override the marginBottom value so that there is a little more space between the divider and the score. Because the style is defined as an object, I can use the spread operator to "spread" the values from the hrStyle object into the style prop here. Then, the additional marginBottom setting explicitly here overrides whatever was spread into the prop object. It's a nice, clean way to do overrides like this on an individual element level.

After that comes the area for the score:

```
<h3 style={{ color:"#ff0000" }}>
  Score: <span id="score" />
</h3>
```

Again, nothing fancy, just a <span> that the gameCore.js code will insert the current score into.

Finally, since Material-UI isn't used here, we have to build a faux-button (I could have used a basic HTML button, of course, but I thought this was a little more fun!):

```
<div onClick={gameCore.startLevel}
  style={{ cursor : "pointer", width : "100%",
    color :"#ffffff", fontWeight : "bold",
    backgroundColor : "#8080ff", textAlign : "center",
    paddingTop : "10px", paddingBottom : "10px",
    marginTop : "50px" }}>Start Game
</div>
```

Yep, nothing but a `<div>` with an `onClick` handler that points to a `startLevel` function, a function you'll see a bit later. Then, it's just some basic styling. There's nothing tricky there, so I'm going to assume you got it and move on to the page query I mentioned earlier.

Querying for JSON-Level Data

As I said earlier, each level of the game will be stored in a JSON file. These will be in the `src/levels` directory (aside from the first one, which is in the `src` directory). One of the two ways we'll get them into our app is to let Gatsby process them so that we can execute a GraphQL query to get at the data. To do this, we have to bring in a transformer that knows how to read JSON, so add this dependency to the project:

```
npm install --save gatsby-transformer-json
```

And, as you saw in the previous project, we'll also need the `gatsby-source-filesystem` plugin to actually read the files:

```
npm install --save gatsby-source-filesystem
```

As you saw when we dealt with Markdown, there's a little bit of configuration that must be added to `gatsby-config.json` to make use of these, and in fact, it looks a lot like the Markdown configuration. Just add two elements to the `plugins` array:

```
"gatsby-transformer-json",
{
  resolve : "gatsby-source-filesystem",
  options : {
    name : "data",
    path : `${__dirname}/src/levels`
  }
}
```

That's it! Gatsby will now source the JSON files in `src/levels` and add them to the internal data model. Once that's done, a page query can retrieve the data:

```
export const pageQuery = graphql`
  query LevelsQuery {
    allLevelsJson {
      edges {
        node {
          totalScreens
          data
        }
      }
    }
  }
`;
```

We'll see the level data later, but you can already tell from this that it has two elements, `totalScreens` and `data`. The `allLevelsJson` element is created by Gatsby and is where the JSON files are found. We just need to dig down through the usual edges/nodes/node structure that is common to most sourced data. The results of this query will be an array where each element in the array is an object defined in each level data file, an object that we'll look at in context later, so it makes some sense.

Note   Just a reminder that the query name, LevelsQuery, doesn't really matter, it can be anything and has no special meaning except to you as the developer.

Before that, though, we have some other code to discuss, the beginnings of the code that constitutes the actual game!

The Heart of the Matter: gameCore.js, Part 1

The `gameCore.js` file is where you find the real meat of this project, the actual game code. It largely follows the basic structure of a Phaser game, which means there is a `Game` object, which is a class provided by Phaser, which is the primary interface into Phaser. There is also at least one `Scene` object, where a game can have multiple scenes (though this game only needs one). Think of a scene as the various screens that might appear in a typical game: maybe a menu screen, a character selection screen if it's an adventure game, then a scene for the actual game (maybe more, depending on the game). This structure is up to you, and in JAMJumper, we'll just need a single Scene.

A Phaser scene has a standard set of methods that you, as the developer, must provide, which Phaser will then call at various points in the lifecycle of the game and scene to perform specific tasks. Most importantly, those methods are `preload()`, `create()`, and `update()`. We'll look at each of those in turn (although `update()` will be looked at in the next chapter). But, before we get to those (and the handful of "support" functions that will live outside of the `Game` and `Scene` objects), let's start from the top.

Basic Structure

The basic structure of the gameCore.js file is pretty typical stuff, beginning with some imports:

```
import Phaser from "phaser";
import level_01 from "./level_01.json"
```

Obviously, we'll need Phaser itself, or we won't get far with this whole thing! After that, you can now see the second approach that I mentioned there was to working with JSON files: you can simply import them! The `level_01` variable will contain an actual JavaScript object, so effectively, the JSON is run through `JSON.parse()` (I don't actually know if that's what the JavaScript engine literally does under the covers, but it's a good bet, and even if it's not what it does, it does the equivalent, which is what matters to us as a programmer). The first level is imported this way, and the rest are sourced by Gatsby and read in via the query you saw earlier. It doesn't make much sense to do one this way and all the rest via query *except* as a way to show you that you *can* do both, which was my only goal here!

Note   The level_01.json file is in the src directory, whereas all the other level data files are in src/levels. This is on purpose: it avoids level_01.json being part of the query results and the player winding up having to play through the level twice.

Module-Level Variables

Following the imports, we have a series of module-level variables to declare:

```
const sizes = {
  tile : { width : 64, height : 64 },
  grid : { columns : 9, rows : 11 },
  astronaut : { width : 54, height : 44 },
  trackPixelsPerIteration : 2
};
```

First up is an object that contains information about the size of the graphics used in the game (which you'll find in the static/img directory that we'll be discussing shortly). The fire in the background and the stone track are created as a grid of tiles. Here, we can see that this grid is 9 columns by 11 rows. Each tile has a width of 64 pixels and a height of 64 pixels. If you do some multiplication here, you realize that the game area is 9*64=576 pixels wide by 11*64=704 pixels tall. Our astronaut has a width of 54 pixels and a height of 44 pixels, which you'll note are even numbers. That allows for an even number of pixels around the astronaut when centered on any tile.

Next, we have to create a configuration object that Phaser will use to create our Game and Scene objects later:

```
const config = {
  type : Phaser.AUTO,
  parent : "gameContainer",
  width : sizes.tile.width * sizes.grid.columns,
  height : sizes.tile.height * sizes.grid.rows,
  fps : { target : 60, forceSetTimeOut : true },
  physics : { default : "arcade" },
  scene : {
    preload : preload, create : create, update : update
  }
};
```

The `type` attribute tells Phaser to choose between its WebGL and Canvas renderer as appropriate for the browser. The `parent` attribute is the ID of the element on the page where the game will be rendered (from `index.js`). The `width` and `height` are, of course, the size of the area the game will take up, and you can see the calculation done as described before. The `fps` attribute tells Phaser how many frames per second we want to render. We target 60 here, and as long as our code isn't terribly inefficient, Phaser will be able to ensure that happens on any halfway decent systems.

The `forceSetTimeOut` option tells Phaser to use `setTimeout()` rather than `requestAnimationFrame()` when rendering each frame. Usually, you would want `requestAnimationFrame()` to be used because it leads to a somewhat smoother gameplay. However, for JAMJumper, it's critical that we know exactly how long each iteration will take, something you can't be sure of with `requestAnimationFrame()` because it is time-based rather than target frames per second-based. Using `setTimeout()` instead ensures that each frame will have exactly 1000/60=16.6 milliseconds per frame, and we can move things on the screen knowing that. It's just a slightly easier way to code movement in graphics, and for a simple game like this, it works well enough.

The `physics` attribute indicates to Phaser that we want the physics engine to run and that we want it to run in `arcade` mode. We'll need physics for one purpose: collision detection. As such, we're not simulating gravity or anything, so the more straightforward `arcade` mode is suitable. There is also a `matter` mode, which allows for much more complicated physics bodies defined for game elements and much more complex activities like simulations of gravity and how it affects different types of physical objects. There is also an `impact` mode, and that appears to be a mode somewhere in-between the two.

Finally, the `scene` object is where you define one or more scenes. This can be an array or an object, and since we just have a single scene, it's just an object here. This object references the three methods I mentioned earlier, referencing functions you'll find in this module and that we'll look at very soon.

Next up, we have variables that will reference the `Game` object:

```
let game = null;
```

And, one to reference the `Scene` object:

```
let scene = null;
```

Those will be created a bit later, but having them in module scope like this ensures that they are accessible to all the functions to follow.

Next, we have an object that stores most of the current state of the game at any moment in time:

```
const gameState = {
  currentLevelIndex : 0, currentLevel : level_01,
  gameRunning : false, score : 0, trackMoveCount : 0
};
```

This tells us what the current level is (as an index into the array that comes from the GraphQL query in `index.js`), as well as containing a reference to the actual object that houses the level data in the `currentLevel` attribute. We also have an attribute that tells us if the game is currently running (`false` before the user has clicked the Start Game button or after they have died), and the current score. The `trackMoveCount` attribute will be described later as it wouldn't make much sense to you right now.

Next, we have an object that will store references to the graphics needed:

```
const images = {
  track : null, astronaut : null, endTile : null
};
```

The `track` attribute is going to wind up being an array of static images, as you'll see soon. The `astronaut` attribute is a sprite, which is an image that has multiple frames of animation. The `endTile` attribute is a reference to the special track tile that is the end that the astronaut must reach to end a level.

Next up, what game is any good without sound? That's right, JAMJumper will have audio too:

```
const sounds = { running : null, jump : null, death : null };
```

There are just three sounds: running, which is a footstep sound any time the astronaut is running (but not jumping). The jump sound is obviously when he jumps, and the death sound is when he meets his early demise. You'll see these loaded later.

Next, each of the fire tiles needs to move in the background, and that's going to be done with tweening, which is a way for us to tell Phaser "change property X of this object over time as I specify." In this case, we'll be telling it to move the vertical position of the fire tiles:

```
const fireTweens = [ ];
```

Of course, this game wouldn't do much if we didn't have some controls:

```
let keys = { left : null, right : null, up : null };
```

Each of these flags in this keys object will get set with the corresponding cursor keys are pressed, as you'll see later, and our code will react accordingly to them.

Speaking of controls, jumping is the one game mechanic the player is in control of, and we have an object named jumpData with all the data about jumping:

```
const jumpData = {
  isJumping : false, direction : null, phase : null,
  jumpTicks : null, tickCount : null,
  DIR_UP : 0, DIR_LEFT : -2, DIR_RIGHT : 2, PHASE_UP : 0.12,
  PHASE_DOWN : -0.12
};
```

Obviously, we need a flag to tell the code when the player is jumping. We then need one to tell us whether they are jumping left, right, or straight up, and that's the direction of the jump. We also need to know whether the player is going up or coming back down, which I term the phase. The jumpTicks and tickCount are values that change as the player is jumping so that the code knows when to switch phases (when they've jumped as high as they can and now need to come back down) and when they land again. You'll see how these are used later. The remaining attributes are simply constants. The value of direction will be one of DIR_UP, DIR_LEFT, or DIR_RIGHT, while the value of phase will be one of PHASE_UP or PHASE_DOWN. The values are specifically chosen here to make the timing of the jump work right, as you'll see later.

When the player dies, they tear a rupture in spacetime. To make that happen, we'll use Phaser's particle system. The key component of the particle system is something called an emitter. Although there's only one, I create an object to contain a reference to it, just for consistency with the images and sound:

```
const emitters = { rupture : null };
```

To avoid doing DOM lookups over and over again when updating the score, a reference to that <span> is cached in the scoreSpan variable:

```
let scoreSpan = null;
```

Finally, we will need a flag to know when a click on the Start Game button should start a new game:

```
let restartGame = false;
```

Obviously, there's still a lot you don't know at this point, so most of these variables and objects don't have full meaning to you. Don't worry, as you see them used, I think it'll become clear very quickly.

And, you're about to see the first such example in the next section!

The init() Function

The `init()` function, if you remember back to `index.js`, is called from the `componentDidMount()` function. It's quite simple:

```
export function init() {
  scoreSpan = document.getElementById("score");
  game = new Phaser.Game(config);
}
```

Until this function executes, there is no game. A new `Phaser.Game` object is created here, passing it the `config` object from earlier. Phaser takes over from there, building the display and taking control of (almost) everything that happens from this point on is, either directly or indirectly. In essence, React is out of the equation at this point, its job done in `index.js` to render the basic layout and the `<div>` that Phaser will render the game into.

Of course, displaying the score is something our game code will have to handle, so here is where we get a reference to the `<span>` as described before.

The preload() Method

The first of the three methods that are needed to satisfy Phaser is the `preload()` method. While you theoretically could get away without this (as well as the `create()` method), that would be a nonstandard way to use Phaser, and you may well run into issues. It's better to just stick with what you're *supposed* to do and provide one:

```
function preload() {

  scene = this;
```

The goal of this method is to load any audio and graphical assets that your scene requires. As such, Phaser will call this first. Remember that JAMJumper only has a single scene, so here we're going to load everything that the entire game needs. For a more complex game, you would limit what you load here to just what a particular scene needs. However, before we load anything, a reference to the scene is stored. This will make some of the code later a lot simpler.

After that, the actual loads begin:

```
this.load.image("track", "img/track.png");
this.load.image("trackBlank", "img/track_blank.png");
this.load.image("trackEnd", "img/track_end.png");
this.load.image("ruptureParticle", "img/ruptureParticle.png");
```

The Phaser Scene object provides a variety of methods for loading various assets, but `load.image()` – along with `load.audio()`, as you'll see – is probably the most used. As their names imply, they are for loading images and audio assets. These make Phaser aware of them and give Phaser a chance to load them. Each image is given an identifier, like `track`, `trackBlank`, `trackEnd` (images for drawing the stone track, or areas where there is no track, and the special end tile that is the teleporter the astronaut is trying to reach), and `ruptureParticle` (an image used to produce the spatial rupture, in conjunction with the Phaser particle system). These identifiers are how you'll refer to a given asset later on when you want to put one of these images on the screen, or use them to create a sprite from.

Now, if you look at the directory structure of JAMJumper in the code bundle, you'll quickly notice that there doesn't appear to be an `img` directory under `src`, like you'd probably expect. So, where does `img/track.png` go to load the image? Well, that's where that `static` directory I've mentioned a few times comes into the picture!

A Quick Detour: The Static Directory

Usually, when you build a site with Gatsby, and you want to use images, you'll import them directly into your code as you would any JavaScript module. Gatsby, in conjunction with Webpack, makes this work. This usually goes for stylesheets too, as well as many other assets a website might need (audio files, web fonts, etc.). This has several benefits. First, these resources are automatically minified and bundled together for efficient loading. Second, any missing files will show up as compilation errors, not runtime errors. Third, the filenames that are used by Gatsby are dynamic (hashes), so that browser won't cache older versions.

However, there are sometimes cases when you want or need to opt out of all of that and handle things yourself. Phaser is one such instance because it doesn't know how to use the bundled resources that Gatsby and Webpack produce. Fortunately, Gatsby recognizes that this is sometimes needed and provides an "escape hatch," so to speak: the `static` directory.

You create this directory in the root of your project, and within it, you can have any directory structure you like (or no subdirectories at all). Every file and directory you put in the `static` directory will be simply copied right into the `public` folder at build time, unaltered. You can then reference these resources in your code as you would any other resources in a plain, non-Gatsby website, because recall that the public folder is where the output from the build process goes.

So, when we tell Phaser to load `/img/track.png`, it will look for an actual file named `track.png` that starts in the `static/img` directory and winds up in the `public/img` directory after the build is completed.

It really is that simple, but it's a powerful mechanism when you need it, as we do with Phaser. As you'll see in the next section, audio files are in the `static/snd` directory and are managed the same way as the images. Remember, though, that Gatsby or Webpack won't touch these resources, so you'll need to minify them yourself. And, remember that if you type a path wrong, you'll get an error at *runtime*, not at build time, so be careful!

Back to the Code!

Next, we have to load two spritesheets:

```
this.load.spritesheet("fire", "img/fire.png",
  { frameWidth : 64, frameHeight : 64, endFrame : 3 }
);
this.load.spritesheet("astronaut", "img/astronaut.png", { frameWidth : 54,
frameHeight : 44, endFrame : 1 });
```

What's a spritesheet, you ask? Well, take a look at Figure 7-2. That's the spritesheet for fire on the left and the astronaut on the right.

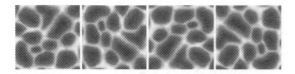 

Figure 7-2. *The spritesheets for the fire (left) and astronaut (right)*

A spritesheet is basically an image that contains multiple frames of animation. Take the fire, for example. To give it a swirling effect, I took the base image, which is the one on the left, and then rotated in 90 degrees to create the second frame, then rotated that one 90 degrees again to get the third, and once more to get the fourth. Note that I've added some separation between the frames to make it a bit more obvious what you're looking at, but there are no gaps in the actual fire.png graphic.

Each frame or animation is the same size: 64x64. So, when the load.spritesheet() function is used, you tell Phaser what identifier to use for this spritesheet, the image filename that contains the animation frames, and then you tell it the frameWidth and frameHeight of each animation frame (while there are options for frames that aren't all the same size, it's often the case that they *are* all the same size just because it's easier to put the images together that way). In addition, you essentially tell it how many frames there are in total with the endFrame value (3 because the first image is 0, so 0–3 for all the frames, with the last frame, or "end" frame, being index 3).

The astronaut is the same, but in this case, there are just two frames of animation. Note that none of this inherently makes any animation occur. It's simply giving Phaser the information it needs to load the image and then slice it up into individual frames. We'll define the actual animations later and activate them. We have to do that because, in a spritesheet, there might actually be several different animation sequences, and Phaser won't know how to use them. For example, if we wanted to have an animation sequence of the astronaut exploding, we might put, say, ten more frames after the two you see, but then frames 0–1 is one animation sequence (running, in this case) and then 2–11 will be the explosion. Having them all in one spritesheet allows for more significant compression and is more efficient, but it means we have to tell Phaser what's going on.

Finally, we have some audio assets to load:

```
this.load.audio("running", "snd/running.ogg");
this.load.audio("jump", "snd/jump.ogg");
this.load.audio("death", "snd/death.ogg");
this.load.audio("beamup", "snd/beamup.ogg");
```

As mentioned earlier, they're just Ogg Vorbis (.ogg) audio files and they are in the `static` directory in their own `snd` subdirectory. It's the same deal as images and spritesheets: call the appropriate loader method on the Scene object and provide an identifier and the filename and Phaser will load them up.

After all of this, these resources are all ready for us to use throughout the rest of the code, and the next method is where we begin to use them.

The create() Method

The second method that Phaser calls is the `create()` method. If you didn't have a `preload()` method, then `create()` would become the first method called. The goal here is to create the elements of the game, and do general setup required.

```
function create() {

  scoreSpan.innerHTML = gameState.score;
```

First things first: an initial score is shown. Since `scoreSpan` is just a reference to a plain old `<div>`, it's nothing fancy: setting `innerHTML` does the job. The `gameState.score` attribute has a value of zero at this point, which makes sense when the game is starting.

From here on out, I'll break this method down into logical chunks, starting with a chunk for creating our astronaut.

The Astronaut

The first step is to figure out where the astronaut is on the screen:

```
const ax = (sizes.grid.columns / 2) * sizes.tile.width;
const ay = ((sizes.grid.rows-1) * sizes.tile.height) - (sizes.astronaut.
                                                 height / 2) -
  ((sizes.tile.height - sizes.astronaut.height) / 2);
```

Since we know that there are nine columns of tiles, figuring out the horizontal location is a simple matter of figuring out the center tile and multiplying by the width of a tile.

The vertical location is a little trickier. Here, we want to place the astronaut one row up from the bottom, so one is subtracted from the number of rows. This is multiplied by the height of a tile, which gets us onto the right row. But, then, we want to make sure that the astronaut is centered on that file, which they wouldn't be if we stopped here. So, we now need to subtract the difference between the height of a tile and the height of the astronaut, and then divide that result by two, so that the space is evenly distributed.

The result of all of this is that ax and ay are coordinates that put the astronaut on the center tile of the second row from the bottom, centered on that tile. That is, it *will*, once we actually create the astronaut! Keep in mind that by default, the coordinates for an object in a Phaser game are based on the center of the object. You can change that, and you'll see how when we deal with the track.

First, though, we'll need an animation sequence for the running animation:

```
this.anims.create({ key : "run", repeat : -1, frameRate : 5,
  frames : this.anims.generateFrameNumbers(
    "astronaut", { start : 0, end : 1, first : 0 }
  )
});
```

Recall that the astronaut spritesheet is two frames of animation. We can create an animation sequence using the anims.create() method of the Scene object (which, remember, is referenced by the this keyword at this point). The key is just an identifier we can use later to activate a given animation. If we had ten more frames, and they represented a different animation sequence (say, the player exploding), then we could define another sequence in the same way for those, all sourced from the same spritesheet, and could then activate them as needed.

The repeat attribute being set to -1 means to repeat this sequence indefinitely. It'll just keep looping between the two frames, which are referenced by the frames attribute. The value needed is what is returned by the anims.generateFrameNumbers() method of the Scene object. We tell it what the first frame and end frame are (taken from the astronaut spritesheet) and which frame the sequence starts on. Finally, the frameRate attribute tells Phaser how frequently to flip through the frames. Remember that the game runs at 60FPS, so the astronaut will appear to alternate between left and right legs 12 times a second, which gives the desired running effect.

Next, it's time to actually create the astronaut, which is a sprite:

```
images.astronaut =
  this.physics.add.sprite(ax, ay, "astronaut");
images.astronaut.body.setSize(1, 1);
```

Because we need collision detection, we have to use the `physics.add.sprite()` method of the `Scene` object (you could also create a basic `Image` instead of a `Sprite`, but then collision detection can't be used). This takes the location coordinates and a reference to the spritesheet. Here, I'm also defining the size of the physics body for this sprite. By default, the physics body will be a square completely encompassing the sprite (it's also possible to define them as more complex bodies that follow the contour of the object – it all depends on the needs of your game). That works in many cases, but here, it would be a problem because as soon as the astronaut is even a single pixel off the edge of the stone track, it would register as a collision with the fire, and they would die. The game would be virtually impossible to play. Instead, the player need some leeway. The easiest way to do that is to make the physics body a single pixel right in the middle of the player (remember, these coordinates are by default based on the center of the object). That way, the astronaut can be off the edges of the track a little bit without registering as a fiery death!

We also need to ensure that the astronaut will be on top of the track and fire graphics (which, of course, haven't been created yet). Similar to HTML, there is the concept of z-index for Phaser objects, called *depth*:

```
images.astronaut.setDepth(2);
```

The fire will have a depth of 0, the track images will be 1, the astronaut is 2, and the spatial rupture particles will be 3. As in HTML, higher-numbered objects are on top of objects with lower numbers when rendered onto the screen.

Finally, we have to deal with the run animation:

```
images.astronaut.anims.play("run");
images.astronaut.anims.pause();
```

As you can see, the `anims.play()` method of a Phaser object allows you to specify the animation to run. But, since the game starts out not playing until you click the button, I immediately pause the animation. When the game starts, `images.astronaut.anims.resume()` will be called to start the run animation (only one animation can be playing at a time for an object, but it can be paused and resumed at will).

The Fire

Now that we have an astronaut, let's go ahead and create some fire. First, we need an animation:

```
this.anims.create({ key : "burn", repeat : -1, frameRate : 10,
  frames : this.anims.generateFrameNumbers(
    "fire", { start : 0, end : 3, first : 0 }
  )
});
```

Giving it a key of burn, I think, makes sense! This animation runs a bit faster than the player's run animation, but otherwise, it's defined the same.

Now, with an animation defined, it's time to create a bunch of fire images, one per space in the grid in the play area:

```
for (let row = 0; row < (sizes.grid.rows + 1); row++) {
  for (
    let column = 0; column < sizes.grid.columns; column++
  ) {
    const tile = this.add.sprite(
      column * sizes.tile.width,
      (row - 1) * sizes.tile.height,
      "fire"
    );
    tile.setOrigin(0, 0);
    tile.anims.play("burn");
```

I'll stop here so you can chew on that. Once more, the add.sprite() method of the Scene object is used. This is done inside two loops that will "paint" fire tiles, so to speak, onto the 9x11 grid of tile spaces from the upper left to the lower right. In this case, though, I call setOrigin(0, 0) on each sprite. This has the effect of making the x and y coordinates of the sprite relative to the upper-left corner of the sprite. This makes the math far easier when positioning each fire sprite.

One important thing to note here is that I'm actually creating one extra row of fire tiles, which are positioned outside the gameplay area, above it. In game development, this is often referred to as an "overscan." Remember that the fire appears to scroll down the screen. This effect is sort of a cheat. The way it works is that all the tiles are moved downward, including that row of tiles above the gameplay area. The bottom row of fire tiles will move down and out of the gameplay area, while those above move into it. When all the tiles have moved 64 pixels – the height of an individual tile – the positions of all of the tiles are reset to where they begin. The effect is that of a continuous scrolling sea of fire. You'll see that reset in the next chapter, but I think giving you the basic idea here makes sense.

Now, you know that tiles move, but how is that accomplished? The answer is this:

```
const t = this.tweens.add({
  targets : tile, duration : 1000, repeat : -1,
  y: { from: (row - 1) * sizes.tile.height,
    to: row * sizes.tile.height },
});
t.pause();
fireTweens.push(t);
```

A tween is a way to animate some property of an object over time. The term "animate" here is a little bit of a misnomer because animation doesn't necessarily mean movement. You could animate the alpha property of an object, for example, to have it fade out over a few seconds. You can do that with a tween. The great thing about a tween is that it is, largely, a "fire and forget" sort of thing: you tell Phaser what to do, and it goes off and does it. In this case, the tweens.add() method of the Scene object creates a tween for us (a reference to which is stored in the fireTweens array, since we'll need to pause the tween later – and just like with an animation, that's something you can totally do with tweens!). We have to tell it the target, that is, what object to animate, and we have to tell it the duration that tween should take, 1 second here (1000 milliseconds). As with animations, repeat set to -1 means keep doing it over and over again. Then, we have to tell Phaser what property to animate. In this case, it's the y location, the vertical position of the fire tile. We tell it what the starting value is (from) and the ending value (to). Since each subsequent row of tiles created here will simply move 64 pixels down and then reset, and since we have that overscan row to consider, the starting position is the height of a tile minus the row number minus one. So, for the first row drawn, row-1 will yield -1, so multiplied by the tile height (64) means that tile will start 64 pixels above the gameplay area, just like we want. The to value is 64 pixels more, so 0 in the case of the overscan row. With each row of tiles having the same positioning logic, we get the desired continuous scrolling effect we're after. But, as with the fire animation, we need this tween not to be going at the start, so it too is paused for now.

The Track

Next up, we need to create the stone track:

```
createTrack();
```

Uhh, wait, that seems a bit anticlimactic, doesn't it?! Not to worry, we're going to look at that in the next section because it's probably the most complicated bit of code in the whole game, so I think it more than deserves its own section. Before that, though, let's finish up the rest of the code in create().

Sounds

While we loaded the sounds in the preload() method, that just prepares them for Phaser to use. In order to actually use them, we have to add them to the scene:

```
sounds.running = this.sound.add("running");
sounds.jump = this.sound.add("jump");
sounds.death = this.sound.add("death");
sounds.beamup = this.sound.add("beamup");
```

References so these are kept in the sounds object so that we can play these later, as you'll see.

Keyboard Input

Obviously, JAMJumper wouldn't be much of a game if we couldn't control the astronaut, so let's set up some key handling here:

```
keys.up = this.input.keyboard.addKey("up");
keys.left = this.input.keyboard.addKey("left");
keys.right = this.input.keyboard.addKey("right");
```

The way this works is simple: any time the up arrow key, for example, is pressed or released, the up attribute of the keys object will be updated. It'll have a value of true when the key is pressed, false when it's not. We can read this value in the main game code later (which you'll see in the next chapter) and react as appropriate. You can hook up as many such key handlers as you wish, whatever your game requires.

The Spatial Rupture

Finally, we have that spatial rupture to deal with. This uses the Phaser particle system. If you've never heard this term before, you've undoubtedly seen it if you've ever played even a semimodern video game. A particle effect is one that uses numerous small images to create a more significant effect than the individual images themselves could produce on their own, and a particle system is a piece of code that produces these effects. Picture an explosion like you've probably seen in many games. That's almost certainly a particle effect: tiny bits of fire and debris fly out from a central point to produce the explosion you see. Sparks on an electrical wire are another typical example. Rain can be created with a particle system. Even the flame on a torch might be produced this way. Particle systems can be extraordinarily complex and the effects they produce very involved.

Fortunately, for the spatial rupture, it's not so complex:

```
const particles = this.add.particles("ruptureParticle");
particles.setDepth(3);
emitters.rupture = particles.createEmitter({
  radial : true, quantity : 1,
  speed : { min : -800, max : 800 },
  angle : { min : 0, max : 360 },
  scale : { start : 4, end : 0 },
  lifespan : 800, visible : false
});
emitters.rupture.pause();
```

First, we have to add an image that will be the basis for the particle effect. The `add.particles()` method of the `Scene` object here references the `ruptureParticle` we loaded earlier, which is just a circle with a little gradient color effect. Then, the depth of it is set so that it will be above all the other graphics of the game.

Note An interesting aside: the term "particle system" came about thanks to 1982's *Star Trek II: The Wrath of Khan*. In that movie, the Genesis video that Kirk, Spock, and McCoy watch used a system of particles to produce the effect of the Genesis "fire" progressing across the surface of a planetoid. Before this, similar results could be created by animators hand-drawing them (see Disney's Fantasia, for example), but Star Trek was the first time this was done via computer graphics, and the first time the term "particle system" was used to describe it.

After that is where the magic happens: a particle emitter is created with the `particles.createEmitter()` method. An emitter is responsible for creating the particles, positioning them, and animating them through the life of the effect. Here, I'm saying that the particles should emerge from the emitter randomly (`radial : true`) in all directions around the center of the emitter between the angles specified by `angle` `min` and `max` (0–360 degrees is all directions around a circle). The `quantity` is how many particles are emitted at each tick of the emitter's animation cycle. One is sufficient for the effect I was after. The `speed` attribute denotes the speed of emitted particles in pixels per second. Here, I gave a range that the values will be chosen from to provide some variation. The `scale` attribute serves a similar purpose to `speed` in that it gives a range from which particle sizes will be chosen. So, we'll get some small particles and some larger ones. The `lifespan` attribute tells how many milliseconds each particle should live for; after which, they will fade away. Finally, setting `visible` to `false` means that none of what we just set up will show up on the screen! Obviously, this should only appear when the astronaut dies.

One last thing to consider: a particle system can be computationally expensive. Maybe not so much in this case, but even still, better to not have all that work going on if the rupture isn't actually visible, so the emitter is paused here, just like an animation and a tween, and will be started up (and made visible) when the time is right.

The createTrack() Function

Now, let's go back to the `createTrack()` function that you saw called from create() and see what it's all about. But, that will be hard to do without one of my world-famous quick detours.

A Quick Detour: Defining Level Data

By now, you've seen level data loaded two ways, but to this point (unless you've looked at the code already!), you haven't seen what's in the JSON files for the levels. Well, time to remedy that!

```
{
  "totalScreens" : 4,
  "data" : [
```

```
  [ 1, 0, 0, 0, 0, 0, 0, 0, 1 ],
  [ 0, 0, 0, 0, 0, 0, 0, 0, 0 ],
  [ 0, 0, 0, 0, 0, 0, 0, 0, 0 ],
  [ 0, 0, 0, 0, 0, 0, 0, 0, 0 ],
  [ 0, 0, 0, 0, 0, 0, 0, 0, 0 ],
  [ 0, 0, 0, 0, 0, 0, 0, 0, 0 ],
  [ 0, 0, 0, 0, 0, 0, 0, 0, 0 ],
  [ 0, 0, 0, 0, 0, 0, 0, 0, 0 ],
  [ 0, 0, 0, 0, 0, 0, 0, 0, 0 ],
  [ 0, 0, 0, 0, 1, 0, 0, 0, 0 ],
  [ 1, 0, 0, 0, 2, 0, 0, 0, 1 ],

  ...three more blocks of 11 arrays each, one per screen...


  ]
}
```

It's just an object with two attributes. The `totalScreens` attribute tells the game code how many total screens there are defined for the level. The `data` attribute is the actual data that corresponds to the pattern of stone pathways on the screen.

Each screen is simply a full set of 11*9=99 codes, one per tile, which in total fills the gameplay screen. Each screen consists of 11 arrays in the data, since there's room for 11 rows of tiles in the gameplay area, and each array has 9 values in it since there's room for 9 columns of tiles. The values are as follows:

- **0** – No track (identifier trackBlank, file: track_blank.png)

- **1** – Stone track (identifier: track, file: track.png)

- **2** – End tile (identifier: trackEnd, file: track_end.png)

The easiest way to make the connection between this and what you see on the screen is to load the game, but don't start it. Then, load the `level_01.json` file and look at the *last* set of arrays. Compare those arrays to what you see on the screen and see how the pattern of the data matches up to what you get on the screen. The data maps directly to the virtual grid of tiles in the gameplay area. If you're still having trouble making the connection, go into those arrays, and anywhere you see a 0, make it a space. You should quickly see that the stone pathway you see on the screen mirrors the 1s still present.

The track images are going to scroll downward, which is why we start with the *last* set of arrays: that's really the *first* screen of tiles drawn. It's where things start at the beginning of every level. As you play the game, the track tiles scroll down, and the next row of tiles above scrolls into view and the one on the bottom scrolls out of view. This happens over and over again until the set of arrays at the top of the level data is what's filling the screen, which means the end of the level has been reached.

Back to the Code!

Now, it's time to build us a stone track! The aptly named createTrack() function is responsible for that:

```
function createTrack() {

  if (images.track && images.track.length > 0) {
    images.track.forEach(
      item => { item.destroy(); item = null; }
    );
  }
  images.track = null;
  images.track = [ ];
```

This first bit accounts for the fact that this function can be called at the start of the game from create(), or when the game is restarted when the user clicks the Start Game button after dying. In the latter case, since we're effectively resetting everything, including this track, we need to destroy any track images that exist. The Phaser Image object provides a destroy() method, which gives Phaser a chance to clean it up and get rid of it. Also, I want to ensure there are no references left anywhere that could cause a memory leak, so I set each item reference to null after that and then set the entire array to null before creating a new, empty array. All of that very much should be overkill and more than is necessary, but when I kill something, I like to make *real* sure it's dead! I mean, I've seen more than enough sci-fi movies in my day to know you don't play games with stuff like this!

Next, it's time to start creating Image objects, one per tile per screen in the level data:

```
let y = -(sizes.tile.height * sizes.grid.rows *
  (gameState.currentLevel.totalScreens - 1));
for (let row = 0;
  row < sizes.grid.rows * gameState.currentLevel.totalScreens;
  row++
) {
  for (
    let column = 0; column < sizes.grid.columns; column++
  ) {
```

At this point in writing the code, I had a choice to make: do I create images for *every single element* in *every single array* in the level data, or do I instead create them on the fly, one row at a time? Essentially, do I create a big, long array of images and make the gameplay area basically a window into it, with tiles scrolling in and out of view all the time but never being created or destroyed during that time? Or, do I do a similar thing as with the fire where only enough images to fill the gameplay area are created, plus one extra row up top to scroll into view, then destroy the row that just scrolled out of view and create a new overscan row?

In thinking this through, two thoughts occurred to me. First, creating them all up-front would likely be a bit simpler to code. I like simpler! Second, I was concerned that continually creating and destroying objects during gameplay might lead to jankiness. JavaScript would be doing garbage collection, and that might impact the smoothness of the game. As an extremely broad, general statement, in game development, it's usually better to avoid object destruction and creation during gameplay as much as possible, especially in a garbage-collected language.

Since memory isn't a real concern with the relatively small size of these graphics, wihch would be the other concern, I opted for creating them all at once. With that in mind, the very first step is to determine the starting Y location of the first row. Since I actually want the last 11 arrays to be visible initially, that means that the first row has to start with a negative Y value so that it's way off-screen above the gameplay area, in effect. The calculation then is just the height of a tile, times the number of rows, times the total number of screens minus one, and negating that result. That gives the proper location for the top row, and each row after that is just that value plus the height of a tile.

After that calculation is done, two loops are started so that we can create the tiles on a per-column/per-row basis.

Next, we create the appropriate kind of tile based on the level data:

```
const tileType = gameState.currentLevel.data[row][column];
let tile = null;
if (tileType === 0) {
  tile = scene.physics.add.image(
    column * sizes.tile.width, y, "trackBlank"
  );
  scene.physics.add.collider(
    images.astronaut, tile, () => gameOver(false)
  );
} else if (tileType === 2) {
  tile = scene.add.image(
    column * sizes.tile.width, y, "trackEnd"
  );
} else {
  tile = scene.add.image(
    column * sizes.tile.width, y, "track"
  );
}
```

Note that for areas in the level data with a zero, you would think there would simply be nothing there, but it winds up being a little easier to code if you do have a tile, but it just so happens to be a blank one. Much more importantly, we need that because without it, we wouldn't have a way to register death! At first, you'd imagine, quite logically, that if the player collides with a fire image, then that's a death. The problem, however, is that collision detection isn't aware of depth. In other words, even though there's a stone tile between the astronaut and the fire, a collision would still be registered because, based on X/Y coordinates, the astronaut collides with the fire.

So, instead, the collision detection is applied on the blank tiles! If the astronaut collides with a blank tile, and if they aren't jumping, then that's the same, effectively, as hitting fire, and we know they're dead.

The collision detection is added to the blank tile using adding a `Collider` to it, which is the other half of the equation (in addition to configuring the physics engine and using the `physics.add.image()` method instead of the `add.image()` method). This informs the physics engine that we want to detect collisions with this object, but only if it collides with the astronaut sprite. When that happens, the `gameOver()` function is called, passing it `false` (the meaning of which you'll learn in the next chapter).

For tho rogular stone track tiles, as well as the special end tile, since no animation is required, they're just basic `Image` objects created with the Scene's `add.image()` method rather than sprites. For all of them, the X/Y location is calculated based on the look values and the width of a tile.

I haven't mentioned how the game detects that the player has reached the end tile, but clearly, it's not collision detection since there's no `Collider` attached to it. Don't worry, that's something else you'll see in the next chapter.

Finally, for each tile, we have a little more work to do:

```
    tile.setOrigin(0, 0);
    tile.setDepth(1);
    images.track.push(tile);
    if (tileType === 2) { images.endTile = tile; }
  }
  y += sizes.tile.height;
}
```

As with the fire tiles, since we're building these images and in a virtual sense inserting them into a grid, the calculations are more straightforward with the local origin of the images being the upper-left corner. And, you already know that the depth has to be set so that these images are above the fire but below the astronaut. Each image gets pushed into an array, and note that this is a plain old array, it's not multidimensional. This makes moving the tiles easier since there's just one loop needed to iterate through all of them (which, again, is something for the next chapter). Since there's only ever a single end tile, and since the logic that determines when the player reaches it depends on having a reference to it, as you'll see, that reference is captured when `tileType` is 2.

Finally, the `y` value is bumped up at the end of each row so that the next row is positioned correctly, and that's how you build a stone track over fire for a thieving astronaut to run away from angry aliens on!

Dealing with a Build Issue

Before we can go any further, we have to address an issue that is present at this point. If you try to build the project now (gatsby build), you'll encounter the same sort of error I discussed in the previous project: the `window` object is not available. Unfortunately, the code that uses the `window` object is Phaser itself, and its core to what Phaser does. So, whereas the code that used window in the previous project was application code, so it wasn't a problem to refactor the code to avoid the issue, going and hacking Phaser code isn't really an ideal solution (and, as it happens, not even possible or Phaser won't work).

Fortunately, there's another solution. It involves adding a `gatsby-node.js` file with the following content:

```
exports.onCreateWebpackConfig = (
  { stage, loaders, actions }
) => {
  if (stage === "build-html") {
    actions.setWebpackConfig({
      module : {
        rules : [
          { test : /phaser/, use : loaders.null() }
        ]
      }
    })
  }
};
```

This code executes when Gatsby builds the Webpack configuration it will use to build the project. This allows us to alter that configuration. The goal here is to make it so that Webpack ignores Phaser entirely when doing the Server-Side Rendering since the `window` object isn't available at that point. So, when Webpack reaches its `build-html` phase, which is when SSR happens, we define a rule that says: "hey, Webpack, when you encounter a resource named `phaser`, don't load it." The `loader.null` is a noop resource loader available in a Webpack configuration, which does exactly what we want: nothing! With this in place, you should be able to do a gatsby build successfully.

If you do that now using the Chapter 7 code in the code bundle, you'll discover that the build works, but when you access the site, the screen appears, and there's some spinning fire, but that's it. The Start Game button does nothing; the cursor keys do nothing; the game doesn't play. That's expected, because if you then examine the code, you'll find that there are three functions that are empty: update(), gameOver(), and startGame(). Those are the remaining three functions that we need to build to make the game work, with update() being the most critical. That's what the next chapter will cover... you know, nothing *too* important, right?

Summary

In this chapter, we began the process of building a little game using Gatsby and JAMstack techniques. You got a look at the Phaser library and how it can be used in a Gatsby/React app. You saw how you can source JSON files in Gatsby, or just import them directly, and you got a look at avoiding a frequent problem with Gatsby apps in terms of objects not available during SSR.

In the next chapter, we'll complete the game code to make it a fully functional and playable game, and we'll also take the game and make it a PWA (whatever that is!) to show that Gatsby and JAMstack are totally cool with being involved in that new hotness!

CHAPTER 8

Completing the Game

In the last chapter, we built... *part* of a game! In truth, it wouldn't even qualify as a game as it stands now because it's obviously not playable. So, before we do anything else, we need to remedy that by adding the core game logic and control handling.

After that, I'm going to take you in a totally different direction: we're going to turn JAMJumper into a PWA, or Progressive Web App. PWAs are a popular topic these days, and I think it's valuable to learn that JAMstack, and the things we've used to build this JAMstack app including React and Gatsby, in no way preclude you from creating a PWA.

So, let's get into making JAMJumper an actual game by completing the code!

The Heart of the Matter: gameCore.js, Part 2

There are just three functions remaining that we have to look at: startLevel(), update(), and gameOver(). These, and update() most especially, are the real core of the game and are what make it an actual playable game. I think you might be surprised by how little code there actually is in them.

The startLevel() Function

Although the update() function – which we'll be discussing in the next section – comes before the startLevel() function in source code order (as does the gameOver() function), I think it makes sense to look at startLevel(), which is the function called to begin the game, as well as a new level, first.

It begins thusly:

```
export const startLevel = function() {

  gameState.gameRunning = true;
  gameState.score = 0;
  gameState.trackMoveCount = 0;
```

F. Zammetti, *Practical JAMstack*, https://doi.org/10.1007/978-1-4842-6177-4_8

This function is ultimately all about resetting everything as it needs to be for the game to begin running. So, the first thing to do is to deal with the values in the gameState object. Obviously, the game is going to be running now, so gameRunning is set to true. The score starts at zero, and the trackMoveCount is reset to zero. The usage of that variable will be seen in the update() method.

Note   The startLevel() function is the only one that is needed outside this module (it's the click handler for the Start Game button), so it must be exported.

After that, we have to deal with the jumpData object to make sure the player isn't jumping:

```
jumpData.isJumping = false;
```

Oops, we almost forgot to actually reflect the zero score on the screen!

```
scoreSpan.innerHTML = gameState.score;
```

Okay, whew, crisis averted! Next, the attributes of the astronaut must be reset:

```
images.astronaut.alpha = 1;
images.astronaut.scale = 1;
images.astronaut.anims.resume();
```

The astronaut fades out when it reaches a teleporter, but to start, he is, of course, at full opacity, which means its alpha attribute is one because the range of that attribute is zero for transparent to one for fully opaque. Similarly, the scale is used to do the jump animation (which you'll see in update() shortly), so it too needs to be reset to one, which means display at regular 100% scale. Finally, the run animation is started up again, since it is paused at the start of the game, and it paused if the astronaut dies.

Next, there's a little bit of difference between what happens when this function is called as a result of the user clicking the Start Game button vs. when it's called because they reached the end of a level and need to go to the next one. The restartGame argument dictates this:

```
if (restartGame) {
  restartGame = false;
  gameState.currentLevelIndex = 0;
  gameState.currentLevel = level_01;
}
```

When the game is being started (or restarted, both with clicks of the button), then we need to start them off on the first level again. And, once that's done (or not done, in the case of restartGame being false), then it's time to create the track:

```
createTrack();
```

You got a look at that function in the previous chapter, so we can move on to resetting the spatial rupture particle effect:

```
emitters.rupture.pause();
emitters.rupture.setVisible(false);
```

The emitter is paused to ensure it doesn't hurt performance by running in the background, and it's hidden again, to be shown once more if the player dies again.

Then, the tweens for all the fire images need to be restarted because, as you'll see later, they get stopped when the astronaut dies:

```
fireTweens.forEach(t => t.restart() );
```

Note that just like with the astronaut's run animation, restarting a tween that is already running does no harm, so there's no worry about this executing when the game first starts.

Then, the running sound needs to be started:

```
sounds.running.play({ loop : true, rate : 0.75 });
```

The sound just continually loops until stopped, and the rate is slowed down by a quarter to, roughly at least, coincide with the run animation.

Finally, the physics engine is turned on so that collision detection works:

```
scene.physics.resume();
```

From that point on, the game is running. Now, let's look at the core code that actually gets run to make it all work.

The update() Method

The update() method is the third of the methods that Phaser requires us to write. Simply put, it gets called once per frame, which means 60 times a second given the configuration from the previous chapter. Think of it like a heartbeat. Phaser calls it, over and over again, and it is responsible for, essentially, everything that happens! It has to move images as needed. It has to handle keyboard input. It has to handle moving the track. It has to handle when the level ends. It has to handle when the player dies or reaches the end. It has to handle jumping.

It sounds like a lot, doesn't it?

But, the amount of code is actually quite small, and it begins with this:

```
function update() {

  if (!gameState.gameRunning) { return; }
```

The important point to remember is that, more or less, from the moment the Phaser Game and Scene objects are created, the clock is ticking, quite literally! The update() method configured for the Scene object will begin to be called, and it won't stop until the program exists. So, if you have a scenario where your game is paused, or otherwise stopped, you need to handle that. For JAMJumper, that's done with the gameRunning attribute of the gameState object. When it's false, execution of update() ends right at this statement. Nothing will move, no keyboard handling will occur, nothing.

Of course, when gameState.gameRunning is true, then execution moves on:

```
images.track.forEach(
  t => t.y += sizes.trackPixelsPerIteration
);
```

The first task to be accomplished is to move the tile images. For every single element in the images.track array – which you'll recall was populated by the code in the createTrack() function – its Y location is shifted downward by the sizes.trackPixelsPerIteration.

The next block of code also deals with the track:

```
gameState.trackMoveCount++;
if (gameState.trackMoveCount === 32) {
  gameState.trackMoveCount = 0;
```

```
    gameState.score += 10;
    scoreSpan.innerHTML = gameState.score;
}
```

The goal here is that every 32 frames, as determined by the value of gameState.trackMoveCount, each tile will have moved down one full row. Or, looked at from another perspective: the player will have safely traversed one entire row of tiles. When that happens, we bump their score by ten points and update the display and, of course, reset gameState.trackMoveCount to start counting toward another ten points.

The next thing we have to consider is whether the level has now been completed. The way this is determined is to see if the special end tile has reached the bottom of the screen. Well, to be more precise, one row up from the bottom. Or, to put it another way: is the very first screen defined in the level data array now fully visible?

```
if (images.endTile.y ===
    sizes.tile.height * (sizes.grid.rows - 2)
) {
    sounds.beamup.play();
    gameState.score += 100;
    scoreSpan.innerHTML = gameState.score;
    gameOver(true);
    return;
}
```

Remember in the last chapter where a reference to the end tile was stored in images.endTile? Well, this is the reason why! Now, we can check whether its Y location corresponds to the second-to-last row on the bottom of the screen by calculating that value based on a tile's height and how many rows there are on a screen. If that condition is met, then a few things occur. First, the beam-up sound is played. Then, the score is updated. Finally, the gameOver() function is called, and we'll look at that in the next section, but suffice for now to say that it either starts the next level or ends the game. Note that in this situation, we do not want anything else in update() to occur, so we return immediately.

Next, jumping has to be handled. You may remember in the last chapter I mentioned that jumping is not done with a tween because a little more control is needed. Now it's time to see that control:

```
if (jumpData.isJumping) {
  images.astronaut.scale += jumpData.phase;
  images.astronaut.x += jumpData.direction;
  jumpData.jumpTicks++;
  if (jumpData.jumpTicks === jumpData.tickCount) {
    switch (jumpData.phase) {
      case jumpData.PHASE_UP:
        jumpData.jumpTicks = 0;
        jumpData.phase = jumpData.PHASE_DOWN;
      break;
      case jumpData.PHASE_DOWN:
        sounds.running.play({ loop : true, rate : 0.75 });
        jumpData.isJumping = false;
      break;
    }
  }
}
```

If and only if jumpData.isJumping is true, then it's time to do some work. Jumping is a two-step process: the up phase, when the astronaut is going up, and the down phase, when they're coming back down. The actual jump is done by increasing the scale of the astronaut sprite during the up phase and decreasing it during the down phase. In Figure 8-1, you can see how the effect looks during a straight-up jump.

Figure 8-1. *A straight-up jump, scale larger than one*

If you look back on the values of jumpData.phase, you'll notice that the values of PHASE_UP and PHASE_DOWN attributes are positive and negative, respectively. That's to make this code easy: it's just a matter of added jumpData.phase to images.astronaut. scale during each frame to make it bigger or smaller as he's jumping up or coming back down.

But, jumping comes in three flavors, so to speak: a straight-up jump, a jump to the left, and a jump to the right. So, in the same way the scale is modified, `images.astronaut.x` is similarly modified with the value of `jumpData.direction`, which is one of three values: `DIR_UP` (0), `DIR_LEFT` (-2), or `DIR_RIGHT` (2). So, for a straight-up jump, since the value is zero, the X location won't change.

Note   The values for PHASE_UP, PHASE_DOWN, DIR_LEFT, and DIR_RIGHT were determined more or less through trial and error. I played the game a bit and figured out what values gave me the amount of jump distance covered I wanted and the amount of change each frame to make it look right. You'll notice as you play that a jump straight up seems to take slightly longer and seems to cover a little more distance. That's what my play-testing determined was an optimal value to make the game not ridiculously easy but also not completely impossible. As a general rule, I don't like using "magic values" like this, which is why most other values throughout the code are calculated. Still, in this case, I didn't see a good, consistent way to calculate the values and have them work out like I wanted, so a few magic numbers snuck in. As John Cleese so elegantly put it in the movie *A Fish Called Wanda*: "I apologize unreservedly."

Now, the actual jump depends on a specific number of elapsed frames, and this is determined by incrementing `jumpData.jumpTicks` each time through `update()`. When `jumpData.jumpTicks` equals `jumpData.tickCount`, then it's time to either switch from the up phase of the jump to the down phase, or else end the jump. `jumpData.tickCount` will be set in the next block of code, but it's simply the number of frames that must elapse for a phase change, or jump end, to occur. This, now is why the interval method was used rather than the `requestAnimationFeame` method in the last chapter: knowing exactly how many ticks of the `update()` method occur and how long each takes is key to this approach working, something that wouldn't be the case with `requestAnimationFrame` (or at least, not without a bunch more code to account for the variability that approach introduces).

Once that condition is met, if the jump is in the up phase, then it's switch to the down phase. If it's in the down phase already, then the jump ends. The running sound needs to be restarted since it will be paused during a jump, and `jumpData.isJumping` naturally has to be set to `false` again.

The `else` branch of the if statement that checks `jumpData.isJumping` is next, and it's where keyboard handling occurs:

```
} else {
  if (keys.up.isDown) {
    sounds.running.stop();
    sounds.jump.play();
    jumpData.isJumping = true;
    jumpData.jumpTicks = 0;
    jumpData.tickCount = 24;
    jumpData.phase = jumpData.PHASE_UP;
    jumpData.direction = jumpData.DIR_UP;
  } else if (keys.left.isDown) {
    sounds.running.stop();
    sounds.jump.play();
    jumpData.isJumping = true;
    jumpData.jumpTicks = 0;
    jumpData.tickCount = 16;
    jumpData.phase = jumpData.PHASE_UP;
    jumpData.direction = jumpData.DIR_LEFT;
  } else if (keys.right.isDown) {
    sounds.running.stop();
    sounds.jump.play();
    jumpData.isJumping = true;
    jumpData.jumpTicks = 0;
    jumpData.tickCount = 16;
    jumpData.phase = jumpData.PHASE_UP;
    jumpData.direction = jumpData.DIR_RIGHT;
  }
}
```

Remember that keyboard handling is simply a matter of flags in the keys object being set by Phaser, so all we need to do here is check those flags and act accordingly. So, if the up key is pressed, then the code does a couple of things. First, the running sound is stopped. Next, the jump sound is played. After that, all the attributes in the jumpData object are set appropriately: isJumping naturally gets set to true; jumpTicks starts at zero; tickCount is set to 24 (that's how many frames a straight-up jump will take); and the phase and direction are set to start the jump off in the up phase and with the appropriate direction.

For a jump left or right, it's precisely the same, except that the value of `tickCount` and `direction` are, of course, different. The `tickCount` value of 16 here means that a jump left or right is eight frames faster than a straight-up jump, which again was just some trial and error to see what worked best.

And, believe it or not, that's all the core logic that goes into making this game work! Granted, it was never a complex game to begin with, so you wouldn't expect any profound logic here, but it still seems like not very much, doesn't it?

There's just one bit of code left to examine, and that's the `gameOver()` function.

The gameOver() Function

Okay, time for the final bit of code in JAMJumper! The `gameOver()` function is next:

```
function gameOver(inWon) {

  if (inWon) {
    scene.tweens.add({
      targets : images.astronaut, duration : 2000,
      alpha: { from: 1, to: 0 },
      onComplete : function() {
        gameState.currentLevelIndex++;
        if (gameState.currentLevelIndex <
          global.levelData.length
        ) {
          gameState.currentLevel = global.levelData[1].node;
          startLevel();
        } else {
          gameState.score += 500;
          scoreSpan.innerHTML = gameState.score;
          restartGame = true;
        }
      }
    });
```

First, we branch on the value of the incoming `inWon` argument. When `true`, it means that the player has reached a teleporter pad. In that case, we need to fade them out. This is done with a tween. The tween itself should look familiar by now, save for one

thing: the onComplete attribute of the configuration object passed to the tweens.add()
method. This is a function that will be called when the tween completes, meaning
when the astronaut's alpha value reaches zero. Here, it's an anonymous function,
and it's responsible for either starting the next level or doing nothing because the
player completed the final level. In the case of starting a new level, the gameState.
currentLevel attribute is pointed to the next level's data, which is found in the global.
levelData array, and then the startLevel() function is called. If there are no more
levels, then we give the player a score bonus and set restartGame to true so that the next
click of the Start Game button will restart the game from the first level.

In the else branch, we cover the case of the game ending with the astronaut's death
(inWon is false):

```
} else {
  if (jumpData.isJumping) {
    return;
  }
  restartGame = true;
  sounds.death.play();
  images.astronaut.alpha = 0;
  emitters.rupture.setPosition(
    images.astronaut.x, images.astronaut.y
  );
  emitters.rupture.setVisible(true);
  emitters.rupture.resume();
}
```

The first thing to consider is whether the player is in the process of jumping. The
issue here is that collision detection will trigger regardless of whether the player is
jumping or not when they come into contact with a blank track tile (remember, it can't
be a collision with the fire tiles themselves if we'd have constant collisions). But, imagine
what happens when a collision occurs and the player is jumping. They need to be safe
in that case, so execution returns immediately. If they're *not* jumping, that's when the
rest of the logic kicks in. That logic plays the death sound, while hiding the astronaut by
setting its alpha to zero, and then starts the spatial rupture emitter and ensures it's visible
(shown in Figure 8-2). The restartGame variable is set to true as well so that clicking
Start Game will start the game fresh.

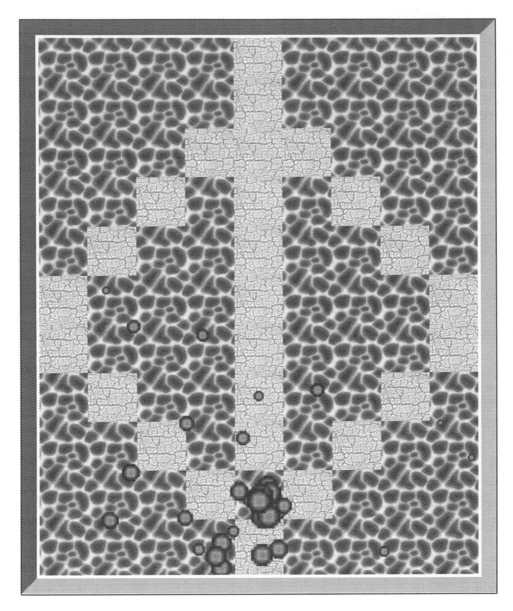

Figure 8-2. *Uh-oh, you destroyed the universe. Well, I suppose someone had to*

After that, there are some common chores that need to be done regardless of the actual outcome of the game:

```
sounds.running.stop();
gameState.gameRunning = false;
scene.physics.pause();
```

```
fireTweens.forEach(t => t.stop());
images.astronaut.anims.pause();
```

The running sound is stopped, physics is paused, the fire tweens are paused and so is the astronaut's run animation. The `gameState.gameRunning` attribute is set to `false` so that the ongoing calls to `update()` will do nothing, and that's a wrap on JAMJumper, at least as far as the code goes!

The Progressive Agenda: PWA-ifying JAMJumper

At the start of this chapter, I mentioned that creating a JAMstack app, whether you use Gatsby for it or not, does not preclude you from creating PWAs, and I said that I would prove that by turning JAMJumper into a PWA.

Well, we've finally reached that bridge, so let's cross it together now!

Of course, there's a pretty important piece of the puzzle missing right now, a piece that is definitely needed before we can continue, so let's deal with that piece right now, shall we?

Wait, Wait, Hold Up… What's a PWA?!

A PWA, or Progressive Web App, is a webapp built with the usual web technologies – HTML, CSS, and JavaScript – but which, to a large extent, looks, feels, and functions like a typical native application. They typically run as full-screen apps, or in windowed environments, they run in windows that don't look like browsers but instead look like regular native applications.

Things like push notifications, background synchronization, the ability to self-update, and being able to install and run when there is no network connectivity are some of the things PWAs bring to the table. In fact, of all the things that make something a PWA, I would suggest that being installable (which means, for example, that there is an icon for the app on the home screen of your phone) and functioning offline is probably the number one capability people think of when they think of PWAs.

PWAs are also sites that are fast and reliable and are responsive, meaning they adjust to the screen and device they are run on. They also, frequently, use newer web APIs that provide access to native device capabilities like local file system access, camera access, and clipboard support.

Almost any website or webapp can be turned into a PWA, which is one of the most attractive parts of it. But, to really make full use of the paradigm, you typically need to develop with a PWA mindset from the start. With JAMJumper, that wasn't really the case, at least not in any specific way, so this is an excellent example of how almost any website can be turned into a PWA after the fact without too much effort, as you'll see.

Note   It isn't necessary for a site to necessarily tick all the PWA marks to be considered a PWA. As I mentioned, offline support is probably the most prominent hallmark of PWAs, and arguably an app that only ticks the offline support can be considered a PWA, so long as it's done the "right" way, which the next section will demonstrate. I only mention this because JAMJumper isn't responsive to screen size, so if every last facet of PWAs had to be implemented, then JAMJumper couldn't be called a PWA for this reason alone. You can almost think of PWAs like you do JAMstack itself: it's not so much a concrete technology stack that you build an app on, it's more of a philosophy and a set of principles (though PWAs are indeed a bit more concrete than JAMstack is, as you'll see shortly).

The Key Bits

There are three keys to PWAs, things you must provide for a site or app to be a PWA: the Web App manifest, the Service Worker, and HTTPS.

The manifest file is a plain old JSON file that controls the way the application is displayed (for instance, whether it's full-screen or whether the URL bar is visible) and how it can be launched. It's a central location for all the metadata about the application (such as starting URL, short name, full name, and icons) that a browser will use to install, launch, and otherwise deal with a PWA.

An elementary manifest file, which usually is named manifest.json (or sometimes manifest.webmanifest) and is in the root of your application, might look like this:

```
{
  "name" : "My Awesome App",
  "short_name" : "MyAwesomeApp",
  "lang" : "en-US",
  "start_url" : "/index.html",
```

```
"display" : "standalone",
"background_color" : "black",
"theme_color" : "red",
"icons": [
  { "src" : "img/awesome-icon-128.png",
    "sizes" : "128x128", "type" : "image/png"
  },
  { "src" : "img/awesome-icon-256.png",
    "sizes" : "256x256", "type" : "image/png"
  }
]
}
```

While I would bet most of that is pretty self-explanatory, and while there are several other options available, I'm not going to go into details here for one straightforward reason: Gatsby is going to do most of this work for us! We won't need to write this file by hand, nor will we need to ensure it's linked to from the index.html page (which is something that needs to occur for the browser loading the page to know this is a PWA). I just want to give you a basic idea of what's involved so that should you ever need to tweak the file yourself, you'll have a rough idea of what to expect.

The second key component that (nearly) every PWA will have is a Service Worker. A Service Worker is a JavaScript file that runs in the background, even when the browser that initially launches it is closed. This worker would be responsible for showing notifications on the desktop when a message is received, for example.

The general idea of a Service Worker can be seen in Figure 8-3.

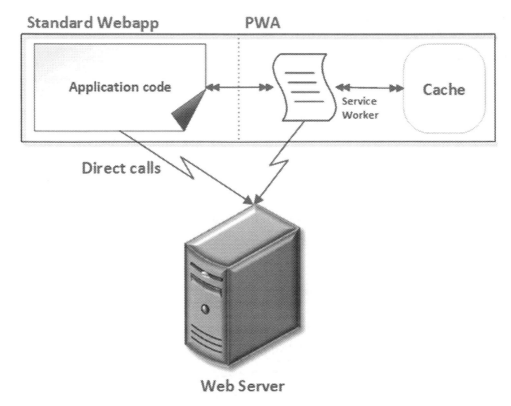

Figure 8-3. *The underlying architecture of a standard webapp vs. a PWA*

In a standard webapp, the app's code makes direct calls to a web server. In a PWA, though, those calls go through the Service Worker. The Service Worker will make a call to the web server if needed, or will serve the requested resource out of a cache on the client instead.

But, perhaps the most crucial chore a Service Worker performs, for virtually every PWA, is to act as a proxy for web requests.

Imagine you load an HTML file, and that file contains an <img> tag. The browser will make a request to the server for that image (assuming it isn't already in the browser's cache). In the case of a PWA, the Service Worker would intercept that request, which allows it to return the image itself. What will normally happen is that when a Service Worker is installed the first time the PWA is accessed, it will cache the resources the app needs (at a minimum it will cache the most critical ones, things like images, other HTML files, whatever the app may need). Then, when the app later requests one of those, the Service Worker can serve it from its cache. You can basically think of it as a browser cache on steroids and which your code is in control of.

This is what gives PWAs their offline capability: if all necessary resources have been cached, after the first load of the PWA, then that app can then function without a network connection, obviously assuming the app doesn't make real-time requests to a server to perform its functions, but ensuring it can work when such requests fail is up to your Service Worker code, since it will intercept all those requests too.

If you think that a Service Worker can be fairly complex in a large app, you would be right. But, here again, Gatsby is going to do a lot of the work for us: it will actually generate a Service Worker automatically, just like the manifest file.

Don't worry, before long, you'll see what relatively little we have to do to get Gatsby to do all this work for us, but the pertinent point is that the manifest and the Service Worker are two necessary keys you as the developer must provide for a PWA.

The third key is HTTPS. PWAs *must* be served securely. You'll find that a browser that supports PWAs will not provide the basic PWA functionality, like being able to install them if they aren't served securely. This can actually make testing PWAs on your developer workstation tricky because you have to use a valid certificate (or else jump through *a lot* of hoops) on a domain you own. While there are ways around this, later on, I'm going to show you perhaps the most straightforward solution: host the site on Netlify, since Netlify, by default, serves all content under HTTPS.

Some History and Perspective

For a little bit of history, the term PWA was coined by Google in 2015, specifically Chrome developer Alex Russell and designer Frances Berriman. But, the original idea can be traced back to a guy you may have heard of: Steve Jobs. In 2007, as part of the initial Apple iPhone launch, Steve described how apps for the platform would be written as webapps rather than as native apps. However, as the reality of the idea was explored, it was recognized for various reasons that the time wasn't right for that idea to take over the world, and a native SDK for iOS was released not long after. As for iOS apps on iPhone (and eventually the iPad), the rest is, as they say, history.

But, the boys from Google saw what Steve was thinking and realized it was actually the right answer, just perhaps a little before its time. So, a few years later, PWAs were birthed, but now using modern web technologies and techniques, essentially supercharging that original idea and finally making it viable. Google has been pushing PWAs hard ever since, and Microsoft, among others, has taken up the mantle strongly too, even allowing PWAs to be offered in the Microsoft Store right alongside native apps and "modern" Windows apps, and unless you know what to look for, you can barely tell the difference between them.

> **Note**   Although it's not often stated in the literature, I would like to officially put
> out there that I think there's a step on the road to modern PWAs that doesn't get
> much focus or recognition and that is Palm's webOS. Release in 2009, the Palm
> Pre smartphone was built on webOS, and perhaps the defining characteristic of
> that operating system and device (aside from the before-its-time-and-probably-
> still-not-matched-today gesture-based navigation system) is the fact that most
> of the apps on it were written using web technologies. They were HTML, CSS,
> and JavaScript through and through. Arguably, webOS represents the first true
> (and successful, to some approximations of the word) implementation of the PWA
> paradigm. I don't recall ever seeing this stated anywhere, but I for one think it
> should be, and the creators of webOS should get at least part of the credit for
> making PWAs a reality too, in my humble opinion.

Ironically, one company that *hasn't* hopped quite as enthusiastically on the PWA train is Apple itself. Especially when it comes to mobile devices, Apple has a vested interest now in not whole-heartedly supporting PWAs: the profit they make from their app store. The iOS ecosystem is a walled garden, meaning Apple controls who can sell apps for it and what apps can run on it, taking a percentage of any profits from those apps. PWAs, on the other hand, can be installed right from the public Web without any control by Apple. As such, there is no chance for Apple to collect profits on PWAs. As a result, Apple has been lukewarm at best in its support for PWAs. At the time of this writing, creating a PWA that runs on iOS is... problematic. At best, you won't be able to use the full breadth of capabilities PWAs typically offer, and at worst, you won't be able to make it work at all. The hope is that Apple will support PWAs more robustly in the future, and there certainly is no shortage of developers and users pushing them to do just that.

We'll see how it goes.

But, for now, if you know that iOS is a definite target for an app you intend to write as a PWA, you may want to do some research and ensure what you're planning to do will work. If it won't, you may have little choice but to create a native app for iOS and a PWA for everywhere else, or forego the PWA approach entirely in favor of a typical website. I'm just throwing all this out there so that you go into this PWA thing with your eyes open.

Okay, Sounds Good, How Do We Make JAMJumper a PWA?

Okay, basic explanation and history lesson out of the way, how do we go about turning JAMJumper into a PWA? Since we've built it with Gatsby, it actually just takes installing two new plugins:

```
npm install --save gatsby-plugin-manifest
npm install --save gatsby-plugin-offline
```

With those added, there's just some configuration in `gatsby-config.js` to be added to the plugins array:

```
{
  resolve: "gatsby-plugin-manifest",
  options: {
    name: "JAMJumper",
    short_name: "JAMJumper",
    start_url: "/",
    background_color: "#6b37bf",
    theme_color: "#6b37bf",
    display: "standalone",
    icon: "src/images/icon.png",
    crossOrigin: "use-credentials",
  }
},
{
  resolve: "gatsby-plugin-offline",
  options: {
    debug : true
  }
}
```

> **Tip**   An essential thing to remember is that the `gatsby-plugin-offline` plug must come *after* the `gatsby-plugin-manifest` plugin.

The gatsby-plugin-manifest plugin is responsible for generating the manifest file for the app. As such, the configuration options available in a manifest file are surfaced into the configuration for the plugin. There are some additional options available, `crossOrigin` being one of them. Setting this to `use-credentials` turns CORS (cross-origin request sharing) on and enables sharing resources via cookies. This setting ensures we won't run into any problems when multimedia assets are fetched during the initial caching if they come from another domain and will be handled the same as our own application assets.

The gatsby-plugin-offline is the plugin that generates the Service Worker for us. There aren't too many options available for this plugin, but an important one is `debug`, which, when set to `true`, causes debug information to be displayed in the browser console. This plugin uses something called Workbox Build (`https://developers.google.com/web/tools/workbox/modules/workbox-build`) to generate the Service Worker code, so most of the options available for this plugin are actually options on Workbox Build. But, I would suggest you not think about altering these options unless you have particular needs. You should find that the default code generated will typically serve you well enough.

With both these plugins and their configuration done, building the app will produce a PWA, just like that! No changes required to the code, nothing extra we need to do. It just works!

Of course, if you run it on your machine using `gatsby develop`, you'll find that the PWA functionalities don't work, and that's because, by default, Gatsby doesn't serve the app via HTTPS. And, it turns out it's kind of tricky to get that set up so that the PWA functionality works. So, instead, we'll use Netlify to test it out and just wait until you see how easy it is!

Hosting on Netlify to See PWA in Action

Okay, you ready for this? Do you remember the screen shown in Figure 8-4?

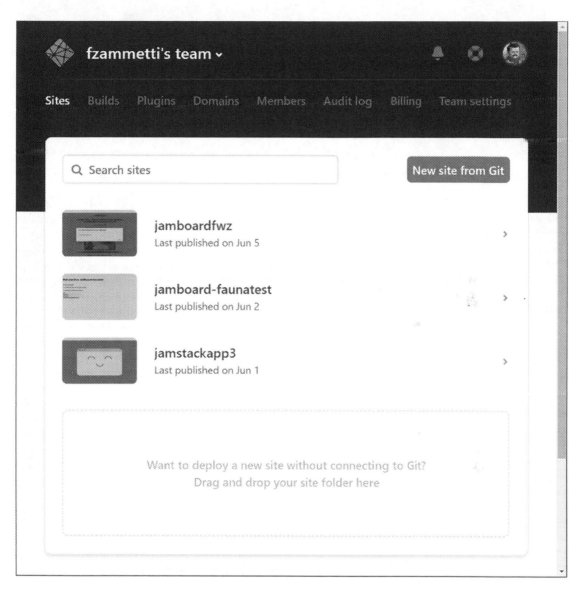

Figure 8-4. *See that big box at the bottom? It's cooler than it looks!*

Previously, you learned how to deploy an app on Netlify when it was sourced from GitHub, and indeed, there's a lot to love about that. But, what about when you're working on a project and just need something swift and easy, even easier than setting up a repo on GitHub? Well, that's where that big dotted box at the bottom comes into play!

Here's what you do: first, execute gatsby build in the JAMJumper directory to do a production build. Next, go zip up the public directory, using whatever tool you usually use to create Zip files. Finally, drag the archive onto that big, dotted box.

Give it a few seconds – like, literally, just a second or two! – and before long, you'll find that you have a new app available and accessible. You just deployed JAMJumper to Netlify!

You can, at this point, click the link that Netlify provides for the app, which you'll notice is served via an HTTPS URL, and at that point, all the PWA goodness you expect should work. If you're using Chrome, you can click the three-dot menu and select Install JAMJumper (in Edge, it's Apps ➤ Install this site as an app, and it looks like Firefox and Opera don't support this function on desktop yet, but they should on mobile, but since the game uses keyboard control, it's not really mobile-friendly… but maybe that's something for you to work on as an exercise?). Once you install it, go to the developer tools in your browser, and usually on the Network tab, there is an option to go offline. If you can't find it, just disable Wi-Fi or pull out your Ethernet cable! Then, click the icon that was added to your desktop for JAMJumper, and you should find that it works exactly as expected, as if it were a native app.

Suggested Exercise

I really have only two suggestions for this chapter, one relatively simple (and honestly not very educational, but I think fun!) and another that might be challenging but quite educational for you.

- **The simple one** – Create a few more levels! This will give you some experience doing level design. Granted, it's a not at all complex game, so the level design is nothing grandiose, but it's still always kinda fun to enhance a game like that.

- **The more challenging one** – Create a function on Netlify that records a high score, and have the game send the final score to that function when the game ends. Then, upon launch, have it call a second function to retrieve the current high score and display it on the start page (it can be the same function even, just with an argument to denote updating or retrieving the top score). That way, you can gain some experience adding an API to the mix. Of course, how you store the high score is something you'll need to determine. FaunaDB is an obvious choice, but Amazon Lambda functions – which is what Netlify functions become, remember – also reuse instances, so can you maybe use that to your advantage? Hmm.

Summary

In this, the concluding chapter of this book, you completed the JAMJumper game, making it fully playable. You then saw how you could take a JAMstack app like JAMJumper and make it a PWA, allowing people to "install" it so they can play the game even when they have no network connection. This shows that just because you're working on the JAMstack doesn't mean you can't participate in the PWA revolution.

I sincerely hope that you have enjoyed your time with this book and that you've learned a lot from it. Hopefully, I have shown you the power of JAMstack, Gatsby, GraphQL, React, and a few other things thrown in for good measure. Now, take all you've learned and charge forth creating the Next Big Thing, whatever that may be. I'll see you on the JAMstack!

Index

A

addComment() function, 195
add.image() method, 273
addMarker() function, 193, 194
add.sprite() method, 264
allMarkdownRemark, 175
Amazon AWS, 203, 222
anims.create() method, 262
anims.generateFrameNumbers()
      method, 262
app.createNavBar() method, 28, 29
app.firstMouseEventDone property, 33
app.js files, 23, 24
Application programming interfaces
      (APIs), 7
app.mouseMoveHandler()
      method, 31, 32, 35
app.resizeHandler(), 31, 33, 35
app.slideIn() method, 33, 34
app.slideVal property, 35
app.start() function, 24, 27, 31
Async/await, 219
attach() method, 110
Axios, 217–221

B

Babel, 130–134
Backdrop component, 226
BitKeeper, 48

Branches, 47
Button component, 160

C

Cascading Style Sheets (CSS), 3
client.query(), 233
Collection index, 210
collection() method, 233
Command-line interface (CLI) tool, 63
componentDidMount() method,
      148, 181, 215, 217
componentDidUpdate() method, 148
Components, React, 112–119
contentInner class, 26, 43
Content Management System (CMS), 10
Continuous deployment model, 8
create() method, 261
createPage() function, 174
Cross-origin request sharing (CORS), 296
CSS Grid, 40–42
currentMarkerText variable, 187, 192, 237

D, E

defaultProps, 142, 143, 146
descriptionValidator() function, 146
destroy() method, 270
Developer experience, 12
Dialog component, 164
DialogActions component, 166

Printed in the United States
By Bookmasters